Peculiar Discipleship

Peculiar Discipleship

An Autistic Liberation Theology

Claire Williams

scm press

© Claire Williams 2023

Published in 2023 by SCM Press
Editorial office
3rd Floor, Invicta House,
108–114 Golden Lane,
London EC1Y 0TG, UK
www.scmpress.co.uk

SCM Press is an imprint of Hymns Ancient & Modern Ltd
(a registered charity)

Hymns Ancient & Modern® is a registered trademark of
Hymns Ancient & Modern Ltd
13A Hellesdon Park Road, Norwich,
Norfolk NR6 5DR, UK

All rights reserved. No part of this publication may be reproduced,
stored in a retrieval system, or transmitted, in any form or
by any means, electronic, mechanical, photocopying or
otherwise, without the prior permission of
the publisher, SCM Press.

Claire Williams has asserted her right under the Copyright, Designs
and Patents Act 1988 to be identified as the Author of this Work

Scripture quotations are from New Revised Standard Version Bible:
Anglicized Edition, copyright © 1989, 1995 National Council of
the Churches of Christ in the United States of America. Used by
permission. All rights reserved worldwide.

British Library Cataloguing in Publication data
A catalogue record for this book is available
from the British Library

ISBN 978-0-334-06306-3

Typeset by Regent Typesetting
Printed and bound in Great Britain by
CPI Group (UK) Ltd

For Ben

Contents

Acknowledgements	ix
Introduction: Peculiar Discipleship	1
1 Trauma, Crisis and Ecclesiology: The need and manner of autistic liberation theology	16
2 Time	47
3 It'll be Alright in the End: Autism, healing and eschatology	74
4 Motherhood and Solidarity	107
5 Community	140
6 Practices	178
Letter to the Peculiar People of God	209
Index of Names and Subjects	213

Acknowledgements

I am grateful to many people for their support with this book, their constructive comments and their encouragement to write. To my colleagues at Regents Theological College, I am thankful for your warmth and your friendship and your depth of scholarship. Thank you for giving advice from your areas of expertise, for challenging my thinking, for welcoming me into the faculty – something I never imagined would be possible.

The Centre for Autism and Theology at Aberdeen University has been a source of much joy and hope. I am grateful to Professor Grant Macaskill for his thoughtful comments and his willingness to invite me to events. Dr Léon Van Ommen has become a good friend and a colleague, always humble but offering brilliant insight. I am extremely pleased to have worked and continue to work with him and am very grateful for his review of aspects of this book. Dr Joanna Leidenhag read a chapter of this book and offered comments and kind words, thank you.

To all the mothers who contributed their thoughts about parenting and autism, you are brilliant and you know and speak about your brilliant children. The attempt to show solidarity between neurodiverse and neurotypical people would not be possible without your standing in the gap.

To Anna, your emails are such an encouragement. From all the way across the globe you bring light and hope to me, you have given me such faith in this process while offering your own experiences. Who would have thought that Jesus could be shown through an email on a computer screen? Your words have done that for me.

To James, words cannot express my thankfulness for your friendship. You have done more to uphold me writing this project than perhaps you can imagine. Thank you for your emails, your post and the gift of your friendship. You are a wonderful ambassador and theologian in your own right. I can't wait to see all that you become in the future.

My family, you have been wonderful. Thanks for believing that a book like this could be written and that I could possibly write it. During the final days of writing this book my mum died of cancer. I think she would have been pleased to see this published. She was always there for me, supporting me in my childhood when my difficulties and struggles could not be described. She adapted and helped. I love her and I miss her. My dad, thank you – your quiet strength is remarkable. To my boys, Caleb, Barnaby, Andrew and Elijah – it is difficult to describe how you have formed me, how without you I was a shadow of what I am today. You are all wonderful young men, full of character and joy. I am extremely proud of you and in awe of you. Thank you that even though you are four boisterous and intelligent boys with plenty to say you keep our home quiet and do it because you know it helps me!

Finally, to Ben, my wonderful husband. Not many people so obviously reflect Jesus as you do. Without you not only would this book be impossible but so would my life. You daily pick me up and help me carry on with little regard for your own self. I find it hard to put into words what you have done and continue to do. I love you and thank you.

Introduction: Peculiar Discipleship

On a Tuesday afternoon in 2018 in a windowless NHS consulting room I sat with my husband and a psychologist. I'd answered a lot of questions, fidgeted with my fingers, doubted myself and gone over questionnaires and artificial scenarios. I had looked at the pictures of fish on a page and failed to make up a story that explained them. I'd not made eye contact. I'd explained that I had no long-standing friends other than my husband and that my childhood and teenage years had been marked by odd behaviours, obsessive anxieties, periods of deep depression and self-harm.

I described my failure to play with my children, setting up strategies for their entertainment that didn't require my own imagination. I explained that I had a script that I worked from when I met new people and that if I was planning a social activity I would play out many different conversations in my head in order to be prepared.

I explained a life that was lived out of sync with the rest of the world, at a peculiar angle, oddly. I noted that I could not bear loud noises, shoes that fit correctly (they need to be too big), lots of different food or being touched. I told the psychologist that this life seemed to be unbearable but that motherhood had been a wonderful blessing because it had given me a world that I could enter and live in according to my own choices. As I faced the time when the children wouldn't need me as much, I explained, I was at a loss as to what I should do.

I recounted a number of failed attempts at employment, at being over-qualified but under-skilled. That I could never imagine what is good and suitable for me, and by failing to do that had made poor choices. By the time I had said all of these things I had run out of any other words and fell silent.

At this point the psychologist reached into her drawer and drew out a pen; she took a piece of A4 paper and signed her name two-thirds of the way down. She explained to me that I was indeed autistic, that my suspicions had been correct and that this piece of paper was my diagnosis. She said that explaining to the GP my guesswork, based on googling, had been the right thing to do. Not only was I autistic but I wasn't the most 'mild' version that existed according to medical scales. I was one up on the severity rating than that. I would need specialist help if I ever had mental health problems, I would face needing to explain myself to medical professionals, and my future for employment was uncertain, and my life expectancy significantly shorter than average.[1]

I came away from that appointment exhausted and embarrassed. I had wanted an explanation, a justification. I had not wanted to be too odd even for an autism diagnosis – a very real fear I had. Now I had it, I wished I didn't. I looked at the students who entered the special school next door to my church and tried to understand how they and I had the same 'condition'. How they seemed quite different to me – neither better nor worse but different – but yet they shared with me a common thread of otherness that placed us all on the outside looking in, discordant with the rest of the world.

It took me 18 months to tell anyone other than immediate family about this diagnosis. I was afraid of being rejected (which did happen), disbelieved (also happened) and of saying words that could never be returned unspoken. That by naming myself as officially in this discordant group, by identifying myself as autistic, I would be consigned to the scrap heap, terminally without friends and community and unable to play at being normal again.

There are many days when I still feel this way but by writing this book for publication I have broken something of the power of my autistic shame. If I am rejected for writing these words I suspect that I will be among a fellowship of similarly forgotten but, by finding those people, a future can be carved for autistic people. A future where they are together at least and hopefully accepted by more people than just those others who strike alongside them their discordant notes.

What I did not explain to the psychologist, and what took a number of months and years to begin to understand, was my relationship with the faith that had formed me and sustained me over the years. I had a diverse Christian background having been all the way up the candle and back down again, born of nonconformist stock but educated in the heart of the Anglican communion at Wycliffe Hall in Oxford.

As an adult I am part of a third-wave charismatic church and have stayed in that community for many years.[2] I began to consider how the functions and ways of being that formed such a Christian community of worship might fundamentally be at odds with the way that I lived. For a long time I had made myself attend home groups[3] despite finding them very difficult, and I had joined in with the worship practices of the charismatic church despite finding them too loud and too unpredictable. However, I had stayed for the sense of belonging, the conviction that God had called people to worship together and be in community with one another.

As I began to consider the implications of an autistic way of being a Christian, I sought out answers to some of these difficulties. I used my journal access from my MA studies to read research papers that suggested autistic people could not be Christians because they were incapable of knowing God. I looked around for other Christians who were saying that they were also autistic and at the time failed to find anyone. I felt quite alone, although not completely alone. Despite the research papers that suggested otherwise, I had always had a very real and strong sense of the presence of God, of the salvation of Jesus Christ, and the life of the Spirit given to me.

I had never truly felt alone throughout all the difficulties of growing up as an undiagnosed autistic woman. This interplay of security in faith but insecurity in faith expression became something of a theobiography for me, although at the time I did not know it. Pete Ward describes his understanding of this as like a story of one's self. As a form of autobiography, he says, theobiography interacts with the calls that practical theologians make for honesty and reflexivity in their research; theobiography accepts situatedness and understands that as significant in theological reflection.[4] I had unwittingly begun a journey of theological reflection that would take my own experiences of an autistic life and bring to bear upon it the life of the church, the promises of doctrine and the world of scripture. As grand as this sounds, it is not a completed task but rather a journey that for me began the moment the psychologist signed the piece of paper that diagnosed me and discharged me from her service.

I re-entered the world at that moment fundamentally the same person but irrevocably changed. My world was formed in the Christian faith, steeped in the creeds, the liturgies of the Anglican church and the new liturgies of the charismatic nonconformists. I could not separate this autistic diagnosis from the faith that was part of my every fibre and sinew. That promised me that, despite the prognosis of an autism diagnosis and believing I was chronically unlikeable and unrelatable, there was a God who did like me, and had drawn me into his presence. What followed was a dialogue with that certainty and the new language I had to describe my being-in-the-world. This book is my attempt to speak out loud these reflections in the hope that they are not only helpful but spark further conversations.

In her *Time for Hope*, Flora A. Keshgegian states that the beginning of her writing stemmed from her own experience.[5] From that experience she hopes for resonances with her story and readers' own. I do not know if I can hope for resonances, although I suspect autistic people who read this book might find some. However, I do hope that the storytelling that underpins the book makes what might be strange slightly familiar. The strangeness, or peculiarity, of the autistic experience compared to neurotypical experience is part of what causes the trauma and difficulty that many autistic people face daily.

If this book does anything towards making the peculiarity less profound, less other, then a large part of the liberative work is achieved. Much of the quest for autistic people, as I shall explain further shortly, is to be heard. The voice of autistic people has long been silenced, whether through difficulty of being understood in the way perhaps non-speaking autistic people might experience, or through communicating at odds with those that speak as the normative voice.

As I shall indicate throughout the book, part of the task of liberation theologies is to draw attention to that which is in need of liberation. By describing my own experiences and drawing on the written and described experiences of other autistic people, this task begins to be undertaken. I do not speak as if my experience is universal for all autistic people. My experience as a speaking, educated, white, heterosexual, middle-class, British woman does not represent a number of other autistic voices. For example, it does not represent black women who experience oppressions of autism differently, nor does it represent the large number of autistic people who are also transgender. Similarly, my voice does not represent the male autistic voice which again encounters the world differently. I do not make claims that I am representative of these experiences but that there is a common thread of experience that is worth giving voice to in the hope that others will join in and a multitude will begin to unravel the autistic experience in the world and in the church.

Introducing the neurodiversity paradigm

I have begun telling my story of autism, diagnosis and the Christian faith. However, alongside my own experiences this book has another fundamental underpinning. The assumptions I make are founded in the belief that autism is not a medical problem that needs to be fixed, nor a disability that is located solely inside the bodymind of the autistic person.[6] Rather I understand autism in line with the belief that it is part of the diversity of human existence and always has been. I will make use of this idea in various ways theologically as I progress through the reflection on autism and theology, but it is fitting here to describe the new way of understanding autism and its place within the broader spread of difference: neurodiversity.

Neurodiversity is the manner in which autism is described and understood. The term was first coined by Judy Singer in 1998 as a socio-political descriptor that eschewed the bio-medical language and pathologization of autism. Singer believed that neurodiversity was similar to biodiversity: it reflected natural variance and the benefit to systems that difference allows.[7] This, and the ongoing development of the idea of neurodiversity, attempts to take away the medical emphasis on failure and dysfunction and highlight that there is no one 'normal' type of brain to which an autistic brain can be compared. Rather, much diversity exists in both the neurotypical brain and the autistic brain, alongside ADHD brains, dyslexic brains, bipolar brains and others; such brains are not 'broken' and should not be subject to value judgements.[8] The neurodiversity movement strives for acceptance and resists treatments that aim for 'cures' of autism. Thus, the movement, and any theology that engages with it, is fundamentally political and social.

One of the issues that the neurodiversity movement regularly counters is the idea that autism is a 'tragedy'. Much is written in popular culture about the rising 'epidemic' of autism. One frequently hears comments to the effect that 'autism didn't exist in my day, we just had to get on with it' or 'we were made to behave' or similar. This view was not helped by the devastating 'research' that linked autism to the MMR vaccine by Andrew Wakefield in 1998.[9] Despite Wakefield's work being removed from the medical journals it was published in, and condemned by professionals in the field, the damage had been done. He had incorrectly made a link between vaccinating children and the onset of autism, at once undoing much of the hard work of the vaccine programmes and identifying autism as something that was 'caused' and therefore could be prevented. Much hysteria followed and even today the worry that surrounds childhood vaccination programmes is testimony to the devil that stalks parents – what if my child 'gets' autism? This reveals the extremely unpalatable truth that many parents would rather their child caught a preventable disease such as measles that can have life-changing consequences, than risk the perceived chance of their child being autistic. Autism is the terrifying possibility, the worst of all outcomes. Autism is the enemy that prowls around looking for otherwise perfect children to devour. The neurodiversity paradigm rejects entirely this depiction.

In stark contrast with the pathologization of autism, the neurodiversity movement has developed its own language, descriptors and campaigns. It has seen the beginning of cultures such as autistic culture and community, and there are now autistic scholars and the beginnings of areas of scholarship such as 'critical autism studies'.[10] The need for this work of neurodiverse community and scholarship indicates that there is still much to be done regarding the acceptance and understanding of autism. As will perhaps become apparent throughout this book, it is not straightforward to argue that acceptance is the only goal here. I fully subscribe to the neurodiversity paradigm but also find that it does fail to account for the things that I find disabling about autism.

The social model of disability with which neurodiversity interacts would suggest that I am disabled by autism because the world I inhabit is not designed for my flourishing. To some extent I think this is true; much of the world is indeed not designed for me. However, it is difficult to account for all my struggles in this way. It may be that I am so socially constructed that even the thought patterns that so frequently trouble me are the fault of this ill-designed social world. But perhaps there is more to it than even that. A theological account of autism would allow for more nuance, but would also accept that there is something fundamentally flawed with *all* human society since the fall and that flourishing is limited until the kingdom of God comes again in its fullness. Therefore, the neurodiversity paradigm is the best fit for an autistic liberation theology because it accounts for the difference that is found in individuals, but places them within the grace and design of God rather than outside of that intention.

Before the neurodiversity paradigm came to be it would have been very difficult to describe an autistic liberation theology that did not rely on medical models of cure and treatment, and did not ultimately find something wrong with the autistic individual. Such 'wrongness' would then require explanations that account for the deficit by relying on predictable notions of sin and human fallenness rather than the gift and beauty of creation. Disability theology today makes similar claims with regard to the neurodiversity paradigm and rejects much of the deficit language; throughout this book I make reference to those texts that aid in the description of autistic liberation. However, the neurodiversity paradigm does not sit comfortably within a pure disability theology framework. It is its own entity as it wrestles with the nature of disability in relationship to autism and the questions, rather than answers, that raises.

The problems and the solutions that are found in disability theology do overlap but not consistently enough, and a new way of understanding is necessary. This new way is autistic theology, the particular and peculiar engagement with God and the world that accounts for and describes theologies of autism and the unique dialogue that is necessitated by that.

The potential for autistic theology

Autistic theology is located in the autistic experience with the assumption that it is in need of liberation. This is in the world, and therefore part of the concern of political and public theologies, but also in the church. Autistic theology is an inheritor of the liberation and practical theology traditions, engaging in conversations with experience and theology, rather than necessarily placing one thing as a priority over another. Although autistic theology has the potential to move in unforeseen and exciting directions I conceive of it as standing firmly within liberation and practical theologies and making use of the tools and well-worn paths of those theologians that have gone before.

Making novel links and sideways moves is, however, a factor in the autistic mind that means that those theological steps made by autistic theologians may well seem to be unrelated and disconnected. This too has precedent, if it is a suitable comparison. Robert Beckford has made for black theology links and categories that were unthought of before he created them.

His dread theology, his links between theology and Rastafarian thought culture, are creative in their liberative potential.[11] It is of a similar category that I believe autistic theology can be: creative, thoughtful, novel and disruptive.

Autistic theology is similar to other theologies of liberation such as womanist and feminist theologies, black theology and the first liberation theologies of the poor in that it seeks to describe the situations of oppression and assumes, usually, that the Christian faith has productive and hopeful resources that can aid in the quest for liberation. It also assumes that the Christian faith has in some way been complicit in the oppression of people. In the same way that the church has utilized its resources to silence and oppress women, black people, poor people and many, many others, so also can autistic lives be understood as victims of these oppressive tendencies. However, despite the poor track record the Christian faith has in understanding autism and supporting autistic people, I believe that the fundamental work of the gospel to demonstrate God's sacrificial love and stance of being 'for us' applies to autistic people and it requires work on the part of the church and from theologians to foreground autistic experience and to explore creative potential for autistic liberation.

The troubling issue of language

The academic field of autism studies is in a constant state of flux. The descriptive task of the field – trying to identify what autism *is* – the ontological status of autism and the nature of the experience of autistic people changes regularly. Any work that attempts to engage in this task must recognize that it is always in that moment. It is provisional and contextual, likely to be in need of revision and editing as knowledge and reflection improve the ways in which the field explains itself. This is primarily an issue of language.

Without delving into the philosophical nature of language itself it is broadly true to say that the language we use reflects our understanding and our cognitive commitments. Throughout this book I use the language that reflects the best understanding I have at this time as an autistic person who has a particular type of lived experience of autism. I recognize that this language is provisional. Throughout the book I refer to 'autistic people' rather than a 'person with autism'. This distinction recognizes that a person is autistic to the core of their being; that it is not a disease that is tacked on to their otherwise 'normal' personhood; and that it is in line with the neurodiverse community at this time. Autistic first language is a commitment to the de-pathologizing of autism; it rejects searches for cures and treatments because it rejects the idea that it is a disease.

However, at points during this book I will consider whether theologically 'person-first' language is *entirely* suitable, as although I do not consider autism in need of a cure nor as a disease, I also do not consider it the main aspect of my identity. This is that I am a follower of Jesus Christ. Thus, I would prefer 'Christian autistic person' if I were to follow the route this discussion of language naturally takes me. However, in order to recognize that many autistic people would certainly *not* see their primary identity as in Christ, I continue with person-first language because of the commitments outlined above. I recognize that this language may change and I ask forgiveness of the reader if the language I choose becomes a difficulty in the reading of this book; and I do hope that the intention and the theology that I sketch will be apparent even within these limitations.

Throughout the book I focus my language on autism rather than on neurodiversity in general. This is because the language of neurodiversity encompasses more than just autism. It would be incorrect to assume that what oppresses autistic people applies to the entirety of the neurodiverse culture.

A note on the title of this book. *Peculiar Discipleship* attempts to adopt the language that would in the past have been used as derogatory and instead redeem it as a positive descriptor for autism. This follows other such attempts including 'crip' as a reappropriation of the negative term 'cripple', and of Joanne Limburg who titled her own book *Letters to My Weird Sisters*[12] where she writes to women in history who were considered

INTRODUCTION

'uncanny', and even indecent by those around them, being that they didn't follow socially assumed norms of behaviour. By claiming the title 'weird' and by taking it out of the hands of those who label and dehumanize, Limburg creates a solidarity with all those who have stood out or been pushed out and reclaims with triumph language that is meant to be cruel. Calling this book 'peculiar' reflects the idea that until recently autistic worship and faith experiences were unspoken; that they were only provisionally researched and largely condemned as either impossible or examples of negative spirituality. Autistic people are thought of as odd and different. By suggesting that our journey in faith might be different too is, I hope, an act of challenge and subversion. No longer is it acceptable to highlight autistic differences in Christian faith and in the world and try to change them; rather, autistic voices will state their own needs and desires and come before the throne of grace in their own peculiar way. And that will be okay.

The book itself

This book of liberation theology winds its way through a path of thought that understands the ontological nature of autism as of political and theological interest. It critiques the demands made upon all people of liberal democratic productive values and describes a theological anthropology that rejects such values.

Chapter 1 is something of a methodological tour, attempting to integrate reflexively the core values of my own theological commitment. There are many ways in which an autistic theology could be undertaken and therefore it is more accurate to say autistic *theologies*, of which this is but one. I outline my understanding of autistic theology in relationship to liberation and practical theologies, indicating where the particular elements of charismatic theology intersect and complicate the relationships. I suggest ways in which this work could be done while recognizing that other liberation theologies have undertaken their theological reflection quite differently.

Chapter 2 begins the theological reflection proper with an understanding of autism and time. Autistic time defies normative standards of productivity. It is subject to 'overwhelmings' in the present and trauma in the past.[13] The resources of Pentecost and Sabbath are brought to this autistic time hoping for the possibility of renewal and reconstruction.

Chapter 3 develops this understanding of autistic time by looking at the future in autism: autistic eschatology. This chapter particularly uncovers ideas about disability and healing and looks to the future and asks, 'Will I be autistic in heaven?' It is at this point that the neurodiversity paradigm particularly impacts the theological discourse.

Chapter 4 is a particularized account of an area of dispute in autism that allows for a theological generalization to be made. Motherhood in the autistic community is a site of disruption; the 'autism as a tragedy' narrative meets the neurodiversity model. Through the theological notion of solidarity I sketch a theological anthropology that offers one way through this particular difficulty, and that also has potential implications beyond it. In this chapter I sought other voices from autistic mothers and mothers of autistic children, which through the very structure of the chapter indicate that discourse is possible and hopeful rather than angry and hopeless.

Chapter 5 naturally develops this argument from solidarity towards community. Suggesting that autism theology must describe the requirements of the church for acceptance of autistic individuals is radical hospitality, not adjustments nor inclusion. Ideas of inclusion are found insufficient for a Christian community; rather, this should be a belonging that is structured by being one in Christ and made in the image of God. Autistic theology expands ideas of community because of the novel potential of autistic thought. It is an example of an autistic understanding of the community of creation as significant in the community of faith.

Finally, Chapter 6 develops this idea of community to understand what it is that the church practises and how that makes statements about the autistic person within that community. Autistic theological practices are sketched theoretically in order to be suggestive of individual choices and preferences.

INTRODUCTION

My prayer is that this book will feel familiar to autistic people, that it provides primarily a sense of 'not aloneness'. I pray that autistic lives of whatever type will see liberation both now and in the coming kingdom because it is evident that God loves autistic people and desires their liberation.

Finally, I would like to end this introduction with the words of a friend of mine, J, who writes as a non-speaking autistic man, who finger spells to communicate. His words do much to summarize the problems and the hopes of autistic theology:

J's spiritual story

I'd like to start with my earliest memory of church. I was in the womb and heard hymns and I knew that God was present. I knew from that time that my life belonged to God. I also knew that my life would be unusual, though I didn't know how. As a baby I understood language easily but soon learned that I couldn't produce it as others could. This was horrible but God made himself known to me. He impressed his presence on me in ways I can't describe with words. Perhaps if I were an artist I could paint or make music to express this experience. I can only say it has been real and profound. I wonder if the great mystics had a similar theophany; I will never know until we all dance before the Lamb.

As a child I was loved in the church but didn't fit in. I couldn't talk and play. I couldn't do sports or join clubs. I needed a friend and Jesus was that for me. He talked to me and we shared jokes and insights. He is really kind and funny and warm. Yes, I heard words and he heard mine. My autism was not a barrier with him. He is my best friend as well as my Lord and King.

Now that I can communicate through spelling, I want to tell the story of his goodness to me. He is real and present in our lives even though most don't see him as I have. He continues to meet me directly, especially in the nave of our church. I somehow see him in light and glory. He tells me he loves us and wants me to proclaim his name. He meets me in dreams and tells me he will give me all that I need. I have learned that he seeks out the broken-hearted and waits for our silence to speak. I don't know why I am so lucky to know him so directly. I hope my story is encouraging to others.

My experience in the church has been largely positive. I always knew I was loved; this is a great gift and foundation. However, there have been problems, too. For example, I think it is a problem when the church segregates people with disabilities into a separate group called 'special needs'. I am wanting to connect with all people, not to be segregated. Our needs are not 'special'; they are needs all humans have: belonging, being loved, connecting, laughter, friendship.

What is needed is for the church to be intentional about including and valuing people who are different. This takes effort and patience, a slowing of time. You cannot listen without waiting and silence. I'd love it if the parish would slow down and wait for us to speak and move and be ourselves. We sometimes do not feel valued because people talk over us. Does the church really honour the deaf and dumb and weak and poor in spirit? Too often the church looks for beauty and status and 'social skills'. Perhaps we are too conformed to the world.

I'd love it if my peers showed an interest in me. I think they are so involved in their own lives they don't notice me. I hope God works in their lives so they can look beyond themselves and care for people who are not cool. It is hard being so weird. I am glad that God values the weird. I am hoping that my story will not elicit pity or guilt, but rather that God's people will see autistics in a new way. Amen.

Notes

1 L. DaWalt Smith, J. Hong, J. S. Greenberg and M. R. Mailick, 'Mortality in Individuals with Autism Spectrum Disorder: Predictors over a 20-year Period', *Autism* 23, no. 7 (October 2019): 1732-9, doi: 10.1177/1362361319827412. Epub 28 February 2019. PMID: 30818975; PMCID: PMC6713622.

2 For more on these types of churches, see Andrew Walker, *Restoring the Kingdom: The Radical Christianity of the House Church Movement* (London: Hodder and Stoughton, 1988); and William Kay,

INTRODUCTION

Apostolic Networks in Britain: New Ways of Being Church, Studies in Evangelical History and Thought (Milton Keynes: Paternoster, 2007).

3 Home groups, cell groups and life groups are all versions of the same faith practice – meeting in people's homes in a group of approximately ten, and over tea and biscuits studying passages of the Bible, talking about one another's lives and praying.

4 Pete Ward, *Participation and Mediation: A Practical Theology for the Liquid Church* (London: SCM Press, 2008), p. 4.

5 Flora A. Keshgegian, *Time for Hope: Practices for Living in Today's World* (New York: Continuum, 2006).

6 Karen O'Donnell suggests the use of 'bodymind' as a way of describing the complete experience of minds and bodies that are united and should not be separated. 'Bodymind' acknowledges our embodiment within the world: that we are holistic beings whose bodies affect our thoughts and spiritual expressions. For more, see Karen O'Donnell, *Dark Womb: Re-Conceiving Theology through Reproductive Loss* (London: SCM Press, 2022), p. 144.

7 Damian Milton, *Neurodiversity Reader: Exploring Concepts, Lived Experience and Implications for Practice* (Charlotte, NC: Baker & Taylor, 2020), p. 3.

8 Milton, *Neurodiversity Reader*, p. 3.

9 Chloe Silverman, *Understanding Autism: Parents, Doctors, and the History of a Disorder* (Princeton, NJ/Oxford: Princeton University Press, 2012), p. 203.

10 Lindsay O'Dell et al., 'Critical Autism Studies: Exploring Epistemic Dialogues and Intersections, Challenging Dominant Understandings of Autism', *Disability & Society* 31, no. 2 (2016): 166–79.

11 For an excellent introduction in his own words, see Robert Beckford, *My Theology: Duppy Conqueror* (Minneapolis, MN: Fortress Press, 2022).

12 Joanne Limburg, *Letters to My Weird Sisters: On Autism, Feminism and Motherhood* (London: Atlantic Books, 2022).

13 Nicola Slee, *Fragments for Fractured Times: What Feminist Practical Theology Brings to the Table* (London: SCM Press, 2020), p. 81.

I

Trauma, Crisis and Ecclesiology: The need and manner of autistic liberation theology

Theology begins with God, even if then it proceeds to particular contextual issues. This book begins with the knowledge of God that is received through the sacrifice of Jesus Christ, and known through the living presence of the Holy Spirit in the lives of believers. It is held in the Spirit-imbued community that interprets the scriptures as the word of God. It is from this beginning that the contextual and practical theological elements of an autistic theology emerges.

Trauma, crisis and ecclesiology: Why autism needs liberation

'Autism is a lifelong developmental disability which affects how people communicate and interact with the world. One in 100 people are on the autism spectrum and there are around 700,000 autistic adults and children in the UK.'[1] Autism is a diverse condition that impacts people in a multitude of ways. It is often conceived as being a spectrum where individuals fall at different points along it; the spectrum itself usually indicates the specific support needs of autistic people.[2]

More recently, autism is conceived of as a form of 'neurodiversity' where the idea of a spectrum is replaced with profiles of needs that acknowledge that there is no 'worse' version of autism and no 'mild' type. In other words, people have varied needs and an individual may have a 'spiky profile' of skills and requirements. This means that individuals may appear to be very capable by neurotypical standards in some areas of their life but struggle to meet their own needs in others. Neurodiversity, first coined by Judy Singer, is a descriptive term that indicates variations in 'the cognitive, affectual, and sensory functioning differing from the majority of the general population'.[3] Neurodiversity indicates that there is more than one way of being-in-the-world; more than one way in which to encounter it and process it, to engage with others and reflect on oneself, the other and God. It indicates that rather than an ideal type of person who acts and thinks in a particular way, there are many types who act and think in many ways. Autism is one aspect of neurodiversity; there are others – such as attention deficit hyperactivity disorder (ADHD) and bipolar disorder.

The alternative to neurodiverse is neurotypical. Neurotypical individuals conform to the predominant model of cognition and behaviour; they comprise the majority. Those who do not conform, who are neurodivergent, are in the minority. In the UK and around the world autism is considered a disability and is medically diagnosed using a deficit model. To be diagnosed, criteria of impairments must be met, but there are three areas that are usually described: social communication, social interaction and repetitive behaviours. Additionally, difficulties with sensory reception and tunnelled focus can be found. These are all understood as deficits, as lacks compared to 'normal'. Autistic strengths are not considered diagnostic. For example, extreme focus to the exclusion of other factors is deemed a negative trait rather than a positive ability to focus on one task until it is complete. Individuals diagnosed as autistic are subject to therapies and treatments in order to conform them to the neurotypical model.

Deviant and deficit models of autism have contributed to the subjugation of autistic individuals, and theology has the resources and motivation to aid in liberation. It is also my contention that an autistic life is a challenging life because of the many intersections. These may be intellectual disability, social isolation or the plethora of additional disadvantages of trying to exist in a neurotypical society – and that it is reductive to suggest that liberation equals, without qualification, a simple acceptance of difference. Liberation cannot only be a recognition that neurodiversity exists; that is insufficient in describing the reality of the challenges faced by autistics. Recognition alone does not make use of the ways in which theology can speak to the lived experiences of difficulty and challenge that make up the daily lives of autistic people. In this chapter I will illustrate the need for liberation for autistic people via stories, autistic writing and academic writing. I will then suggest some methods for theological reflection that are situated in my own theological disciplines, and go on to draft potential autistic models for liberation theology that take into account the multiple stakeholders who engage with autism.

Manners of disadvantage

The types of disadvantage associated with autism can be split into three categories: disadvantage in society; disadvantage experienced individually; and disadvantage in the church. These categories intersect and suffer the limitations that are typical of typologies, but they are useful as a starting point.

In society, autism is subject to a tragedy narrative, a condition that should be cured, endured and prevented; as Steve Silberman puts it, 'society continues to insist on framing autism as a contemporary aberration'.[4] Research into autism is often accused by the autistic community of seeking social and genetic causes with a view to eradicating it. Recent research initiated by Cambridge University was paused when autistic people criticized the collection of genetic material.[5] Collecting genetic material sounded like the first steps towards eugenics, the critics argued, for what other reason would there be for finding the genetic origins of autism? Whether or not this is accurate is not the main point; rather, it is the narrative that is debated between medical research and autistic individuals: that research seeks to problematize autism and then treat it.

Hanna Bertilsdotter Rosqvist, Nick Chown and Anna Stenning say that the word 'neurotypical' is constructed as an ideal ethical type – that it is considered, to the disadvantage of those who do not conform, as the correct way to rationalize and to behave.[6] Those who do not conform to the ideal type are considered 'deviant' and are medically, socially and economically ostracized. Ostracization results in stigma and then shame, argues Gordon Gates.[7] He finds that autistic people are traumatized by the shame that they experience compared to most others. Trauma also comes from experiences that are invalidated; for example, adults who seek diagnosis will often have to convince medical professionals of their need for it. Gates argues that invalidation is frightening, causing fear responses and ultimately more trauma. It is a 'threat to our humanity' to experience invalidation, which is compounded when the trauma from that invalidation causes further autistic 'behaviours' that are stigmatizing (for example, stimming – repeated behaviours or actions that are soothing for autistic people). Further differences in communication and facial cues can lead to traumatic experiences for autistic people who are then stigmatized – often unintentionally – by neurotypical people who do not respond in the same ways to autistic cues.[8] Pervasive and continual 'othering' is a traumatizing experience – in other words, being treated as intrinsically different from others. Social situations become fraught with triggering and re-traumatizing experiences and the cycle of trauma continues.

Autism makes engaging in society as it is constructed a challenging experience. This is evidenced in the statistics for employment for autistic people – only 22 per cent of autistic people are in any type of employment.[9] Employment makes many demands upon an individual. For example, expectations are placed on employees. This is difficult if an autistic person is demand avoidant or anxious because offices and workplaces are sensorily out of the control of the autistic person; workplaces are full of unwritten social rules that must be navigated; time-keeping and regular productivity are required and no exception is made for any irregular output of autistic people. In addition, stimming is not socially acceptable and therefore cannot occur in a workplace. These and many other reasons make employment a challenge for people on the autistic spectrum.

Personal experiences of autism disadvantage vary. It is often assumed that autistic people are incapable of relationships, or at least their ability to form and partake in them is substandard.[10] This leads to low expectations or rejection for people who are autistic. The reality, though, is that autistic people *do* desire relationships and *do* have them, but their requirements and their navigation of such relationships are different. Eilidh Campbell remarks upon her son's ability to navigate her husband's dry humour; it takes him a minute to understand it.[11] I can appreciate this as many a time I have listened seriously to a conversation and taken part in it, only to realize hours later that it was a joke. One that I didn't get. Not only this, but autistic individuals may be non-speaking, either all the time or episodically. Relationships based on speech and communication via speech – as is typical – will not work in these instances. Loneliness and isolation are significant issues among autistic people primarily because of the challenge of navigating relationships such as I have described.

Autistic people process the world through their senses differently, as has already been indicated. They are likely to be either sensorily sensitive or seeking. This means that our environment is likely to be ill-equipped to manage our needs. For me, shopping centres are bright, smelly and loud. Doctors' surgeries require phone calls to make appointments, which is difficult if auditory processing is problematic. Public spaces do not accommodate shouting – nor stimming. Standards of dress, and even fashion, are implicit and unwavering even if many of these clothes are uncomfortable. Sensory processing impedes the way that autistic individuals navigate the world, how they interact with others, and with systems. Sensory processing can vary in the way it manifests in individuals and the way that it causes disadvantage. It may be as seemingly innocuous as a strong dislike of Guy Fawkes night to as extreme as pervasive nutritional deficiencies as a result of restricted eating.

Churches are places that are not well equipped for autistic people.[12] They are in every Christian tradition places where implicit behaviours are assumed, but rarely explained. My experience of charismatic worship is a useful example. Charismatic worship is unpredictable. It reflects the leading of the Holy Spirit which can make time-keeping unreliable in church services. It can often change tack as the discerned movement of the Holy Spirit dictates. It is relational, founded on small groups and friendships. It is loud; charismatic worship services are noisy. These are situations hard to navigate for those with sensory sensitivities and a need for predictability and stability. It is not just the charismatic church, though, that is difficult to exist in. The fluid and interpretive nature of liberal Anglican communities is also problematic. I find the theological ambiguity of such institutions unpredictable, with liberal theology's commitment to cultural relevancy and a desire to show the gospel to the world as compassionate and responsive (extremely good aims I might add). This is difficult to square with my need for clear boundaries and straightforward thinking. These are just two examples from my own experience that are indicative. In the same way, theology has not been accessible for autistic people; it has traditionally sought to explain autism or to find analogies to it in scripture. This can result in dangerous associations with demonic possession or other unhelpful and inaccurate analogies.

Rosqvist, Chown and Stenning find that neurodiversity has been subject to academic 'othering', requiring a reorientation towards embracing and engaging with neurodiverse voices. It is the task of books such as this one to take some of the first steps in the discussion about autism and theology. This is not just liberation for those held captive to autism, but to the intersections of disadvantage, rejection, trauma and disability that accompany most, if not all, experiences of autism.

An imaginative example of neurodiversity

In the words of Micah Campbell:

> Having autism doesn't necessarily mean that you are extremely hard to take care of or will always have trouble managing things. But I feel as though being diagnosed with autism is challenging, so it's a strange thought being different from other people.[13]

I find myself agreeing wholeheartedly with Micah's clear and articulate words. Micah is the son of Eilidh Campbell, author of *Motherhood and Autism*, and he describes the purpose of this chapter very adeptly. Autism is not necessarily a problem; it is a different way of being, a different type of existence – one which, as it intersects with the neurotypical world, can create interference in the neurodiverse brain. An imaginative example is helpful to illustrate the different narratives and the intersections of the neurodiverse and neurotypical worlds and their competing demands.

A little boy is visiting his grandparents with his family. It is bedtime and the parents are tired, looking forward to not having to do the daily bathing, changing, brushing and reading tasks they would usually do. Perhaps they can simply sit down and put their feet up. Any parent of young children is likely to be familiar with this strong desire. Suddenly, though, the little boy is screaming and shouting and has locked himself in the bathroom. His parents are distressed, his grandparents too. Much effort is made to calm the child down, coax him from the bathroom (and subtly remove the key from the lock), and resume a routine more conducive to sleep. Much adaptation and manoeuvring is needed to help the child get back on track for bedtime. Eventually the boy's mother takes over the bedtime routine and sits in his room until he falls asleep – little sobs escaping now and again as he calms down and drops off, completely exhausted. The mother loses two hours to this process and the evening is nearly over.

How can this scenario be understood? Perhaps a medical

model, inclined to tragedy narratives, would describe the difficulty that the parents had trying to get even one evening off to rest. Perhaps the disruption the child caused by shouting and screaming is noted. The grandparents' inability to be involved in a basic element of the child's care might be highlighted. All the adaptations will be noted, along with the steps towards safety – such as removing the bathroom key. Ideas about autism and sleep and the troubles that children can have with entire nights is highlighted. These observations are all to some extent *true*. The little boy has had what is typically called a 'meltdown'. The adults involved in raising him have helped him overcome this meltdown in order to go to sleep. However, a neurodiverse narrative might be different and is illuminating. The little boy is in an unfamiliar house. He does know this, but it is a fundamentally different environment. It smells different and there are lots of items around that look old and a bit frightening: ornaments and pictures that are strange, but ones that his grandparents like and sometimes tell him about. He enjoys the stories but finds the items uncanny, they appear strange, old and unfamiliar. Many things that he has done that day aren't the same as usual. He woke up differently, with his grandparents' cat scratching at the door and noises from the radio; neither of those things are usual. Then he had a very tiring day when lots of fun activities happened but he feels odd and unusual and can't quite understand why. Breakfast and lunch were okay but the bread was different at lunchtime. Dinner was bad. He didn't eat it and everyone was pretty upset and cross. At home, he would usually sit and watch TV after dinner but today he played a game with his grandad. He liked the game, but he wouldn't usually do that. Bedtime is a scary time. He has to stay in one room on his own for a long time. He worries that he might be awake all night (which is often the case), and sometimes he is scared of the dark. When it gets round to the time he would usually go to bed nothing happens. Some time passes and he is still up, and this might be good because bedtime is scary, but also bad because it is different. Suddenly his grandmother announces bedtime and sweeps him up to the bathroom. Everything becomes far too scary at that point. He wants his mother, he feels terrible, and he is frightened. He feels lots of feelings and they all crash down at once. The bath is running and there is a strange-smelling soap. He doesn't like the sheets in his borrowed bed as they have bobbles on them. The cat is still in his room. It all becomes too much, and out of him burst all his feelings in a big, loud scream.

This example is only slightly a figment of my imagination; it is a patchwork of my childhood rewritten, my troubles with bedtime, and my reflections upon that now as a parent. Two worlds collide in this story. They are the worlds of the parents and the world of the child who is autistic. Both have needs and both have stories, but the child's needs and story are largely unspoken and unknown. It has happened to me on a few occasions that I can remember when I have been given the opportunity to quietly explain to a parent what might be causing their autistic child's meltdown ('of course she is upset, you told her she had to return to school to get her coat and she usually comes straight out'). Often, autistic children do not have the words to explain to themselves – never mind anyone else – what is causing them concern. This may apply to autistic adults too. The need for language and explanation is just one of the many ways in which neurodiverse and neurotypical worlds can come into conflict.

This brief survey is limited in its scope. It is not possible to chart all the ways in which the lives of autistic people need liberation. I have not examined intersections of other disadvantage – such as race, gender or sexual orientation. I cannot speak for those people and their experiences of being doubly or more othered. I hope that what I have achieved here is illustrative of the myriad ways in which autism affects people. In summary, autistic people are victims of oppression because of difference. They 'suffer' not from autism but from a construction of the world that does not fit them. Yet God offers to bind up the broken-hearted and to set the captives free (Isaiah 61.1–3) and therefore it is fitting that theology attempts to find out and show how God's liberative purposes for the world also apply to autistic people.

Characteristics of liberation theology

Liberation theology seeks to free oppressed peoples from their situations of oppression. It is grounded in the work and lives of ordinary humanity.[14] It is also situated in the life of the worshipping church. Christopher Rowland describes liberation theology thus:

> It is theology which, above all, often starts from the insights of those men and women who have found themselves caught up in the midst of that struggle, rather than being evolved and handed down to them by ecclesiastical or theological experts.[15]

Rowland notes that despite the sophisticated language and methods of liberation theologians, it is a theology that is fundamentally grassroots, concerned with the outworking of liberation and the associated practices of those who are oppressed. Liberation theology, according to Clodovis Boff, is a 'suffering with' those who are poor.[16] It is a commitment to comradeship and alongsiding, to do theology 'with' instead of 'to'. It is a two-stage process: liberating action fundamentally changing and improving the lives of the poor, followed by the second: theological reflection upon the action taken.

Liberation theology commits first to seek action. Leonardo and Clodovis Boff say that it must go beyond the tried and failed techniques of 'aid' and 'reformism'.[17] 'Aid' tries to fix the problem by doing things to a group that is pitied. The action of aid is unhelpful in autism because it is othering. For Boff and Boff, it creates a belief that the poor are simply those who lack and have nothing, rather than those who have been made to lack by others. It also removes their agency and their value as people who can change their own situations. 'Reformism' lacks because it seeks renewal of the situation from within the structures that already exist. Their example is the reformism in Brazil, where it improved its economic rankings from 46th in the world in 1964 to 8th in the world in 1984. This was achieved by huge industrial growth that changed the material circumstances only of those who were already well off. The rich were made richer. The poor remained poor. In light of these failed methods Boff and Boff suggest 'liberation' as the category for change. It is liberation because it is located at the site of oppression and the agents of change are those who are oppressed. The poor work together to change their situation. They undertake 'conscientization', which means understanding the modes of their oppression, the opportunities for challenging those modes, and the actions that they will undertake. This is the first move of liberation theology.

The second move of liberation theology is the move of theological reflection towards practice.[18] Theological reflection must be the second move because action must take priority. In the opening chapter of their book, Boff and Boff describe a woman who went to a cathedral with her small children. Approached by a bishop who feared that the woman's baby might be dead or dying, he told her to feed it. The woman cried that she could not. When the bishop insisted, she opened her blouse to show that her breasts were bloodied, and when the baby tried to nurse all it drew was blood. She had no milk to give because she was starving.[19] It cannot be that the first act for those who wish to see the liberation of the poor is to advance theological reflection. Hungry mouths must be fed.

This second move of liberation theology is that the church places itself in solidarity with the poor. Boff and Boff witnessed the churches, base communities and religious of South America working alongside the poor, with the poor inspired by the life, works and death of Christ. They were motivated by the gospel witness that saw Christ eat with the sinners and outcasts in society, being alongside them: 'The gospel is not aimed chiefly at "modern" men and women with their critical spirit, but first and foremost at "nonpersons," those whose basic dignity and rights are denied them.'[20] Hannah Lewis writes in *Deaf Liberation Theology* of methodologies and methods for the liberation of d/Deaf[21] individuals.[22] Deaf individuals have similar overlaps with neurodiverse individuals, although many differences make each situation unique. Neurodiverse people are considered by some to be disabled but do not always consider themselves so. There is a range of disadvantage associated with neurodiversity and the many ways in which society embraces them (or fails to do so) affects the lived experience of neurodiverse people. This is similar to the account that Lewis gives of d/Deaf experience. The world is designed for hearing, and deafness is constructed as a lack of hearing rather than a different encounter with the world. In the same way that autism is sometimes described as a 'different operating system', so also d/Deaf people can reject the deficit model and argue for an alternative. Lewis proposes that d/Deaf people are invisible to the church; that they are used as negative metaphors and are pitied.

Lewis proposes that Deaf liberation theology challenges the dominant narratives of theology and reorients theological discourse from particular standpoints, which in this instance is the Deaf community. She finds that knowledge is constructed and is an instrument of power that is sometimes wielded against those who are without. To construct a theology for Deaf people that is meaningful, it should be written, spoken and enacted by the Deaf community itself. So also should a theology for autistic liberation. A liberative theology for autism should reflect these concerns: to allow autistic individuals to speak and be heard and for the autistic community to play a leading role in the construction of theologies that concern them. Theology should be, according to Lewis, life-enhancing rather than destructive. It is necessarily contextual in that it favours and regards particular contexts as being in need of liberation. It cannot simply be an academic enterprise but must be rooted in the lived context within which communities exist.

Lewis expresses the common concern of liberationist theologians that traditional sources of theology are complicit in the repression of the marginalized. Texts, including scripture, are viewed with suspicion as they are used by those who have abused their power or neglected the vulnerable and have made use of these texts to validate these actions. Compared to Lewis's concerns with traditional sources, Rowland finds liberation theology to be rooted in deep and hopeful accord with the Bible. Books such as Revelation 'become a vehicle of hope and insight in these situations of oppression and deprivation as new hope in God's purposes are discovered'.[23]

It becomes clear that the issue of sources for liberation theology methodology is a live question with different liberative traditions and individual theologians taking different approaches. I shall, therefore, attempt to explain my own process which will be reflected in the rest of the book.

Charismatic/Pentecostal liberation theology

As a charismatic/Pentecostal theologian committed to reflexivity and transparency I wish to articulate a liberation theology that is situated in my own confessional tradition. As a member of a new apostolic church, I am a charismatic in praxis and am employed as a lecturer in a Pentecostal college.[24] My theology is always situated in the traditions from which I emerged but is informed by the wider theological heritage of my education and experience. The sources for this liberative theology for neurodiverse people are therefore wide, ranging from the Roman Catholic tradition, through to many Anglican theologians, and also the offerings of the relatively recent and emergent Pentecostal and charismatic traditions. Pentecostal theologies exist in a different key; they contribute to the wider conversations in theology with new and constructive ideas and it is the case that there are some (but relatively few) Pentecostal theologies of liberation. However, those that do exist express clearly the distinctive elements and contributions that are possible from the Pentecostal world. Selina Stone offers one such contribution in her reflections upon political engagement. Stone argues against the traditional view that Pentecostals are 'too heavenly minded for any earthly good', describing a change from the early Pentecostal view that Christ would soon return and that social action and change were of little value. This was in particular compared to the belief that saving individual souls was the greatest priority and mission of the church. However, says Stone, Pentecostals are formed as disciples who are political.[25] Pentecostals are political because they are citizens, and as citizens even inactivity is agency in the polis. However, they are also political because of the nature of Pentecostal discipleship.

Pentecostal discipleship is political because it is empowering for those who are victims of inequality and those who are disempowered.[26] Pentecostalism was formed from the margins and is a grassroots movement that has never existed as an established church. It is a working-class movement that has 'thrived among the underprivileged'. Discipleship in Pentecostal churches raises up to positions of influence and power people who would have had no such opportunity elsewhere.

Amos Yong describes the opportunity that Pentecostalism provides to equalize diversities of privilege and power. The Dalit community in India is an example of such change.[27] The Dalit community is the lowest caste in Indian society, considered unclean and untouchable. They are seen as lesser humans and ostracized from society. Many Dalits converted to Buddhism and Christianity partly to avoid this. From the 1920s, Dalit Pentecostals were able to experience the mutual fellowship in communities with Syrian Christians in a way that is liberative. Yong recounts the story of Robert Cook, a Church of God missionary who identified deliberately with the Dalit community by baptizing a leper and laying hands on him. Women were given roles in Pentecostal churches; as Dalit women they were the 'outcasts among the outcasts'.[28] Pentecostalism, according to Yong, has a holistic soteriology as individuals and communities encounter the Spirit of God and are given 'spiritual life; bodily healing; communal koinonia; the transformation of material, social, political and historical circumstances ...'[29] Yong finds that Pentecostalism is connected to the poor and the disenfranchised, the 'marginalized of the world', and is in its nature liberative.

In this liberative potential is the discipleship that Stone identifies. The equality that is contained within the church is validating because difference is acceptable by all who are welcomed in the Spirit. She shows how this happened in Pyongyang in the revival that occurred in 1907. This removed barriers between Koreans and Europeans and is modelled back to the early stages of Pentecostalism at Azusa Street where the primary actors in the revival were black – for example, William Seymour.[30] Stone finds this is liberative as all are given a role and a voice:

Empowerment comes to congregations of poor disciples and marginalized leaders through new experiences of God's Spirit which challenge existing power structures and make room for faith from the margins to become central to the future of the Church.[31]

The example of Pentecost, which is of course a motif of importance for Pentecostal Christians, is that all are united: 'And how is it that we hear, each of us, in our own native language?' (Acts 2.8). Language here is an important illustrative metaphor; not only is it spoken languages that God overcomes at Pentecost, but communication difficulties. Communication, at the heart of the diagnosis for autism, is one way in which the neurotypical/neurodiverse divide is exacerbated. Pentecost, and the faith that seeks to model that inbreaking of the Holy Spirit, is liberative in this way as well as in many other ways that I will pick up on in Chapter 6. Pentecostal communities re-humanize those who are outcasts and, as I have indicated at the beginning of this chapter, this re-humanizing work is necessary in the experiences of many autistic individuals.[32] I will develop this idea further in the coming pages.

Liberation theologies and Pentecostal theology have many similarities. Both intend salvation to be more than simply inner change, but instead a wholesale transformation of circumstances. They are founded in small and local communities that are centres of healing and prophetic action. The concrete reality in which they find themselves is an important source of theological reflection. Lay leadership and the absence of a significant hierarchy are common features as well as the belief that these communities have a biblical mandate to change societies. As such, the potential for Pentecostalism to be part of the liberative theological discourse is significant.[33]

Sources of Pentecostal theology are suitable for liberative and creative expressions such as this reflection upon neurodiversity; however, they do have particular qualities that may conflict with other liberation theologies and therefore should be examined here. As highlighted above, liberation theology construed in feminist/womanist terms, and as exampled in Hannah

Lewis's work has a problematic engagement with traditional sources of theology. This is not the case for Pentecostal theology and consequently any liberation Pentecostal theology also. Pentecostal epistemology is necessarily experiential because it is rooted in the worshipping community's praxis; it is not an abstract knowledge but one that is created out of communal worship in the Holy Spirit.[34] Pentecostal epistemology is also concerned with truth.[35] Truth, according to Simo Frestadius, is not a relative term for Pentecostals but instead refers to objective reality. It is a form of theological realism that has three distinct features:

1 Reality exists independently of the human mind.
2 There can be a significant link between truth and beliefs that can be said to 'correspond'.
3 It is possible to have both 'true' and 'false' beliefs.[36]

This is a significant and not unimportant difference compared to some other liberation theologies (although not all, as I shall show). The subjectivity of knowledge described by Lewis does not correspond to this interpretation. To this I say there must be a plurality of liberations for neurodiversity and as such there will be many different epistemologies. This epistemology that I will attempt to sketch corresponds to my Pentecostal and charismatic roots. It is only one articulation, one that I believe is imaginatively and potentially liberative – but one that some others will not.

The key critical move that Pentecostalism makes that is controversial is the access that humanity has to truth. The access that can be claimed is partial and corruptible, in keeping with the fallen nature of humanity and the disruption of the Imago Dei.[37] False belief has the potential to exist in Pentecostal epistemology, and with that comes the need for discernment in the Spirit as part of the resources available to Pentecostal knowledge. However, the work of the Holy Spirit means that access to revelation of God can come both through scripture and through the lives of individuals and the church.

A Pentecostal theology relies upon sources of knowledge from the received tradition. It does not necessarily engage with the level of hermeneutical suspicion of other liberation theologies. However, I do not see that as a shortcoming; instead, I see it as a different route to the same liberation potential. For although this suspicion is not widespread, the notion of Pentecostal discernment is. Discernment, as exercised as a spiritual gift, can work as a questioning and critical spirit, similar to a hermeneutics of suspicion. It is contra to a hermeneutic of cessationism; instead, it acknowledges the active presence of the Spirit in the questioning and knowing of the believer. The Bible, in most evangelical Christian expressions, is a key source of knowledge of God. The potential of the Holy Spirit to facilitate knowledge of God allows for the expansion of these sources to include the sources of historical theology. Theological realism means that there is the potential for theological claims to correspond to truth, both now and in the past.

The received tradition for Pentecostals, which is primarily the Bible but also the pneumatological experience of the community, is interpreted in, by and for the community. In the same way, experiences are interpreted as encounters with the divine, breaking into the human situation which at times can be construed as liberative experiences. Simo Frestadius suggests a model for Pentecostal hermeneutics, based on the model of Acts 15 where the early church gather to understand and negotiate novel experiences and their received traditions. This is a methodology of community, experience and scriptures and he calls this 'an epistemic practice of discernment'.[38] Frestadius intends this for biblical hermeneutics but it can also be applied to experiential knowledge. Indeed, Pentecostals must employ discernment in all things that are deemed to be acts in and through the power of the Holy Spirit. Drawing on William P. Alston's 'Theory of Appearing', Frestadius argues that Pentecostal experience can be understood as correlation to truth, which critically encounters the realism Pentecostals believe is accessible to them. Alongside this should be a 'strong dose of fallibilism' which allows for the fallenness of humans and a limit to their ability to perceive the actions of the divine.[39]

There is potential in Pentecostal epistemology for the novel voice. Historically, Pentecostalism has enabled surprising and underrepresented figures to gain platforms. An example of this is Aimee Semple McPherson's preaching in 1920s Los Angeles; a woman leading a church at that time was unusual and she became nationally famous as part of Pentecostalism.[40] This is just one example; every day in Pentecostal congregations individuals stand and testify to their lived experience of being transformed by God. This use of testimony is a form of storytelling and is a powerful example of liberation. In my own experience in charismatic congregations I have listened to the testimonies of many marginalized people who witness to the transformative power of the Spirit of God. James K. A. Smith relates this to the Pentecostal narrative quality that places individuals and communities in an eschatological grand narrative:

> Pentecostal spirituality is enlivened by a vision for a coming kingdom that imagines the world otherwise – a world no longer plagued by racism or disease or poverty – the world as envisioned at the end of the book of Revelation.[41]

Pentecostalism has the imaginative potential for liberation theology; it anticipates the kingdom of God as being without borders or discrimination and then enacts that kingdom now.

For a liberation theology, concerned as it is with the balances of power and the situation of the marginalized, a strong, clear and forceful discernment process is necessary to protect the most vulnerable. Pentecostalism is vulnerable in this area; those in power and those with a voice are most able to assert their experience of the Holy Spirit most clearly. However, as Stone has indicated, those who have access to power in Pentecostal churches are those on the margins elsewhere, so already the potential for the upending of inequalities is present. Combine this with a theory of discernment, and Pentecostalism has liberative potential. Frestadius says that the practice of 'testing the spirits' is part of the pragmatic route of Pentecostal epistemology. This is a process of referral to scripture as a yardstick for validity, believing that God does not contradict himself. This protects the religious experience, and by extension liberative theological discourse, from abuse. Held within an interpretive community this pneumatological discernment process, albeit undertaken by flawed human beings, has the potential for epistemological protection for the most vulnerable in society.

This very brief sketch of a Pentecostal liberation theology is indicative rather than summative. However, what it does allow is a working method for the progression of this particular book in keeping with my theological convictions.

Autistic, charismatic liberation theology

A neurodiverse liberation theology has specific features. These are particular to the liberation it seeks. These are: the raising awareness of the situation of autistic and other neurodiverse people; the championing of liberative acts by neurodivergent people for their own liberation; the joining in of these acts by the church that confesses Christ as the saviour for all who seek him (which of course includes neurodiverse people); and drawing upon the traditions of the church to inform those acts and reflecting upon them in a way that is uniquely neurodivergent.

Mary Grey says that feminist liberation theologies seek to achieve four things: new awareness; new academic discipline; new culture and ethics; and new spiritual quest.[42] New awareness highlights the fact that religious institutions also suffered from gender blindness, and that Christian churches failed to protect people from it. For autism, liberation awareness is a crucial component. Autism is badly understood and poorly described. It is buried deep in medical terminology, distorted by interest groups that do not look for the interests of autistic people, and plagued by a history that distorts the members of the group and questions their sanity and value.[43] Awareness needs to show that non-verbal autistic people can communicate and that they are valuable.[44] It needs to show that autistic parents are good parents and that autistic children are acceptable and not problematized. This is following on from Elisabeth Schüssler Fiorenza's aim to show that feminist theology must uncover theologies and institutional practices that are unjust and that deny full humanity to those they persecute. Autistic liberation theology must act similarly; it must uncover those theologies that deny full humanity to autistic people and it must show those institutional practices that do the same. By so doing it reveals the injustice that is hidden in the church and in society.

Autistic liberation theology must champion liberative acts in the manner that the first liberation theologians championed liberation for the poor. This will have many outworkings; it will see the church come together alongside those who are neurodiverse, to stand with them and not separate from them. This will be a significant act of solidarity with a group that is traumatically and systematically othered. It will seek accessibility and hospitality that does not look like accommodation, but instead is a radical acceptance. Radical acceptance does not make reluctant change to marginal institutional practices; rather, it makes significant, wholesale and systematic change. Liberative acts of solidarity and radical acceptance will view autistic children who shout and yell as wholly, fully and completely part of the community of faith instead of a patronizing accommodation. It will structure relationships in the church so that autistic people belong in a fundamental sense; not as an outsider looking in, but as an ontological member in Christ. It will champion the cause of autism in society in full solidarity, seeking structural change and improvement so that the rights and experiences of autistic people are centred.

The traditions of the church in all their depth and diversity will be used as tools in this liberation. The Bible, the doctrine and history of the church, the resources of the Christians who have gone before, can all be drawn upon in a liberative way. This will look differently depending on many factors. I have sketched one such option from a Pentecostal perspective, and others will hopefully take up the challenge from alternative Christian traditions. These traditions can be examined for their potential to offer freedom for autistic people; this will be in the same way that Christology was described by Leonardo Boff: Christ as Liberator. For Boff, it is not sufficient in Christology to simply know what others have known. Rather, Christ brings to each situation his potential and power. This was, for Boff, the liberation of the poor. It is Christ's humanity and divinity freshly revealed, when stripped of historic titles and represented to the concrete situation faced by Boff and others. What does this look like, when the resources of Christology are turned towards neurodiversity? Boff says that the titles of Christ, the Christological statements, must be critically reviewed. A critical review via neurodiversity might look towards a neurodivergent Christ, a Christ who stands on the social margins, a Christ who is unattractive to those who are in the majority and interpret those ideas, fully compatible as they are with tradition, in a new light for neurodiversity. This is one example of the resources of the tradition shining new light on the oppression of a people group. It is a hopeful act, one that believes that the gospel, theology, has potential for liberation. It is a faith-filled commitment to working with a group of people for their own good believing that the possibility is found in (and through) theological resources.

An autistic liberation theology with a charismatic hue must engage with the debates that surround the acceptable voices in theology, and question whether it is viable to talk of a 'starting point' in autistic theology. This is a debate that has characterized practical theological discussions about methodologies. Practical theology is both an inheritor of the emphases and priorities of liberation theology, and a discipline in theology that actively engages with lived experience. As such, it is the most suitable theological discipline for autistic theology to locate itself within. This is because an autistic theology will prioritize hearing the voices of autistic people where so often they have not been heard before. It will make sure that the theological work is done in keeping and in reflection with the lived experience of autistic people. This can be a troubling dynamic for a theologian who wishes to do this work from an evangelistic and charismatic background. For many theologians from this church tradition, the emphasis upon the lived experience threatens the priority of scripture as the revealed word of God and the first and final authority in theology.[45] It is a tension that this work, as a reflexive and honest piece of theology, should attempt to wrestle with. Methodologically I will move in a direction that is similar to Pete Ward's suggestions: that the progress through stages of theological reflection that require separation of types of information such as experience and scripture inhibit the reality of the theology that we seek to inhabit.[46] Questions about the priority of experience over scripture, or the role of authority in the generation and descriptions of theology, limit the task that is set before the theologian. For an autistic theology to ignore experience would be to become complicit in the silencing of autistic voices. For an autistic theology to be theological it must take seriously the voices of authority within the field, and for a charismatic theology this means both scripture and the influence of the Holy Spirit. This does not necessarily mean that priority is given to one or the other, but instead it needs mutually informing dialogue to take place.

The impact of the contextualization of theology, developing an academic interest in a person's lived experience and how this can be construed as theology, is in itself the task of a practical theology. Indeed, rather than separating the lived – in the case of this book – experience of autism from theological abstraction, I follow Clare Watkins's view that the realities of experience and theology are assumed to be coherent, that they are part of a multifaceted reality.[47] Following Ward, I resist the atomization of theology, separating theology from other disciplines or modes of knowing.[48] For autistic theology, the necessary conversation and dialogue partners in the generation of theology are both the autistic community itself as well as research with (and about) autistic lives. Autistic experience is rich in theology, generative of theology itself and critical in the conversation that develops in autistic theology. Without autistic experience it is neither liberative theology nor autistic theology. However, a simple methodological diagram of autistic experience or research, plus theological reflection that equals autistic liberation theology, falls short of the complex interplay between both my own theological thought processes and the inability to find a starting point in theology. None the less, the necessity of beginning when writing does artificially create a start that betrays this complex process.

Most of the chapters in this book begin with autistic experience, especially articulated in written research or books. This is a necessary beginning that aids the unfamiliar reader with the autistic situation. However, the process by which this beginning came to be may not have been with experience of autism, but with a theological idea that I found reflected in autistic experience – or a tangle between the two. To attempt to articulate a beginning for autistic theology oversimplifies and removes the complex web of thoughts and ideas that I have tried to untangle and re-weave into something that can be followed by others. In other words, I believe an autistic theology is theological reflection, theological beginnings and autistic experiences all nested together and artificially ironed into the linear processes necessary for writing and communicating. I am perhaps fortunate that as an autistic person I can straighten up my disorganized and unpredictable thinking in a way that is understood by others. I apologize, though, for those moments when the thinking isn't straight, but also submit this as neurodiverse and perhaps beautiful in its own right.

Theological reflection for a liberation theology of neurodiversity will have a particular flavour. Hannah Lewis notes that academic theology creates a barrier to d/Deaf people by making only certain forms of discourse permissible. Academic theology prefers analytical, empirical and written forms of discourse. Other forms are discarded or rejected. Lewis draws attention to educational elitism where oral and signed forms of discourse are not acceptable. Her sources, she says, are not necessarily logical but are poems, accounts and notes of feelings.

Autistic people do not, by definition, think in the same way as neurotypical people, and this will have an impact on their academic work. This affects children in schools who cannot write, students at university who struggle with the curriculum, and academics in the field of research. I have experienced this myself, having academic work rejected after peer review and revisions. The particular work was noted by the editor as having been written by an autistic author and comments made about autistic communication were passed on to me. However, despite my revisions the work was rejected. It may indeed not have met the standards required anyway, and I do know that my written work is non-linear and assumes knowledge that I have and other people do not. However, this is a barrier for acceptance within academic research that a liberation theology needs to help overcome. It cannot be that I, and others like me, have to change the way that we know and process information to meet a standard not designed for us. That is not a liberative process; that is a hurdle before even beginning.

A liberation theology for autism will accept as legitimate fragmentary, disorganized and non-verbal communication as legitimate and acceptable theological discourse. It will actively seek those theological voices that haven't been heard – or have actually been silenced. It will promote those voices that write not only on autism and theology, but on all aspects of theology. All aspects of theology should be drawn into this conversation because all are connected to one another. All theology is situated, say practical theologians, and all situations should be represented.[49] Theology students – from those entering theological education as undergraduates through to doctoral students and those in ministerial training – should have access not only to work written by neurodivergent people on all aspects of theology, but also to systems and procedures that reflect different types of cognition.

Theological reflection has developed in recent years to accommodate different forms of the written word; writers such as Heather Walton and Nicola Slee have both advocated for the use of autobiographical, poetic and literary forms of theological discourse.[50] These advances in the borders of theological expression are welcome, pushing as they do at the boundaries of not only what is acceptable but what is welcome, legitimate, life-giving and informative. Autistic expression is different again, sometimes verbal and sometimes not, sometimes clear and logical and pattern-oriented, and sometimes not. Scope for different articulations and expression in theology is there but does not filter down to the grassroots of theological expression. It is possible, and indeed invited, to be avante garde with theological expression in a PhD thesis but even then it must sit within certain categories and frameworks. It is much less possible in an undergraduate assessment or a theological reflection for formation. Yet, if we agree with Nicola Slee that classroom work is a 'meditating, enabling, priestly ministry', then how does that account for autistic students?[51] Presiding in a classroom, as Slee constructs it, involves directing the company of learners and enabling them to learn. If the systems of theological discourse do not reflect diversity of cognition and expression, then the classroom experience is not enabling. Students are not drawn into the presence of God, but instead are restricted. Better a millstone around our neck!

This should be a significant concern for those in theological education and formation. Slee advocates for the participatory learning that is fluid, 'a shared enterprise'. This is precisely the sort of learning that should embrace neurodivergence. It should accept differences in understanding and expression. A number of instructive examples spring to mind: making students participate in role play can be troubling for autistic people; expecting strict standards of logical and rhetorical written work may make assessments a hurdle, let alone the anxiety and lack of control that exams cause. Formation for ministry should be accessible to all, including those who have not performed in the narrow way that the British educational system assesses.

Autistic liberation theology is a grassroots, participatory enterprise that values the contribution of all autistic people to their own liberation. It is to be hoped that the resources the church holds collectively in scripture and tradition can have a relevant and pertinent voice, a voice that – once examined critically – can rail against the injustice in neurodivergent experiences.

Hermeneutics of charity – many dialogue partners

Boff and Boff advocate a liberation theology that expects the church to stand in solidarity with the poor. They write of the many Christians who are co-labourers with the poor, Christians who work alongside the poor for their liberation:

> ... if we are to understand the theology of liberation, we must first understand and take an active part in the real and histor-

ical process of liberating the oppressed ... We have to work our way into a more biblical framework of reference, where 'knowing' implies loving, letting oneself become involved body and soul, communing wholly ...[52]

This means that liberation theologians such as Boff and Boff envisage the places where the community of faith are in inter-disciplinary groups, as well as doing the 'book work' of the typical theologian. This cross-discipline, community-oriented approach is suitable for autistic liberation theologies also.

There are many voices at the table of autistic discussion that are secondary to autistic voices but still crucial to the liberation exercise. There are medical researchers, doctors, speech and language therapists, occupational therapists, specialist schools and residential care. There are parents, many of whom have tirelessly advocated and supported their children, there are social services and government policy-makers. All of these groups and people are invested in the understanding and support of autistic adults and children.

There are parents such as Eilidh Campbell, who has encountered life as the parent of an autistic child as a life of challenge as well as of love and blessing. She explains this conflict:

> Attention to the everyday, particularly the everyday lived maternal experience of a condition such as autism that so significantly and profoundly affects daily living, demands a recognition that life is messy. It is complex, it is shaped by social, political and theological debates that are interwoven into knots impossible to detangle.[53]

Lived experience of the day-to-day life of mothering a child on the autism spectrum is shaped as a source of knowledge and site of 'liberatory potential' by Campbell. She uses the phrase 'being in the struggle', as described by Ada Isasi-Díaz, as a centre for the reflection upon this quotidian existence; in other words, that small and seemingly insignificant acts take on liberatory potential when understood in the light of adaptive and creative mothering of autistic children.

Campbell describes the complicated and contradictory world

of autism research as one that does not definitively explain any one individual, but stands as a foreground to learning.[54] She describes mothers who must actively 'learn' their children in order to assist in their engagement with a neurotypical world. For example, Campbell's son Micah needed compression clothing to make his school uniform comfortable and his shoes were a constant source of tension until they were switched to sandals. This adaptive and attentive reflection is a source of theological knowledge that interacts with the medical model of disability and the medical research itself, but is not beholden or restricted to it:

> I propose that what is currently absent, and what is needed, is a theology that attends to life as it is and does not attempt to silence experience it cannot neatly explain within the accepted discourses available to it.[55]

Campbell acknowledges that she has attended to the voices of mothers in her work, excluding those of fathers and of autistic people themselves. This, however, is a strength to her work and to those that seek liberation. It demonstrates the many agents and stakeholders in neurodiversity – those who are neurodiverse and those who live, love and exist alongside them. I believe that to deny these voices in the accounts of liberation is a limitation. It is my intention in this book to propose a different conversation with sources. I will prioritize where neurodiverse voices exist; however, I will not silence those who are speaking about neurodiversity from neurotypical perspectives. They are the mothers, fathers and medical professionals who are attempting to widen and further understanding, and ultimately to achieve autistic liberation. This is not a blanket acceptance of all neurotypical input into neurodiverse worlds. There are nuances and caveats to my charitable hermeneutic. Those who engage in the tragedy narrative wholesale (as described at the beginning of this chapter), those who are unwilling to navigate the ambiguities of autistic life but seek only a 'cure', are not voices that contribute to liberation. They are voices that seek to eliminate rather than liberate.

However, a note of caution; many in the autistic community find their voice has been silenced. Many a child has been subject to treatments that they do not want or, historically, sent away from their family for residential care. The shaming and ostracizing of the autistic community means that their voice, in whatever format it can be shared, should be heard. It is this priority that causes Hannah Lewis to say of deaf liberation theology:

> I am really not interested in what hearing people, however involved with Deaf people they might be, have said about what Deaf people think and what a theology of Deaf people might look like.[56]

Although I appreciate similar arguments for autistic rights and justice I believe that a different outlook is necessary. This is because of the principles of Boff and Boff's liberation theology but also because of a broader understanding of the body of Christ.

There are many potential autistic theologies of which I have sketched a range of possibilities. I have engaged with my own theological convictions and sought to demonstrate the fecundity of them for liberation theology. I have situated autistic theology within the family of liberation and practical theologies that seek to set the oppressed free and to attend to lived experiences and voices that have been unheard. I sketch the peculiarities and oddities of autistic theology in order to show it has creative and novel potential and I urge the rest of the church to be involved in the process of liberating autistic people from that which is oppressive.

Notes

1 National Autistic Society, 'What Is Autism?', https://www.autism.org.uk/advice-and-guidance/what-is-autism (accessed 25.11.22).

2 For more on this, see Sue Fletcher-Watson and Francesca Happé, *Autism: A New Introduction to Psychological Theory and Current Debate* (London: Routledge, 2019).

3 Hanna Bertilsdotter Rosqvist, Nick Chown and Anna Stenning, eds, *Neurodiversity Studies: A New Critical Paradigm* (London: Routledge, 2020).

4 Steve Silberman, *NeuroTribes: The Legacy of Autism and the Future of Neurodiversity* (New York: Random House, 2016), p. 511.

5 change.org, 'Stop Spectrum 10K', https://www.change.org/p/university-of-cambridge-stop-spectrum-10k (accessed 25.11.22).

6 Bertilsdotter Rosqvist, Chown and Stenning, *Neurodiversity Studies*.

7 Gordon S. Gates, *Trauma, Stigma and Autism: Developing Resilience and Loosening the Grip of Shame* (London/Philadelphia, PA: Jessica Kingsley Publishers, 2019).

8 Gates, *Trauma*, p. 63.

9 National Autistic Society, 'New Shocking Data Highlights the Autism Employment Gap', https://www.autism.org.uk/what-we-do/news/new-data-on-the-autism-employment-gap (accessed 25.11.22).

10 John Swinton, 'Reflections on Autistic Love: What Does Love Look Like?', *Practical Theology* 5, no. 3 (January 2012): 259–78.

11 Eilidh Campbell, *Motherhood and Autism: An Embodied Theology of Motherhood and Disability* (London: SCM Press, 2021), p. 31.

12 For further reflections on how the church has interacted with autism, see Stewart Rapley, *Autistic Thinking in the Life of the Church* (London: SCM Press, 2021); Grant Macaskill, *Autism and the Church: Bible, Theology, and Community*, first issued in paperback (Waco, TX: Baylor University Press, 2021).

13 Campbell, *Motherhood*, p. 178.

14 Christopher Rowland, *The Cambridge Companion to Liberation Theology* (Cambridge: Cambridge University Press, 2008), p. 1.

15 Rowland, *Cambridge Companion*, p. 2.

16 Leonardo Boff and Clodovis Boff, *Introducing Liberation Theology* (Maryknoll, NY: Orbis Books, 1987).

17 Boff and Boff, *Introducing Liberation Theology*.

18 Boff and Boff, *Introducing Liberation Theology*, p. 6.

19 Boff and Boff, *Introducing LiberationTheology*, pp. 1–2.

20 Boff and Boff, *Introducing Liberation Theology*, p. 8.

21 Lewis writes, 'I have used "Deaf" to refer to people who would describe themselves in this way, "deaf" to refer to people and situations that are clearly referring simply to the question of hearing loss, and d/Deaf when it is either not clear which I should use or I am referring to all d/Deaf people regardless of how they see themselves', https://ereader.perlego.com/1/book/1633605/8 (accessed 13.10.2022).

22 Hannah Lewis, *Deaf Liberation Theology* (London: Routledge, 2007).

23 Rowland, *Cambridge Companion*, p. 2.

24 William Kay, *Apostolic Networks in Britain: New Ways of Being Church* (Milton Keynes: Paternoster, 2007).
25 Selina Stone, 'Pentecostal Power: Discipleship as Political Engagement', *Journal of the European Pentecostal Theological Association* 38, no. 1 (2 January 2018): 24–38, https://doi.org/10.1080/18124461.2018.1434727 (accessed 25.11.22).
26 Stone, 'Pentecostal Power', p. 26.
27 Amos Yong, *The Spirit Poured out on All Flesh: Pentecostalism and the Possibility of Global Theology* (Grand Rapids, MI: Baker Academic, 2005), p. 54.
28 Yong, *The Spirit Poured*, p. 6.
29 Yong, *The Spirit Poured*, p. 80.
30 Stone, 'Pentecostal Power', pp. 30–1.
31 Stone, 'Pentecostal Power', p. 32.
32 Stone, 'Pentecostal Power', p. 32; Harvey Gallagher Cox, *Fire from Heaven: The Rise of Pentecostal Spirituality and the Reshaping of Religion in the Twenty-first Century* (London: Cassell Publishers, 1996), p. 315.
33 For further reading on the interface of liberation theologies and Pentecostalism, see John Mark Robeck, *Towards a Pentecostal Theology of Praxis: A Case Study* (Lanham, MD: Lexington Books/Fortress Academic, 2021).
34 Yong, *The Spirit Poured*, p. 79.
35 Simo Frestadius, *Pentecostal Rationality: Epistemology and Theological Hermeneutics in the Foursquare Tradition*, T&T Clark Systematic Pentecostal and Charismatic Theology (London: Bloomsbury T&T Clark, 2021).
36 Frestadius, *Pentecostal Rationality*, p. 167.
37 Frestadius, *Pentecostal Rationality*, p. 169.
38 Frestadius, *Pentecostal Rationality*, p. 182.
39 Frestadius, *Pentecostal Rationality*, p. 194.
40 For more on Aimee Semple McPherson, see Cox, *Fire from Heaven*, chapter 7.
41 James K. A. Smith, *Thinking in Tongues: Pentecostal Contributions to Christian Philosophy*, Pentecostal Manifestos (Grand Rapids, MI: William B. Eerdmans, 2010), p. 84.
42 Mary Grey, 'Feminist Theology: A Critical Theology of Liberation', in Rowland, *Cambridge Companion*, 2nd edn, pp. 105–22.
43 Sara Luterman, 'The Biggest Autism Advocacy Group Is Still Failing Too Many Autistic People', *The Washington Post*, 14 February 2020, https://www.washingtonpost.com/outlook/2020/02/14/biggest-autism-advocacy-group-is-still-failing-too-many-autistic-people/ (accessed 25.11.22). See also Silberman, *NeuroTribes*.
44 Douglas Biklen et al., *Autism and the Myth of the Person Alone*,

Qualitative Studies in Psychology (New York: New York University Press, 2005).

45 For summaries of these questions within the field, see Helen Morris and Helen Cameron, *Evangelicals Engaging in Practical Theology: Theology that Impacts Church and World* (London: Routledge, 2022); Helen Collins, *Reordering Theological Reflections Starting with Scripture* (London: SCM Press, 2020).

46 Pete Ward, *Participation and Mediation: A Practical Theology for the Liquid Church* (London: SCM Press, 2008), p. 35.

47 Clare Watkins, *Disclosing Church: Generating Ecclesiology through Conversations in Practice* (London: Routledge, 2020), p. 10.

48 Ward, *Participation and Mediation*.

49 John Swinton and Harriet Mowatt, *Practical Theology and Qualitative Research* (London: SCM Press, 2016).

50 Heather Walton, *Writing Methods in Theological Reflection* (London: SCM Press, 2014); Nicola Slee, *Fragments for Fractured Times: What Feminist Practical Theology Brings to the Table* (London: SCM Press, 2020).

51 Slee, *Fragments for Fractured Times*.

52 Boff and Boff, *Introducing Liberation Theology*, p. 9.

53 Campbell, *Motherhood and Autism*, p. 148.

54 Campbell, *Motherhood and Autism*, p. 150.

55 Campbell, *Motherhood and Autism*, p. 175.

56 Lewis, *Deaf Liberation Theology*.

2

Time

Time begins my discourse on a liberation theology because it encompasses much of the dispute, differences and disabling conditions that autistic individuals encounter in their daily lives. Time concerns future hopes of fulfilment and acceptance, along with past stories of rejection and trauma by both the world and the church. It concerns ways that living neurodivergent lives affect neurotypical notions of productivity, rest and time management. It also has significant theological overtures: God was and is and is to come; Christ is the future hope of the world; and the kingdom of God invades our world now by the power of the Holy Spirit. There is much that has excluded autistic people that can be described as occurring with a neurodiverse time. Therefore, there is much that needs to be done to redeem autistic time. The gospel of the good news of Jesus Christ came in time, for all time, and this brief sketch illuminates some of the good news that I perceive theology can offer in particular for the liberation of autistic experiences. This chapter is part one of two chapters. In the next chapter I hope to engage more fully with the eschatological issues raised in disability studies, but here I make a first foray into autistic theological time.

Today is a bad day. I am unhappy and I can't comprehend it. I catch glimpses of a reason as it filters through my disordered brain. My stomach hurts, I've been sitting staring out of the window far too long, I am lonely, I talked to too many people yesterday, my clothes are uncomfortable; in other words, a myriad of small annoyances amount to an intolerable and urgent halt. It could be those things are causal, or they might not be. However, today is a bad day. Sometimes days are good days. In the same way as the bad ones, they are unfathomable.

Perhaps that day my stomach doesn't hurt, or I had a conversation with someone that went well. I was especially productive with work on a Friday and can enjoy a celebratory glass of wine with a sense of achievement. Maybe none of those. Good days are conversational days; I can start and sustain words with others. Good days result in many achievements that I observe are standard for neurotypical people. On the flip side, bad days are not those things. The air feels thick, words are unutterable, people are other and my body fully hurts. I loathe the bad days, their unpredictability, their unknowingness. Bad days cannot be described except through tears on the phone to my husband in between A-level classes and assemblies. *I just feel so awful.* Time is the only thing that continues to slope onwards despite the good days and the bad days. My experience of that time – despite the clock assuring me that it is regular and predictable – is in a constant state of flux. The days that are bad drag interminably; they are worse in winter when the sun refuses to lighten its gaze. I get nothing done, I have wasted my time being unproductive, and I am therefore less valuable in my own eyes. The good days are over in a flash and are fragile, fleeting, like the arrival of the perfect temperature for walking without a coat in autumn. Good hours, of intense and directed work, of creativity and productivity, or of lying still in bed utterly comfortable and with nothing hurting or itching or buzzing or ringing. Those good hours are there, worth waiting for, but fleeting, ephemeral; I cannot produce the right conditions for them. Time progresses without my permission, changing things: the seasons that require me to adjust to light and temperature; the hours, which are better in the morning, worse in the dark evenings, and awful on Sundays; the days – Fridays are the best days, Sundays the worst; holidays much anticipated but unscheduled and usually trying. The marking, observing and existing in time are fast and slow. Hurried and lagging.

When I was pregnant with my fourth child I once again encountered the debilitating form of sickness called hyperemesis gravidarum. My days were confined to lying as still as possible in order to prevent nausea from rolling through my stomach and radiating out to the hairs on my head and the ends of my toes. It was all-consuming. The sensory experience, at the time unknown as such, evaporated all sense of anything else. I would stare, crippled with panic as the clock did not tick through the hours as it usually would. Nine months was a time that I could not exist for. The catastrophizing horror of allowing time to pass slowly while I had to exist in it was terrifying. Never before had I feared the slowness of time in a way like that. I fear that even now I cannot communicate the anxiety I felt about the passing of time. Nothing could speed it up and I couldn't cease to exist until it was over. I simply had to pass through it. I existed on a different plane to the rest of the time around me. I was in stasis, always suffering, confined to a body that was feeling too much, and the solution was the passing of time. All I had to endure was nine months – or eight and a half as the beginnings of nausea negated any medical confirmation of pregnancy – the beautiful and terrible signs were there from early days. The battle with my body was catastrophized as a battle with time; it was never the fault of the baby and I rarely even blamed my body. I simply encountered the endurance of time as the impediment. This war that showed its colours was not one that I could win. I explained to my midwife when 28 weeks pregnant that I just wanted the pregnancy to be over. She sent the mental health crisis team around. I failed to communicate that I needed the conflict with time to be won. Time had slowed down during this suffering.

This may appear an arbitrary judgement upon time and autism. After all, are not these fragments of my life that I have written about more properly described in terms of sensory sensitivities rather than temporal sensitivities? These stories could be told again with that emphasis; however, I propose that it is in reality sensory processing as it intersects with time that I describe above. Time, as I hope I have suggested, is particularly challenging for autistic people. Most classical descriptions or, in popular imagination, the striking autistic relationship with time concerns routine. The relevance of routine and ritual is in relationship to the broader theme of time. My suggestion is that time is an important consideration for understanding how to help and accommodate neurodiversity in a neurotypical environment. As such, theological resources about time should be bought to bear here to articulate the problems encountered by people who are autistic, and propose theological suggestions that are constructive.

This chapter first considers future time as concerned with future hope and productivity. It critiques the view that values applied to people should be anchored to their ability to be productive and also that future choices are only given to those who can communicate according to social norms. Instead, I propose the adoption of 'crip time' theory (see below) and the generation of 'autistic time' which understands production and future hope differently. The second section of this chapter considers autistic pasts as traumatized by neurotypical expectations and existence in a world that is not designed for them. Autistic past is theorized as having a traumatic spectral shape which persists into autistic presents and futures. However, making use of Johann Baptist Metz's 'dangerous memory of Christ' allows for constructive theological work on remembering that is helpful for traumatic autistic pasts. Finally this chapter describes autistic present time as overwhelming and uses the biblical narratives of Pentecost and Sabbath as a way of resistance.

Future

My first encounter with theories of time that I related to autism was reading Alison Kafer's book.[1] Kafer writes about 'crip time'. Crip time is to do with time, futurity and disability. Kafer draws attention to perceived futures and their interaction with disability via the story of a girl called Ashley X.[2] She describes the growth attenuation and sterilization of Ashley. Ashley's story involved her parents and doctors medically intervening to slow her growth and to render her infertile. Among the many commentators and critics of this development, Kafer draws some suggestive conclusions. The causes of Ashley's 'disability', in the view of those who treat her, is a 'disruption in the temporal field'.[3] She will not grow 'normally', nor will she ever fully leave childhood. Her future imagined self was troubling, and steps were undertaken to resolve this temporal fracture. She was 'treated' in order to remain small and easier to handle manually. Her hysterectomy prevented the development of her breasts and reproductive organs. Her body was prevented from running away from her mind. Kafer describes this as being 'outside of time'. Both her disability and the treatment of it affected her interaction with time; she was outside of time because of the difference in her mental and physical development, and 'further out of time' because of her medicalized stunted growth.[4] Much of the motivation for the treatments that Ashley was subjected to were in order to encourage a better future for her and her caregivers. The treatments were undertaken to prevent Ashley having to live her adult life in care. Kafer illustrates the futurity of Ashley's case by stressing the unknowability of Ashley's future. The treatments may or may not improve the quality of life for Ashley and her caregivers; and the unknowability of her future is significant for theorizing time. Normative future is hoped for, and imagined, in the minds of those who seek to edit Ashley's life. This is enacting a belief about childhood development that is linear, says Kafer: that children must all progress predictably and sequentially from one approved stage to another. Eventually they arrive at their destination: adulthood. For those whose destination is unsure, whose adulthood might be unacceptable, measures must be taken and interventions made so that the imagined future is hopeful in normative terms.

'Normative time' is developmental, productive time. Adults are those who are able, having completed childhood unscathed, to move on to the other achievements associated with 'normal' development: romantic relationships, child-rearing, employment, eventual retirement, the trappings of the 'good life'. Here also is an association that Kafer makes with productivity. 'Normal' development is associated with an increasing ability to produce. Value in the liberal democracy is tied to the ability to earn one's keep. Time is spent producing things that are useful – this usually means employment, although care duties are sometimes acceptable. Time and value are preoccupations of society, so those who cannot produce are found wanting.

Ashley was described by one doctor as a Cadillac with a Chevrolet engine.[5] She is not what she seems and she is not good enough, a cheap model that could have been expensive. Normative future time is the imagination of productivity.

Many proposed interventions and treatments for autistic children operate with the future in mind. The child's future self is imagined – how will they live alone? What about secondary school? What will happen when they die? Therapies are designed to try to train the child to behave in such a way that they can 'manage'. The difficulties with such enforced conforming are numerous. Stemming from the medical model of autism (as a problem with an individual that must be solved) and introducing elements of pragmatism, these children are coerced to fit in in order to protect their futures. These elements of pragmatism can be as small as being taught to make eye contact as the necessary requirement for social engagement, or as invasive as applied behavioural analysis. In Chapter 6, I outline the differences between practices in churches that are liberative and practices in churches and in the world that are oppressive. The same distinction could be applied here. Parents who seek to protect their children from harm by others or themselves are morally significantly different from parents who engage in abusive practices such as those described below. The distinction between the two types of parenting perhaps comes down to motivation, or outcomes, or to the wellbeing of the child. This is not a straightforward distinction but one that must be examined carefully to achieve the best future possible for an autistic person.

Applied behavioural analysis (ABA) is a system of manipulating a child into conforming to society's behavioural guidelines. Steve Silberman describes what this looks like in the life of a child whose parents had recently begun ABA with her:

> The slightest signs of autistic behaviour were no longer tolerated. 'Day by day we grew more relentlessly demanding of her,' Catherine [the mother] wrote. 'No gazing into space, no teeth grinding, no playing with her hands, no manneristic touching of surfaces, no *anything* that looked autistic.[6]

Eventually, after a period of time in this programme and getting older, the child in question, Anne Marie, was declared to be no longer autistic. Silberman goes on to describe other children who are exposed to restrictive diets to 'cure' their autism. One description involves a child being subject to electrical current along his spine, and of course many children were prevented from being vaccinated.[7] The futures of these children are being edited and engineered in search of a cure. The hope of the parents is that their child will be 'normal': will eat normally, will be educated normally, and will progress normally. It is easy from my position to appear judgmental about these attempts, but they do not appear to be enjoyable for the children involved. It is the society in which these parents and these children attempt to have futures that is responsible for engineering futures. There is no space for neurodivergent hope for these families and that is a profound lack.

In a similar way it is noted that autistic girls and women also train themselves to fit in through a process called masking. Masking is the practice of pretence. It involves careful observation of other people's behaviours and habits and their careful integration into one's own repertoire. My experiences of this are legion. In most cases I have come to note that my watchfulness of other women in order to mimic their behaviour is with a future self in mind. There is a future aspect to all practices of masking. Each time a behaviour is mimicked it becomes refined, improved and integrated into the self. Where I begin and my lifetime's acting ends is not clear. I am a tapestry of my own self and of those strands of other lives that I have woven into my habits.

> We don't give up, resilient queens that we are. We try on different personalities, accents, religions, cultures, the way that neurotypical girls might try on clothes at a department store.[8]

This is a cheerful description of a difficult and uncomfortable process. Michelle Garnett describes it as a quest for integration of the self, which is ultimately more successful the earlier an autistic girl understands herself as being autistic.[9] This arrests the development of a camouflage of pretence that is prevalent in autistic women. It also testifies to the difficulty with the imaginative future self and future time in autistic women.

Returning to Ashley's story, Kafer says, one issue that recommended Ashley's treatment was her inability to communicate. Yet Ashley was able to communicate in ways that showed she was bored, confused, and also that she enjoyed particular types of music. However, this was judged inadequate communication.[10] This is a familiar narrative for autism. Verbal and written communication is something that is unpredictable or non-existent. Kafer highlights the permanence narrative that suggests Ashley may never communicate in a way that is acceptable. She then questions the interventions of communication devices such as aides or technology that assist forms of communication. They are controversial, she says, but do raise the issue of whether communication is static or changing.[11]

Verbal communication in autism is something of a Rubicon. Those who regularly speak are considered to be 'high functioning' compared to those who do not speak who are not considered to be 'high functioning'. This is reductionistic for all concerned. Speech is neither the key to understanding functioning nor the quality by which someone should be judged. The personhood of the individual who does not speak is disregarded, considered unable to show their value or their own ideas, thoughts or opinions. In *Autism and the Myth of the Person Alone*, Biklen and his contributors robustly challenge this narrative. Rather than presuming both contentment and isolation, he explores the model of disability that entraps these individuals.[12] The book is an encounter with silenced voices, an insightful and disarming journey into the worlds of those who have graciously made use of neurotypical tools of communication to draw others into their community.

The American Psychiatric Association's diagnostic category DSM-IV describes one of the qualifying characteristics of autism to be 'qualitative impairments in communication' which can involve problems with initiation of conversation, language, lack or difficult spoken communication and stereotyped language.[13]

Lack of words, silence or communication that is considered autistic is judged and found wanting. Yet throughout *Autism and the Myth of the Person Alone*, the communication of the individuals who are designated autistic is profound. Each contributor to the volume has been 'rewarded' with a 'pessimistic prognosis' where their future self – as described to their worried parents when they were children – was categorized as being 'unfit'. Their access to education was limited; Richard describes himself as being poorly educated at various points, despite eventually winning awards for his writing.[14]

> Unable to express myself fluently in speech, I found myself in the same dilemma that I have been in countless times before, of people unable to conceive that I have thoughts in my head. Because of my inability to put voice to them, I had no command over my life.[15]

Richard Attfield's written words demonstrate the expectation of others impacting his future self. He has been determined to have no worthwhile future hope and has therefore no control over his own choices. Fractured futurism is prevalent in the medicalized model of autism and speech is both a literal and metaphorical symbol for such imposed prognoses. The ability to produce speech is a normative criterion of productive potential. The inability to produce speech is damning, rendering the hope for a future blindly optimistic at best and unlikely at worst. This is not liberative for autism and I will go on to suggest that theology has tools for silence as valuable; I will explore this further when I discuss practices and tools for future hope that are neither medical nor psychological, but fully theological.

I find speech a troubling notion. I was not mute as a child (unlike the experiences of many autists who go on to speak), nor am I non-speaking as an adult. I write now from a very particularized experience of speech. Sometimes I speak too much, a rush of letters, language and remembered speech that floods the room and drowns out all else it encounters. I retreat from such situations embarrassed and ashamed of my performance. At other times I speak not at all, the words don't come, communication stops before it starts, and my desire to reach others with words or language disappears. I sometimes associate these silent times with tiredness, with trying too hard, and therefore suffering the exhaustion that is a result of this. The silence is not always accountable to my own explanations and many a friendship has not survived my failure of speech. I have attended church services with my head in my hands, an intense charismatic experience assumed, but even the speech to God is stunted. I am trapped in my mind, the possibility of reaching others or God is mute. The hope of speech and a future that is possible because of it is absent in that moment, and the knowledge of whether it will come back has also gone.

Autistic future is uncertain. My future as illustrated by speech fluctuates. I cannot guarantee my friendships; I worry about my relationships with my children as they grow. I wonder if I will say the wrong thing or not enough and lose employment. Will my exhaustion that is associated with the production of speech become permanent? Autistic regression is a process that is much discussed in autistic communities and less researched in medical ones. Autistic regression is usually precipitated by events that overwhelm the individual, leaving them unable to perform functions or skills that they previously mastered. One particular way this manifests is with speech, loss of words, repetition, substitutions and – when writing – odd sentence structures.[16] This type of regression can be temporary or permanent:

> Sometimes the loss is temporary – a period of a few weeks or months – after which a person regains the lost abilities. Other times the deterioration in skills or coping mechanisms takes place over years. It may become permanent or semi-permanent, with skills being regained but not to the level at which they previously existed.[17]

The future looks mixed when presented with autistic regression, especially when combined with ageing. For me, this is particularly noticeable in my ability to meet sensory demands. This fluctuates: sometimes the irregular tapping of one of my children's feet while they watch TV is tolerable, other times it is not. Speech is a particular and useful example of this type of regression because it is observable and impactful on the autistic person's ability to construct their own future. The expectations and hope for others around them becomes problematic as nobody can predict what will happen the next day, or the one after that. Even those, like myself, who regularly speak and write and appear to communicate in a neurotypical way have fluctuating futures determined by their autism.

'Crip futurism', Kafer says, addresses the failure of imagination that pervades the treatment of disabled and queer people. Both, she says, are subject to 'treatment' in the desire to remedy a disordered self:

> Both are failures of the imagination supporting and supported by the drive toward normalcy and normalization. Not wanting to cultivate queerness, or to build institutions supporting that kind of cultivation, is intertwined with fears about cultivating disability.[18]

Future self and future productivity are issues of hope. Theology has much to offer to the conversation about 'crip time'. Crip time recognizes that much of disability studies concerns the mapping of impediments to proper use of time, and symptoms are described as chronic, intermittent, terminal or improving.[19] The value of another person based upon their words, their ability to produce and their future flourishing should be dismantled. The myth of progress declares that constant, observable, conditional and neurotypical improvement is the only future that exists. To not have this 'improvement" is to have no 'good' future. Crip time is called such as an act of reclamation by disabled people. The potential for autistic time is similar, and this is something I attend to in the next chapter. For now, it is sufficient to raise awareness of autistic time and to throw down the gauntlet for hopeful neurodiverse futures – futures that can be aided by a truly liberative autistic theology.

Past

Time also intersects with trauma.[20] Traumatic moments in the lifetime of an individual impact on the way in which they experience time. They are stuck forever in the 'after' – the after of the event or trauma, or even, as Shelly Rambo suggests, stuck forever in Holy Saturday.[21] Autistic individuals are very often traumatized or live with the effects of PTSD. This trauma is a particular type. It is unusual, socially constructed and related to invalidation and rejection.[22] As autism often presents as non-typical, those who enter the social world to become 'other' by their acts of difference – for example, stimming, social behaviour, embodied differences. This contributes to rejection and therefore shame.[23] This functions as a non-normative trauma; it is not traumatic in the way that trauma is recognized.[24] To be non-normative even in the experience of trauma compounds and extends the shame and traumatization.

Rambo describes trauma as an encounter with death.[25] This is not simply the encounter with death that occurs during near-miss or near-fatal illness, but an encounter with the death of self. An internal fracture. There is no return to the before. The impairments of the medical model of autism do allow for a descriptive model for this trauma. First, sensory overload, or understimulation, is connected to feelings of safety. This is not a reductive type of unsafety, an uncertainty or discomfort, but fight or flight responses to perceived danger. Whether or not that danger exists to observers is irrelevant to the autistic subject who is unsafe. These daily encounters with danger are traumatizing and cumulative. The body of the autistic person carries with it the damage of repeated encounters of non-safe sensory environments.

Social interactions bear the load of a history of unhappy relationships, broken friendships and misunderstandings. The autistic person lives with the consequences (and likely unwarranted guilt) of such fractures. This is constructed as part of the self: the belief that the person is unlovely, unwelcome and unacceptable. The autistic person alone may well be a myth best resigned to academic history, but it is the personal history of many autistic people that as they encounter the world they are forecast to always resist being alone.[26] This type of alone-ness might be because of lack of voice; because they are non-speaking; lack of autonomy and freedom because they are restrained in an institution against their will; or lack of relationships for mutual flourishing. Whatever type of alone-ness an autistic person may have encountered this contributes to the shame and trauma of being other.

Finally, flexibility and rigid thinking, described medically as a deficit, is unacceptable in the modern world. Change is constant, and the rapid pace of modern life – so frequently decried by news outlets and commentators – has a devastating effect on those who want to encounter the world with stability. Repeated change in life, a good example being the Covid-19 pandemic and the fluctuations in lockdowns in the UK, means that new situations are approached with the damage from previous changes. This is best illustrated with an example. When I encounter a new situation, a new job for instance, the previous times when I have tried – and failed – to adapt to difference in my daily schedule haunt me. The spectres of failure, the attempts to engage with a new way of existing and not being able to, are all obstacles to me when trying to complete transitions on another occasion.

Trauma in autism is linked to the person's encounters with the world around them. It is a fracture of the fundamental self because it is linked to the core of identities (relationships), and to the embodied navigation through time (change) and space (sensory sensitivities). As such, the emotional and physical are embraced by the ghosts of past trauma and traverse future hope. Accompaniment by such ghosts is unwelcome and restrictive. The past cannot be left behind. The residing in the middle, as Rambo describes it, means that the future and the past are entwined, and autistic time must fully wrestle with this ever-present past.

God knows and receives the past of a traumatized autistic individual. My attempt here is to weave together critical descriptions of trauma and autism alongside liberative and political theology. This is a preliminary sweep of theological possibility; much more could – and should – be written on this subject. The potential of these ideas for a constructive theology of autistic past is located in their descriptions of the suffering human subject, the acknowledgement of the suffering autistic person (notwithstanding the sources of that suffering, whether it is through disability, social conditions or combinations of these) and the hopeful Christian discourse that reconstructs the autistic individual. This reconstruction does not attempt to resolve a situation. This is in keeping with trauma theology and its commitment to reside rather than repair, to be attentive rather than remedy.

Johann Baptist Metz in his liberation and political theology perhaps offers some theological tools for navigation accompanied by the ghosts of trauma. Unlike Kafer, Metz constructs the middle-class subject as a-historical rather than future oriented. He understands this as part of the Enlightenment dialectic that at once embraces futurism as the source of potential, but also removes time from the process by the logic of evolution and historical materialism.[27] This creates timelessness because increased control and progress are emancipatory, or at least illusions of emancipation that are formed through oppression, control and dominion.[28] The modern post-Enlightenment subject is timeless and therefore dislikes tradition and is incapable of acts of memory such as guilt or sympathy. This is inadequate as a formation of subject, so Metz turns to the formation of the suffering subject. This is found in a history of freedom: 'The essential dynamics of history consist of the memory of suffering as a negative consciousness of future freedom and as a stimulus to overcome suffering within the framework of that freedom.'[29] This is a peculiar construction of freedom, one that definitively moves away from the modern understanding of it.

Memory of suffering situates us in history with a past and allows a future with hope. This is parallel to theologies of trauma that consciously divert from resolution futurism. Metz understood in his own terms is complementary to trauma theology rather than divergent from it. This is because his programme is liberative. A liberative programme is capable of acknowledging trauma and trauma theology without negating its commitment to seeking structural and theological change that prevents further trauma. Metz's theological commitment to freedom allows for the past to be reconstituted, while maintaining the traumatic spectral shape (and therefore not denying or silencing it) as a human freedom.

Human freedom is one that is allowed a place in history – that is, freedom to suffer and to understand others' suffering. This he achieves with 'the dangerous memory of Christ'.[30] Modern theories of emancipation fail because they are abstract and not historically constructed, they do not engage with the acts of remembering. These acts of remembering are the encounters with the narrative of Christ found in the New Testament: 'In the dangerous memories of suffering, time is lived apocalyptically – as discontinuous, as rupturing.'[31] Rebecca Chopp utilizes Metz's thoughts, showing there is solidarity with those who suffer, because we are in solidarity with Christ who suffers. We are to be in time rather than to be timeless, and Christianity contributes to this understanding because it is encountered as praxis. It is not the dogmatic or the propositional that allows for a better appreciation of the past and the suffering in the past, but the praxis of Christianity. The following of the way of Christ that interrupts the world and converts it does not accept the world nor prophesize to it, says Chopp, but changes it towards timefulness.[32]

Chopp finds Metz's categories, solidarity, memory and narrative to be the theological tools of worth in his theology. They make theology reorient towards those who suffer and away from methodological and critical concerns. This is therefore truly liberative and works to aid the liberation of autistic time, and in particular autistic past. Theology, says Chopp of Metz, is the concern with the narrative memory – in particular the narrative memory of suffering. Rejecting the use of theory this type of narrative unites suffering and history. The two tasks that Metz finds for theology are the hermeneutical – transforming individuals through the memories of suffering; and the critical, as these memories deconstruct the structures that form the world. As Chopp suggests, Metz does not elaborate on how this reorientation allows for real change in society, so it is therefore helpful to suggest what this theology does do in the quest for autistic time.[33]

Autistic time requires a constructive theology that takes into account the trauma of autistic pasts. That trauma creeps into the consciousness of the autistic subject and is part of their existence in history. Making use of Metz we can interpret the dangerous memory of Christ. Keshgegian tells us that we inhabit time and time inhabits us; in other words, that time is told by the re-telling of stories.[34] Hope comes from the telling of these stories, such as the stories of the Christian tradition; however, hope is threatened when these stories do not help or no longer feel true. The progressive narrative, much like Metz's logic of evolution, no longer helps, says Keshgegian; this is because it must end with achievement or accomplishment. Against the Christian tendency towards triumphalism or 'all's well that ends well' we should reject the authority of a meta-narrative. Keshgegian appears to embrace process theology in her work with time, speaking as she does about the uncertainty of God in the incarnation, and therefore in time. I do not wish to follow that theological path. However, Keshgegian, as well as Metz, speaks of the need for attentiveness to suffering in the past in constructing a person. These sufferings are ruptures in time that prevent us going back to where we were before. We cannot understand autistic time alongside histories of progress or triumphalism. Rather, autistic past time is in solidarity with the sufferings of Christ and the ambiguity of incarnational theology: that which embraces corporeality and concrete pasts that encroach on the present.

Present

The first particularly suggestive theological move with relationship to time concerns Sabbath. Many of us are familiar, as Kafer suggests, with *more* time in relation to disability and neurodiversity. Students sitting examinations are given more time; there is *more* time available to arrive at a destination; *more* time to get situated and find an appropriate place at a venue. Yet for disability, Kafe says, time is not just *more*:

> Crip time is flex time not just expanded but exploded; it requires reimagining our notions of what can and should happen in time, or recognizing how expectations of 'how long things take' are based on very particular minds and bodies. We can then understand the flexibility of crip time as being not only an accommodation to those who need 'more' time but also, and perhaps especially, a challenge to normative and normalizing expectations of pace and scheduling.[35]

Drawing from the radicalizing and political reclaiming of the notion of crip time I wish to present the autistic present. Autistic time is necessarily flexible. No two autistic people will have the same time requirements. My use of time is fluid: sometimes I work extremely fast, achieving academic work much quicker than expected; at other times I need significant rest, having been made tired by things that are not usually considered physically tiring – such as talking to people for long periods. Other autistic individuals will have different time requirements.

Autistic present can be characterized as overwhelming. This appears negative but need not be. These moments are sometimes called 'meltdowns' when they include visible responses such as calling out, rocking or running away, or 'shutdowns' when the response is not visible to others. Overwhelming autistic joy is a recently constructed phenomenon in the autistic community which refers to the pleasure obtained from immersion in special interests. Special interests are a type of autistic behaviour, usually described in negative terms by academics and medical theorists, that are all-consuming focused pursuits. The traditional example is trainspotting, but it could be anything that attracts and holds the attention – maybe mathematical problems, crosswords, music, breeds of dogs, even theology! However, alongside this positive description of overwhelming is the negative side: when sensory stimulation is unpleasant, when pressures of time and change or space are constricting and oppressive. This is the negative, dark side of autistic overwhelming and it can be crippling:

But he himself went a day's journey into the wilderness, and came and sat down under a solitary broom tree. He asked that he might die: 'It is enough; now, O LORD, take away my life, for I am no better than my ancestors.' Then he lay down under the broom tree and fell asleep. Suddenly an angel touched him and said to him, 'Get up and eat.' He looked, and there at his head was a cake baked on hot stones, and a jar of water. He ate and drank, and lay down again. The angel of the Lord came a second time, touched him, and said, 'Get up and eat, otherwise the journey will be too much for you.' He got up, and ate and drank; then he went in the strength of that food for forty days and forty nights to Horeb the mount of God. At that place he came to a cave, and spent the night there. Then the word of the LORD came to him, saying, 'What are you doing here, Elijah?' (1 Kings 19.4–9)

Nicola Slee reflects upon a 'theology of overwhelming'.[36] She cites David Ford, who says that modern life is naturally a state of being overwhelmed. He suggests that this is not a state to be avoided but one to be embraced. Not only do we sometimes feel overwhelmed by negative things but it is also possible to feel overwhelmed by positive things. We hear talk of being overwhelmed by love. For example, there have been occasions as a parent when the love for my children has quite literally taken my breath away. We can be overwhelmed by beauty, autumn being a particularly good season for natural beauty to flood our senses.

To be overwhelmed is to have an experience that is totalizing. The experience of being overwhelmed, whether positive or negative, is of being caught up, carried along or bowled over by some event, force or person, over which one has no control.'[37] It takes over all our senses, our body and our mind, our emotions and our consciousness. The negative versions of this in philosophy have been variously called existential dread, anxiety and even 'the threat of non-being' (following Tillich). More recently, theology has looked at trauma and considered the way in which it overwhelms our personhood. Slee makes the link between trauma and overwhelming – for example, when women are accused of telling 'unstories' (and therefore not believed) when they speak of their experiences of abuse.[38] The denial of self and the invalidation of autistic trauma rears its unsightly head in the present as situations of overwhelming.

All this is to say that there are times when what is hard and trying in this world, the state of our fallen selves, encompasses our vision and takes away our hope and our joy. This is not unlike how it was for Elijah. The constructive response to this is presented by Slee and I wish to put something of a Pentecostal spin on it. Slee suggests that we must give ourselves fully to the immersion of the experience. This is an act of consent – 'I am overwhelmed and I'm not acting against it'. This is intrinsically an optimistic and hopeful stance: the belief that God is present and at work in the midst of the situation. We can also hold the tension of being in a negative space, live in the intersection of a difficult time with the hope that a new and better reality can emerge from it. Finally, Slee suggests giving it attention, a prayerful stance where the situation is brought to God in the life of the church. The attention is given not just as an individual one, but within the body of Christ as all who pay attention to one another – as we are told to in Galatians: to bear one another's burdens.

There are theological metaphors for overwhelming that allow for it to be reframed positively. Baptism is one such instance of overwhelming, where the waters rush in and over and the new creation emerges as the water recedes. A particularly Pentecostal reading of overwhelming can come in the form of the presence, life and gifts of the Holy Spirit. When the disciples gathered in the upper room the experience of the Holy Spirit was an overwhelming, and unexpected, event:

> When the day of Pentecost had come, they were all together in one place. And suddenly from heaven there came a sound like the rush of a violent wind, and it filled the entire house where they were sitting. Divided tongues, as of fire, appeared among them, and a tongue rested on each of them. All of them were filled with the Holy Spirit and began to speak in other languages, as the Spirit gave them ability. (Acts 2.1–4)

This experience is particularly aptly described as overwhelming. The Spirit is auditory, visual, linguistic, sensory and completely present in the space and time that the disciples are in. They cannot move away, look away, or exist outside of the presence of the Spirit in that moment. They are overwhelmed. However, it is a positive and liberative experience. They are given a fresh voice, new opportunity and greater hope in the time that follows the overwhelming. It is a positive version of the effect that trauma can have on a person – the 'time before' can never occur again. The disciples cannot go back to their previous selves because God has overwhelmed their present and moved them into a new future.

To be overwhelmed can be an ordeal, and to be autistically overwhelmed is perhaps a normative experience in this community. Anxiety is severe and debilitating for autistic people.[39] Sources of anxiety can be sensory – unpleasant textures or smells, loud noises; it can be linked to change; social encounters can be difficult to navigate, or related to alexithymia (finding it hard to identify emotions in oneself or others).[40] However, if modern life (and also autistic life) is a series of overwhelmings as David Ford suggests, then our faith has a solution, or a reply.[41] The spirit of God offers us to be overwhelmed by the love, care, sacrifice and divine attention of God. In a way, that is for us and for our good.

This draws me back to 1 Kings and Elijah's encounter with God in his despair. God is not found in the noise and external action; Elijah does not have a dramatic and charismatic encounter. The inbreaking of God in the moment of hopelessness is quiet and still and appropriate for Elijah's state. Yet God is still active and present in the life of the believer. God offers a hopeful encounter via presence. Elijah participates by being fully himself in the moment of his misery and accepting the encounter. The divine act is not negatively overwhelming; it makes no particular demands upon Elijah but is gentle and probing. It is an act of love and of knowing; it is accepting.

Slee says that by definition we cannot choose when we experience overwhelming. The account in Acts is similar: the people in the upper room had no expectation that the Holy Spirit would present to them in the way it did. As such, autistic present time should 'attend to the shape of living' in a way that corresponds to the particular autistic bodymind.[42] Attentiveness in the autistic life might be a slowing down, a waiting in the midst of, an acceptance of the 'meltdown' or 'shutdown'. It might mean accepting the unpleasant experience of the overwhelming in order not to contribute to it with feelings of shame. Thus, says Slee, the unexpected nature means that there cannot be answers to the problems associated with overwhelmings, only postures. This is being attentive to the diversity of autistic experience that is so often constrained to normative behaviour patterns. Postures of response to overwhelmings in the present allow for a narrative, descriptive response that is fluid and adaptive to the diversity within diversity.

Slee recommends naming the experience of overwhelming. This is significant in theologies of liberation (see Chapter 1); the silence must be overcome and the specific conditions of oppression made clear. This description can be in the form of lament, in keeping with the psalmists or with Job, says Slee. However, the challenge of language and unreliable speech means that this type of naming of overwhelming needs to be a community undertaking. No one individual should be responsible for autistic speech. Rather, the autistic cry for liberation comes from the community of the oppressed. The overwhelming of the Holy Spirit resulted in the ability for the disciples to speak to many people in a plurality of languages (Acts 2.8–12). The theology of overwhelming can positively lead to communication and expression between normative and non-normative experience. Speech, whether signed, typed, finger spelled, written or drawn, is a theological model of communicating the good news of God in Christ that liberates those who are captive. Naming the autistic experience of overwhelming is made possible by the overwhelming of the Holy Spirit who draws all in equality together into a community that is empowered to present the word of God and the word of truth to one another. The liberating potential for naming is remarkable. This draws us back to the notion of attention. The ecclesia can give attention to the overwhelming as an act of pastoral care, says Slee. This is a safe attention, one that everybody in the body of Christ deserves.

Time should be understood as God's time, inclusive of autistic time. As such, it is fruitful to embrace resources ordained by God to understand and inhabit time. In this I would like to incorporate the Sabbath into an autistic description of time. The biblical paradigm of time is intricately linked with Sabbath and rest. When time was first ordered and noted, when it was divided and partitioned, one day was given over to rest. Genesis 2.2 tells us that time is both productive – the six days of creation – and restful. It is the rest that is designated 'holy'. Holy time is the time when production does not occur, rather than when it does. Creative endeavour is deemed good; the results are pleasing to God, but the time that is sanctified is the time when endeavour ceases and rest occurs. Autistic time embraces all that I have said about the difficulties with production, expectation, bewildering disturbances and past trauma. Sabbath-keeping can be resistance.[43] This is resistance of the liberal democratic programme of value in keeping with crip time. Walter Brueggemann presents Sabbath-keeping as subversive; it throws off the demands of production and reconditions identities with the creator God.[44] Brueggemann's Sabbath is offering liberation for those who are weary, for those who are forced to conform socially, for those who battle the economic expectations of this age.[45] Sabbath has liberative potential theologically for those who are oppressed by the neurotypical time-thick demands of their current lives.

On that one rest day, identities of production and world time-keeping are shucked off and resisted. This is a declaration of identity found in divine descriptions. The value of the individual is declared to be found elsewhere. This is especially pertinent to autistic people whose identities are so carefully navigated. Some autistic people are comfortable in an autistic identity, others not so. However, all who come to God in the rest of the Sabbath do so via Christ. Christ offers a new yoke, one that is easy; this is in contrast to the heavy yoke of Roman rule. Like Pharaoh before them (Exodus 16.13–21), the secular ruling powers impose unmanageable production demands on the people. In contrast God – both in Exodus and Matthew 11.29–30 – offers an alternative. The Sabbath for the slaves under Pharaoh was a decisive act of resistance. It was the first liberation theology, a theocentric understanding of the world and the world's construction that subverted the attempts of humans to control, oppress and subjugate. Identity for an autistic individual is as one who is caught up into the divine, who is hid with Christ, who is known and loved by God. That identity is enacted in the keeping of the Sabbath in a particular way for the autistic person. To forget the Sabbath for a Jew was to forget their entire history, the story of their salvation, and instead return to the striving and labour of life under Pharaoh.[46] Those who are deemed unproductive and without value embrace the holy time that is deliberately unproductive. The value that is enacted in this Sabbath rest is the value found in God.

Sabbath also offers rest from the practical demands of autistic life. Anxiety can be resisted in Sabbath time. Anxious overwhelmings and societal expectations are part of the autistic experience for which Sabbath offers redemption. God commands rest from the 'anxious production' of the ex-slaves of Egypt.[47] It is a rest from anxiety because all production stops; urgent scrabbling for resources, hoarding and shoring up must cease. Trust in the provisions of the God of the Sabbath have to be sufficient. Sabbath illustrates that God does not demand things of us. A. J. Swoboda argues that Sabbath is rest that comes before work. Humanity was made on the penultimate day of the week, and the following day was the Sabbath.[48] The people had done nothing, achieved nothing, not worked at all. They were simply existing and God led them into his rest. There is no need for anxiety in the time that God ordains; the sacred time of Sabbath is time that is fully immersed in the goodness and generosity of God who created humanity and let them simply be.

The God of the Sabbath is lord over time. Swoboda identifies the polemic against the Ancient Near Eastern creation myths which had the gods swarming over the world demanding labour and production for the human race. Conversely, Yahweh not only rested, he invited the world to rest with him. This God is a God who is in sovereign control over everything that happens; he creates, he sufficiently provides, and he orders time to include resting.[49] Time is God's sacred creation, something that he has given to the world. The world has confused this creation and has corrupted it for its own ends. Autistic time that is subject to the corruption of trauma, productive demands and delayed or distorted future hope needs reorienting to the fullness of what theotime offers. The time that is created by God is not a time that damages; keeping the Sabbath and remembering the liberative potential of it helps autistic people recognize that the world is not as it should be, that theologically it needs to be reordered, and that we must remember that God is the one who orders time.

Keeping the Sabbath and using the Sabbath as a metaphor helps us find liberation and develop an autistic understanding of liberative time. Liberative time, theotime, is time that does not require productively uncertain futures. Sabbath requires trust because we must cease from our labour and believe that there will be enough. As I write these words I am struck by my inability to achieve this. I keep writing, reading, note-taking, for fear that the waters of academic demands will flood over me. If I cannot produce my thesis drafts, mark my students' work, keep publishing articles, I will not be productive enough. I repeat the cycle of working in a way that cannot be divorced from my autistic self because my working actions become obsessive and repetitive while the quality of my output ever diminishes.

Sabbath keeping makes me trust that my wellbeing and my time are not constrained but instead belong to God. I do not need to produce or worry but I can still my anxious thoughts before God. When the overwhelming worry of the future interrupts the flow of the present, when the past traumas accompany our steps, Sabbath-keeping reorients. It does not resolve, it cannot provide solutions, it does not produce answers or productive values. The power of the Sabbath for autistic theology is that it does not do any of those things, but in so being it resides in the middle – just as Rambo says trauma does. The middle space of the Sabbath is uncertain but peaceful. It is this uncertainty that provides liberation; autistic futures are unscripted (and often painfully short because of reduced lifespans) but the God of all time holds them in his hands. Autistic past is traumatized, but the God of all time resides within that trauma. Autistic present is overwhelming, but rest comes in the keeping of the Sabbath.

Future, when conceived as productive, predictable, financially viable and stable, is not necessarily an autistic future. Some of those elements may exist in autistic futures but they are not givens. However, autistic futures are flexible, unproductive, responsive and stimulating futures that are God-ordained. A Christian view of time specifies that God created, ordained and laid it out before humanity as a gift. Time that is God's time does not require measuring and managing, increasing or decreasing, as death or taxes impose their demands upon it. Autistic time is encompassed in that gift. Autistic time does not need to be constrained by clock or calendar to be received as a gift from God. It is liberated by productive understandings of future earnings or value and of timekeeping and regulation. The present is not managed by meeting the needs of others who hold stopwatches and diaries. The present is a fluid construction for neurodiversity, filled with sensory challenges and flexibility difficulties that present themselves with the intersection of autism and non-autistic worlds.

The past, filled with trauma and pain, is liberated in a theological understanding of autistic time. It may be a past that is permanently entangled in a form of Holy Saturday, or a past that returns to the present frequently with traumatic reliving, but it is a past that can be accepted into God's knowing and receiving. It is not a resolved past that is fixed or healed, but a past that is re-encountered daily and accepted within the boundaries of traumatic remembering and theologies of trauma. Present is a present that is navigated ambiguously; overwhelmings both positive and negative occur frequently. Theological resources of Pentecost and Sabbath proffer reflective and pragmatic potential for reconstructing autistic presents with grace and hope.

Notes

1 Alison Kafer, *Feminist, Queer, Crip* (Bloomington, IN: Indiana University Press, 2013).
2 Kafer, *Feminist, Queer, Crip*, p. 48.
3 Kafer, *Feminist, Queer, Crip*, p. 48.
4 Kafer, *Feminist, Queer, Crip*, p. 53.
5 Kafer, *Feminist, Queer, Crip*, p. 54.
6 Steve Silberman, *NeuroTribes: The Legacy of Autism and the Future of Neurodiversity* (New York: Random House, 2016).
7 Silberman, *NeuroTribes*, p. 75.
8 Artemisia, 'Identity: A Beautiful Work in Progress', in *Spectrum Women: Walking to the Beat of Autism*, ed. Barb Cook, Michelle Garnett and Lisa Morgan (London/Philadelphia, PA: Jessica Kingsley Publishers, 2018), p. 50.
9 Barb Cook, Michelle Garnett, and Lisa Morgan, eds, *Spectrum Women: Walking to the Beat of Autism* (London/Philadelphia, PA: Jessica Kingsley Publishers, 2018).
10 Kafer, *Feminist, Queer, Crip*, p. 63.
11 Douglas Biklen et al., *Autism and the Myth of the Person Alone*, Qualitative Studies in Psychology (New York: New York University Press, 2005), p. 8.
12 Biklen et al., *Autism and the Myth of the Person Alone*.
13 Biklen et al., *Autism and the Myth of the Person Alone*, p. 11.
14 Biklen et al., *Autism and the Myth of the Person Alone*, p. 219.
15 Biklen et al., *Autism and the Myth of the Person Alone*, p. 240.
16 Cynthia Kim, 'Uncooperative Words and Where I Go from Here', Musings of An Aspie, https://musingsofanaspie.com/2013/12/11/uncooperative-words-and-where-i-go-from-here/ (accessed 22.10.21).
17 Cynthia Kim, 'Autistic Regression and Fluid Adaptation', Musings of An Aspie, https://musingsofanaspie.com/2013/12/11/uncooperative-words-and-where-i-go-from-here/ (accessed 22.10.21).
18 Kafer, *Feminist, Queer, Crip*, p. 45.
19 Kafer, *Feminist, Queer, Crip*, p. 25.
20 I have written more on trauma in a chapter in Karen O'Donnell and Katie Cross, eds., *Bearing Witness: Intersectional Perspectives on Trauma Theology* (London: SCM Press, 2022).
21 Shelly Rambo, *Spirit and Trauma: A Theology of Remaining*, 1st ed, (Louisville, KT: Westminster John Knox Press, 2010).
22 Gordon S. Gates, *Trauma, Stigma and Autism: Developing Resilience and Loosening the Grip of Shame* (London/Philadelphia, PA: Jessica Kingsley Publishers, 2019).
23 Gates, *Trauma*.
24 Marcia Mount Shoop, 'Body-Wise: Re-Fleshing Christian Spiritual

Practice in Trauma's Wake', in Eric Boynton, ed., *Trauma and Transcendence: Suffering and the Limits of Theory* (New York: Fordham University Press, 2018).

25 Rambo, *Spirit and Trauma*.
26 Biklen et al., *Autism and the Myth of the Person Alone*.
27 Rebecca S. Chopp, *The Praxis of Suffering: An Interpretation of Liberation and Political Theologies*, (Eugene, OR: Wipf & Stock, 2007).
28 Chopp, *The Praxis of Suffering*, p. 72.
29 Quoted in Chopp, *The Praxis of Suffering*, p. 74.
30 Chopp, *The Praxis of Suffering*, p. 76.
31 Chopp, *The Praxis of Suffering*, p. 77.
32 Chopp, *The Praxis of Suffering*, p. 77.
33 Chopp, *The Praxis of Suffering*, p. 80.
34 Flora A. Keshgegian, *Time for Hope: Practices for Living in Today's World* (New York: Continuum, 2006), p. 2.
35 Kafer, *Feminist, Queer, Crip*, p. 27.
36 Slee, *Fragments for Fractured Times: What Feminist Practical Theology Brings to the Table* (London: SCM Press, 2020).
37 Slee, *Fragments for Fractured Times*.
38 Slee, *Fragments for Fractured Times*, following Riet Bons-Storm, The Incredible Woman (Nashville, TN: Abingdon Press, 1996).
39 For an introduction to autistic anxiety, see https://www.autism.org.uk/advice-and-guidance/topics/mental-health/anxiety (accessed 14/01/2022).
40 National Autistic Society, 'Anxiety', https://www.autism.org.uk/advice-and-guidance/topics/mental-health/anxiety (accessed 14.01.22).
41 As cited in Slee, *Fragments for Fractured Times*.
42 Slee, *Fragments for Fractured Times*.
43 Walter Brueggemann, *Sabbath as Resistance: Saying No to the Culture of Now*, new edn, with Study Guide (Louisville, KT: Westminster John Knox Press, 2017).
44 Brueggemann, *Sabbath as Resistance*, p. xiii.
45 Brueggemann, *Sabbath as Resistance*, p. xv.
46 A. J. Swoboda, *Subversive Sabbath: The Surprising Power of Rest in a Nonstop World* (Grand Rapids, MI: Brazos Press, 2018), p. 6.
47 Brueggemann, *Sabbath as Resistance*, p. 27.
48 Swoboda, *Subversive Sabbath*, p. 7.
49 Swoboda, *Subversive Sabbath*, p. 10.

3

It'll be Alright in the End: Autism, healing and eschatology

The previous chapter attempted to describe an autistic theology of time. Future hope is a significant aspect of autistic time, especially in contrast to the liberal democratic hope described previously. To fully articulate such autistic time, a section devoted to considering autistic lives in relationship with Christian eschatology is useful. Christian eschatology, among many other concerns, relates to the perfection or healing of all things. Eschatology contemplates the end of human time, the resolution of all fallenness, and the hope of something that is unknown but improves upon the world as it is now. Disability theology and autism theology will trouble the assumptions that eschatology tends to make about what the world to come, the resolution of all things and the return of Christ, might involve for individuals and communities.

To start, however, a brief discussion about the ways in which autism is described and how this relates to theologies of healing is necessary. Theologies of healing presuppose problems in need of solutions. Autism is variously described as being a problem to be solved or an identity to be embraced. As I shall hopefully show, this binary is troubling and unhelpful because it ignores the lived reality of so many autistic people. Suffering is a reality of autism. Whence this suffering comes is impossible to fully describe. The ontology of autism is contested and insecure. However, the reality of the suffering is not. As such, any theologies of healing must wrestle with the uncertainties of this ontological conundrum. Such theologies must approach the issues that are complementary to suffering and theology, deal with future hope and the question of healing, and ask what a future hope is if it is not to do with the normativity of neurotypicality and the hope that all autistic people will ultimately be healed?

Shifting paradigms

The relationship between autism and disability is complicated. It is a situation that is unresolvable and intractable because to understand the relationships between the two means navigating the complex environment of suffering and identity. The multiple stakeholders that exist in the world of autism increase the confusion. This ranges from autistic individuals who wish to be understood as different, not less, to those autistic individuals who would accept a cure if it were offered to the parents and medical professionals involved in the care of children and adults. This is a complex and multivalent situation. It incorporates the variance that one individual may feel daily. There are days when I am pleased with the way my brain works; I might even think that it makes me interesting, endearing or fascinating. Those days are rare though; many days I wish that I was not the way I am. The crippling anxiety, the repetitive thoughts, the difficulty with sensory issues, plague my waking hours.

J, who wrote his own story on pages 13–14, notes that stimming can be getting stuck in repetitive actions that he cannot escape from. Years of silence when he could not communicate were profoundly significant for his faith, but that silence was not through choice, but circumstance. J was long assumed to be significantly cognitively impaired. It was only once he was able to spell to communicate that he was able to show the reverse. Yet who would I, or J, be if autism was removed? Virginia Bovell writes in her ethical analysis of autism cures that some parents and autistic people still seek a cure.[1] This, I believe, is understandable. However, there is nuance in this that cannot be overlooked. Bovell calls this debate the 'treatment versus acceptance polarity'. This refers to those who campaign that autism should not be cured but accepted, versus those who believe it is realistic and preferable to continue to seek medical interventions that alleviate the undeniable suffering that accompanies autism.

Jim Sinclair has stated:

> Autism is a way of being. It is pervasive, it colours every experience, every sensation, perception, thought, emotion and encounter, every aspect of existence. It is not possible to separate the autism from the person.[2]

When Sinclair wrote this he was changing the way that people understood autism. Instead of it being regarded as a separate medical condition – such as flu – that infects the person and could be removed by proper treatment, he suggested that autism had essential characteristics. This suggested a change in the way autism and the individual related; that there was potentially something that *should not* be cured and treated. Until this time, treatment, cures and segregation were the standard measures for autistic 'care' as a result of the seemingly insurmountable challenges associated with autistic existence. Autism was, for those individuals who were 'afflicted' and their families, regarded as a tragedy. It caused them to be unable to function fully in society and was a drain on the resources of both the state and relatives. In the earliest days when autism was beginning to be described, the suggested care plan was institutionalization, with parents told they could always have another child. These children, it was suggested, should be placed into facilities and forgotten by the world.[3]

The treatment versus acceptance polarity is a difference in ontological understandings. Autism was (and is) primarily a medical concern when first encountered. It is named by doctors, identified through psycho-medical testing, and described using neurobiological discourse. This neurobiological discourse tells us that autism is the result of faults in the brain. It assumes a standard 'normal species functioning', Bovell says, that finds normative brain and behaviour and then describes deviances from that norm. Autism has variously been described using biological and cognitive terms: 'weak central coherence' (Frith and Happé, 1994), executive dysfunction (Ozonoff, Pennington and Rogers, 1991), 'mindblindness' (Baron-Cohen, 1995), and many evolving theories alongside.[4] All of these, say O'Dell and colleagues, assume the existence of a 'normally functioning social brain'. Testing that involves MRIs to view the dysfunction in the brain indicates the belief of biological causes and possible remedies.

Attendant to these medical models is the assessment of needs. The term 'support needs' is replacing the previously contentious terminology of 'functioning'. Since the removal of the term 'Asperger's syndrome' from the diagnostic manuals in 2013, ways of differentiating autism have changed. It was long the case that if an individual appeared to the world as 'normal' but was also autistic, they would receive an Asperger's diagnosis. If the autism couldn't be hidden, then it was plain 'autism'. This is no longer the case; all autistic people are simply autistic. To describe the help and support that autistic individuals might need has relied upon functioning labels. Functioning labels attempt to describe the level at which a person is able to exist in the world without support. These functioning labels are now condemned because they are reductive for those who are described as 'low functioning' and deceptive for those who are 'high functioning'. In the place of these labels, language has adapted (and likely will continue to do so) to 'support needs'. This is, as with all language, a difficult path to traverse; support needs vary across situations and are not always apparent but often assumed. Autism, according to medical terminology, is replete with degrading and problematic language. However, it is also language that is necessary in order for autistic people to receive help should they wish to do so. Autistic people will often find that they need to access services and support, but without diagnosis and descriptive tools at hand this support is non-existent.

It is apparent that the ontological questions about autism are not abstract but relate in a pragmatic sense to the lives of individuals, both in terms of their own identities and the ways in which they receive help. Parsing the nature of autism, is it a problem that requires a solution, a difference that can cause suffering? Can it fall into the category of 'disability', or is it something separate? Attempting to answer these questions, or at least engage with them, allows for the answers that the Christian tradition might offer. In simple terms, if the problem is not understood then the solution cannot be offered. The alternative ontological understanding for autism is neurodiversity, though this has already seen troubled solutions offered to autism when it is described as a medical *problem*.

Neurodiversity

The neurodiversity paradigm developed in order to counteract the medical model of autism. It also makes use of brain and neurological terminology, but in this case to depathologize them.[5] It depicts humanity as having extensive variation in brains and minds. Diversity speaks to a positive understanding of difference rather than a deficit model. Rather than understanding autism as a condition in need of a cure, or a condition that exists independently of the individual, neurodiversity describes autistic people as part of the infinite variety of human existence. However, Woods, Milton, Arnold and Graby say, as a consequence of neurodiversity, there are contested understandings of the ontology of autism. The paradigm shift that this brings about troubles the understanding of essentialist medical models. Rather, in association with social models of disability (see below), it asserts that suffering and problems that correspond to autism have their source not in the autistic individual, but in the society that disables. Society is responsible for the neglect and stigma, the emotional wounding and isolation and shame that autistic people feel.[6] Indeed, Bovell finds that the suffering that personal accounts of autism describe is associated not with the essential features of autism, but with the additional challenges that surround it.

The neurodivergence thesis also assists in naming that which is not autism,[7] thus highlighting normative assumptions, particularly of psychological and behavioural normativities. Those who do not fit into these constructions of normativity are labelled as 'deviant' and found to lack.[8] This normative understanding has a troubling history, defined in modern times 'by way of the prerogative of psychologists who were living in the shadow of eugenics'.[9] There is an ideological type of person which becomes both a typology and an ethical stance. The rationality of the subject is considered to exist in a particular way so described; and the implications for those who do not exist in this way, post-Enlightenment, are that they – to a greater or lesser extent – lack humanity.

Bertilsdotter Rosqvist, Chown and Stenning identify this as resulting in minority status that perpetuates oppression. They speak of 'neurominorities'. Also connected to this is the current person-first versus identity-first language debate. Bertilsdotter Rosqvist, Chown and Stenning prefer identity-first so as to remove the sense that these divergences are somehow external and an 'interruption' to the existence of the individual. As I will describe in Chapter 5 on community, I find the person-first identity discourse a troubling one theologically. This is not because of a problem with the theorization of neurodiversity, but with the primacy it places on sourcing identity in one particular realm that is at odds, as I understand it, with identity found primarily in Christ. However, pragmatism temporarily overrides this concern and as such I have maintained 'identity first' language throughout this book.

The paradigm does not minimize the reality of lived experiences. Suffering, understood to be sourced not in the essential individual self but the community at large, is prevalent. Bovell finds the treatment versus acceptance polarity to be a false dichotomy. Most autistic individuals, she finds, will accept interventions that are particularized and useful.[10] These treatments do not carry the same ethical imperative when understood through the neurodiversity paradigm. Rather, the imperative is flipped; not only should the autistic individual be given help to adapt to the world that surrounds them, but so too should the world adapt to them. It is insufficient to train the autistic individual to adapt and, in some cases, is actually unethical (see Chapter 6) without the reciprocal adaptations of the neurotypical world.

The impact of critical autism studies

Critical autism studies is a developing field of academic enquiry. It questions the medicalized models of autism and draws attention to their dominance in the field.[11] It incorporates a requirement for emancipation – not just discussion and the predominance of autistic voices in the field itself. It advocates for an understanding of autism culture. Critical autism studies advocates a move away from the deficit model towards a 'critical abilities perspective':

> We take as a starting point valuing the skills and agency of people with autism and work to demonstrate the ways in which dominant assumptions do not fully account for the skills, abilities and identities of people with autism.[12]

This allows for the acknowledgement of the complex personhood of the autistic subject and 'critical re-formulations of normative assumptions of "ability"' particularly in relation to employment.[13] O'Dell and colleagues state that they wish to understand the 'neurologization' of autistic and non-autistic discourse that occurs through the conventional scientific narratives. As such, they reject the use of the word 'typical' because of the identity-forming narrative that such terminology forms. Following Ian Hacking's idea of 'looping' they say that classifications define not only categories but also the populations themselves.[14] This is an unresolved conflict that nonetheless highlights the difficulty that all language and attempts at liberation from oppression have in the continued oppression of people groups. Critical autism studies, as described by O'Dell and colleagues, believes that autism is 'materially and discursively produced'.[15] This highlights once again a further ontological question about autism.

Dan Goodley highlights the difficulties with the social model of disability. Both impairment and pain are unaccounted for in the social model of disability and the correspondence with race and gender.[16] He describes the link between ableism and disablism that results in their necessary correspondence. Disability is 'haunted by the spectre of ability' because 'ability needs disability to be by its side in order to speak of what it is not'.[17] However, ableism is a term that is stretched beyond its limits. He suggests instead the split term dis/ability, which allows for the engagement with both ideas and the acknowledgement that they are reliant upon each other. It rejects binaries of ability and disability and considers that there is a spectrum that incorporates the liberal democratic views of production and questions them. It incorporates stakeholders in their own variance, parents and children, reminding us that the parent too has been politicized in the politics of disability.

This is also a difficulty that I find in the neurodiversity paradigm. If such a paradigm seeks only to account for difference and plurality of neurotypes as the different computer processors metaphor is used, then it achieves this well.[18] However, it does not give us language for either suffering or hope. Goodley makes a political statement but it is my belief that it is also a deeply theological one. The situation of the human condition and the value placed upon all people is something that has always concerned theological investigation. Woods and colleagues suggest that reliance upon a social model of disability

> ignores how autism runs in families, the flourishing distinctive autistic culture and the importance of self-diagnosis to autistic persons' sense of well-being.[19]

The significance of this is the recognition, perhaps forgotten somewhat in the neurodiversity movement, of the nature of difficulty in the experience of autism. Although critical autism studies would reject the deficit narratives of autism, they would also not necessarily contribute to the 'celebratory approach to autism' that can come from over-emphasis on autism being solely difference.[20] In the same vein, Chloe Silverman highlights that no amount of inclusivity or autism research (making sure that autistic people are represented in the field of autism research) nor public understanding of autism – things that in particular the neurodiversity movement would reach for – can alleviate the very real difficulties encountered by autistic people:

'The most unsettling of them stem from the reality of dependency and of suffering that can't be ameliorated by changes in the social or physical environment.'[21] Silverman suggests that the social construction of autism, the notion that autism is only a problem within a neurotypical social model, perhaps misses the reality of autistic lives who cannot adequately adjust to their environment. Similarly, Francisco Ortega suggests that 'emancipatory discourse' risks the reduction of autism primarily to an issue of identity politics.[22] Both identify the actual suffering that autistic people experience, and suggest that this alone is not removed simply by changing the ontological status of autism.

One of the issues that an eschatology chapter should consider is suffering. A liberation theology seeks to liberate those who suffer. Neurodiveristy and critical autism studies both suggest that it is not *from* autism that the liberation should come, but from oppression. However, I find it difficult to locate all the suffering that occurs with the autistic life entirely in the social realm without qualification. For example, my difficulties with sensory stimulation could sometimes be caused by living in a neurotypical world, but not always. If our theological notions of hope and healing locate the suffering attendant to autism entirely in the social realm, then this is perhaps a false dichotomy. It even perpetuates the misunderstandings that have existed thus far. We reject talking about people being 'with autism' so it seems that we should also reject people as being 'with social lives', for example. We are autistic people and social people. We cannot be a person with a social world but are in fact social people who are fundamentally social in their existence in the world.

No matter how we parse the cause, autistic people and neurodivergent people persist in finding aspects of life difficult even if the paradigm shifts noted above change the language that we use and the causes that we accredit to autism. Although we wish to remove ideas of deficit, illness and the power of normativity from the agenda, I also want to propose a realistic view. Being autistic can be extremely hard and theology should be able to offer something that helps. Theology is fundamentally concerned with that which is ultimately hopeful, and it is to that hope that I now turn.

Autism, disability and healing

Frances MacKenney-Jeffs raises the important critique of such a move in theologies of disability, one that is potentially reductionist, equating disability with any other type of suffering, as well as dangerous by association with the typically charged relationship between suffering and evil.[23] Making a sharp and concise distinction between suffering and evil – and ending the association of suffering with ontological evil – is necessary. I do not, will not, associate autism with evil, or even the privation of good or any other construction of evil. However, I will associate autism with some suffering because to be diagnosed as autistic requires the use of a deficit model that in turn implies an amount of suffering. Self-diagnosis similarly stems from a recognition of at least 'difference', though more often it is felt as 'difficulty' and the suffering that is a result of that.

Theological accounts of healing necessarily raise questions of divine providence and the nature of seeking help from God. When God does not heal (or does, but only after prolonged suffering), when God seemingly allows unreasonable or disproportionate suffering, the pervasive question remains: to what extent does God command our steps and to what extent can we ask him to change them? Is this within the control of the divine presence? Liberation and charismatic theologies trouble each other with accounts of the sovereignty of God. They do so in such a way that they are not neatly resolved. It is not the intention of this chapter to move towards a particular solution; such a solution would be in the realms of theodicies and outside the scope of this book. Rather, the questions as they apply to autism and neurodivergence should be asked, problematized, and directions of thought indicated.

I do advocate for belief in the reality of petitionary prayer as a mode of seeking divine help, and of its reception by God. The belief held by charismatic Christians, and confirmed by my own academic research alongside commentators such as Christopher G. Woznicki, that Pentecostal/charismatic Christians believe in answered prayer do account for experiences of it, and do hold in dynamic tension suffering and the value of petitionary prayer. It is the case of course that prayer has many descriptors, such as Simone Veil's 'attention' and the monastic practices of contemplation that still have profound value today. Especially in times of suffering, being able to draw near to God without task, outcome or solution is incomparable.

Karen O'Donnell, in her moving and theologically exceptional work on reproductive loss, delves into the meanings and purpose of such moments.[24] O'Donnell reconceives petitionary prayer as invalid and unhelpful in the way in which it casts the divine as unjust, answering some prayers while ignoring others. Rather, apophatic theology, saying what God (and consequently prayer) is not, is O'Donnell's proposal. Taking this cue, what is it to bring to God our desire to fit in better; to not feel the cold as if it is pain; to be able to speak; to have a friend; to restore broken relationships; and to feel that these prayers are not answered? Whether or not an individual wishes to be 'healed' of autism (and I would advocate strongly to *not* pray that prayer, although empathize with those who do) there are associated prayers that go unanswered. These associated prayers are symptoms of the socially constructed disability that autism can be; these prayers are the prayers of autistic bodyminds that do not fit in to the world in which they exist. Sometimes it is not necessary to pray these prayers, and on those days – rejoice! However, often these prayers are necessary, not because autism is a fault that needs repair but because suffering exists – and often exists in correspondence to autistic experiences in neurotypical worlds. O'Donnell suggests that rather than understanding the agency of God in the process of biology, we should understand human agency and divine love as the mode by which biological processes come to be. Therefore, these elements are not credited to God, in O'Donnell's instance the causes of miscarriage – but to biological processes that the divine is not in control of. This leads to a place of ambiguity, where prayers are for the comfort and peace of individuals rather than for divine intervention in mechanical processes. This is a reassuring avenue of theological dialogue, one in which neither the pray-er nor the divine is held to account for failures of prayer.

However, I am somewhat uneasy with this account of providence because of the questions that remain over God's sovereignty. I desperately want to understand God as present and active in the life of believers, as well as account for suffering and unanswered prayer in the lives of autistic individuals. The only way in which I can accomplish this is to fail to do so. I offer here threads and patchwork that do not assemble to create a whole; rather, they are suggestive of a particularly charismatic/Pentecostal reading of prayer, trauma and autism.

I am inclined to turn to theologies of trauma to unpack and unweave these complicated elements. I do so cautiously because I do not wish to imply that all autistic people are traumatized (although I do think this is conceivable) and I do not wish to abandon the traditional notion of Christian hope. Instead, I want to examine that Christian hope with a clear mind, taking into account the distressing lack of answers faced by autistic individuals, and the persistent hope that autistic Christians must cling to while acknowledging that in their experience the negotiation of autism, social worlds and theology is troubling. It is ever my intention to do theological work that is of use, work that directly benefits those who read it. However, the usefulness of this chapter must ultimately be in the questions that it raises and the acceptance of those readers who find that the answers do not readily appear. However, hope remains. It is this hope, in the risen Christ Jesus, that makes the work possible and have potential, even if this potential is not realized as quickly as we would like.

Discourses on healing: a very brief Pentecostal introduction

Pentecostal and charismatic churches are infamous for their healing ministries. In formulations of core Pentecostal doctrine, healing exists as a key tenet, part of the fourfold or fivefold gospel: salvation, sanctification, baptism in the Spirit, divine healing and the coming kingdom of God.[25] Wolfgang Vondey describes this as the theological narrative by which Pentecostalism interprets the biblical story and applies it to current life. With autism's troubled relationship with medical deficit models it might be unsuitable to consider theologies of healing, for what do we seek to be healed from? Indeed, Grant Macaskill questions the notion of applying biblical narratives of healing, as Pentecostal and charismatic Christians do, to the lived experience of autism. Healing, as conceived of by Pentecostals and charismatic Christians, correlates with the origins of the Pentecostal story. Existing in places of oppression, be it racial or gender oppression, Pentecostalism grew out of the margins of society.[26] In situations of relative powerlessness Pentecostals gathered and, consequently, subverted power structures, forming communities of marginalized people who experienced the power of God in their midst. Set within this framework, Pentecostal emphasis on healing takes on a slightly different hue for it was part of the dynamic of resistance and the move of God in the midst of those who were powerless to stop their own suffering or pain, but powerful in the Spirit to transform their lives. Despite this beginning, the emphasis on healing in Pentecostalism and charismatic offshoots has taken a less palatable turn. As I have noted elsewhere, it is the divergent elements that seek inappropriate healing that do damage to the subversive practice that prayer for healing once was.[27]

Pentecostalism originally had an anti-materialistic stream that rejected all earthly troubles as fleeting and imminently to end because of the return of Christ.[28] However, as time went by this emphasis changed and two new emphases emerged from the realized eschatology. This realized eschatology said that although the coming kingdom was still coming (although maybe not as soon as originally expected), the kingdom was also a present reality. In this eschatology, formulated through readings of Acts 2, which indicated the Spirit was present and operative now in the body of believers, the kingdom has very real power for change: for the charismata to be demonstrated. Two different paths emerged from this realized eschatology that have shaped the movement, and those who have come from it, both negatively and positively. The first, which we shall look at now, was the prosperity gospel, and the second was the liberation dynamic in Pentecostalism.

The twentieth century brought about a correlation in Pentecostal theology and practice with American values of success and the larger evangelical movement.[29] As a consequence, the movement became less marginal and more socially acceptable. Alongside this political and sociological move there was the continued interpretation of Acts 3.6, 16 and 4.10 as passages stating that vocalized faith would bring about healing. This faith was based in the healing work of Christ via the atonement. It also interacted with theologies of sin and the demonic, accounting for much suffering by crediting it to a personal and active devil that operates in the world today.

Sprung from these narratives came the Word of Faith movement and its offspring that persist in, I hope, the margins of Pentecostal and charismatic churches today. The Word of Faith movement claimed that suffering from sickness, situation or condition was not what a Christian should accept in their life today. Cast in the light of spiritual warfare, these conditions are deemed unacceptable to Christians who have Christ living within them and have rejected the impact of evil in their lives. If an individual is sick, then they are healed by 'naming and claiming' their healing. Their healing is possible because of their level of faith. It must be spoken out, this word (often called a 'rhema' word), in order to give power to the faith and enact it in their life.[30] In this 'theology' the lived experience of those who suffer is viewed as guilt for lack of faith. If words must be spoken correctly, then those who cannot speak cannot be healed. Sin correlates closely with those who suffer; if a person is considered in deficit, then they are likely to be so because of their sin. Healing here is not life-giving but condemning; it does not offer freedom from the oppressions of the world but adds to it with salvation accompanied by works of 'faith' that are restrictive and judgemental. This theology takes its place alongside the history of Christian theology that represents disability as a condition and consequence of sin. Found both within and outside the Bible, the moral association of disability and sinfulness (e.g. Leviticus 21.17–23), or inability to access the temple for rites, correlates a moral dimension with a physical reality and finds both wanting.

This is 'disabling theology', as Nancy L. Eiesland calls it.[31] Accompanying these ideas is the notion that suffering is virtuous, and a divine image that is connected to a conception of physical that is not disabled, says Eiesland, and I would add mentally 'perfect' or at least normative. Therefore, not only is disability a profound theological lack in the lives of those who 'suffer' it, it is also a condition that the church must act towards. Spatially the disabled person is placed on the outside: they are outside the moral acceptability of God; they are outside the church as agents who can act on their own behalf, but rather are subject to charitable and organizational works. As I shall argue in the next chapter concerning community, this space is not divine space; it is space that 'others' those who are placed within it. Pentecostalism, when it wears its triumphalist wealth and health garb, joins the sad ranks of church tradition that objectifies and judges those it construes as other.

This is a long way from the original Pentecostal theologies and has tarnished that which is good in the theology and movement. Amos Yong rightly highlights the consequent difficulties of interactions between disability studies and disability theologies and Pentecostal theologies. Two obstructions to dialogue exist: the lack of political interest that Pentecostalism is (mis)interpreted as having, and the emphasis upon healing. Political interest for Pentecostalism and autism relate to understanding autistic lives as in need of political liberation from liberal democratic oppression.

Peculiar healing and the difficulties of language

Language critiques are helpful for the progression of this argument, particularly in drawing out the nature of the political oppression of autistic people. In British disability studies there is a distinction between disability and impairment; this distinction is to highlight the socially constructed element of disability, the communal responsibility, and the distance from particular individuals.[32] This is a useful distinction theologically, allowing for a similar separation, founded in language but explored in social and community discussions between suffering and healing. Although they do not map perfectly on to each other, suffering can be correlated with disability, and impairment with healing. Correlating disability with suffering is an acknowledgement that social constructions cause the disabled person to suffer; in other words, they might not suffer if they were not in the social situation they are in. If healing and impairment are linked it is because an individual situation can be regarded with an eye towards that which needs change. If an individual is neurodivergent and in their own particular existence finds no need to be healed, then there is no theological case for intervention by the community of faith for healing.

However, this allows also for the muddy, difficult and particular in this discourse. It is sometimes the case that healing is sought by individuals who are neurodivergent for their particular circumstances. By this I do not relate healing to a fundamental change of self – that is, prayer for change in neuro structures (although I can imagine that these prayers are sometimes uttered and I feel profound sympathy for those praying them) – but prayer for healing of trauma, pain (such as is felt with sensory sensitivities), healing into speech (if it is so desired), healing of relationships and other things that are particular and individualized. Suffering, as it is linked to this communal and societal understanding of disability, is that which is imposed upon a person from the construction of the social world that they inhabit. This is the responsibility that the church has in order to theologically recognize the structures that prohibit freedom, that restrain fulfilment, and oppress autistic and other neurodivergent people from flourishing in the way that they are divinely ordained to do.

I have presented the case in the previous chapter and elsewhere that autistic lives have the potential to be traumatized lives.[33] They can exist on a plane of trauma because of the stigma of autism, the social relational difficulties that exist in communities and families, and the sensory and physical encounters with the environment around them that are objectionable to them. Autistic trauma is *peculiar trauma*; it is peculiar because it is non-standard in its experience and description. It does not necessarily fit the usual understandings of trauma and it is peculiar because the individual is encountered by the world as *odd, strange and uncanny*. Trauma is a fundamental fracture with self. It can be a traumatic incident, one that changes the life of the individual in such a way that there is no return to the time that existed before – for instance, a serious car accident or a sexual assault. The life that preceded this traumatizing incident can never again be re-lived; the self is changed. For autistic trauma this self is, very early on, separated in the individual. Each encounter with the physical and social world is troubled, and as such the self is found to be outside of the world in which it is inside – an impossible position. This impossible situation, however, is possible and lived by those who are autistic and this leads to fracture, a rending of personhood into pieces that cannot be rebuilt in a meaningful way.

When an autistic person is unable to connect with those around them, if they struggle to engage in church services, to maintain relationships, to be employed or to be understood, they feel they are ostracized both from God and from other people. Their relationality is impacted. This damaged relationality is elemental to traumatic lives; the autistic person is disintegrated, their self no longer is whole. In the same way, an autistic person rarely feels safe; they are at risk at all times. This risk is perceptual – fight or flight responses triggered in sensory processing – and it is effectual, being that more risks are associated with autistic lives through economic, sexual and violent means. This 'un-safety' is also traumatizing.

Despite the uncertainty and the reluctance to claim 'disability' labels for autistic lives, there is value in employing generous language for constructive work in theology. By 'generous', I mean language that accounts for many experiences without requiring strict definitions and precise and scientific diagnoses. Whether autism is a disability or not is unclear when societal disability models are applied to autistic experiences. However, as Marcia Mount Shoop notes, the ability of theologians to 'know it when we see it' allows for us to make use of disability, trauma, suffering and pain theologically in order to use language helpfully and profitably for discourse.[34] No standards are required to be met in trauma theology; it is not necessary to meet criteria in order to engage with the discourses of trauma theology. In the same way I do not want language to become prescriptive in autism theology; instead, it must be generous and gracious. This means that those who use identity-first language are able to engage with those that use person-first; that those who identify as disabled are not separate from those who do not. This allows for a conversation about future hope and healing not to be inhibited to participants via the language of disability and deficit. I reject such deficit language but I embrace generous conversations that allow for many participants to question and trouble the oppressive normativity that autistic people are subject to.

Making use of language available to describe trauma and suffering allows for constructive theological work. Healing is also described generously, incorporating many different facets of struggles and pain that can be healed by divine intervention. By restricting notions of healing to deficit models of autism, the potential for theology to positively intervene for the good of autistic people is greatly reduced. However, if generous language is used which incorporates much lived experience of autistic people themselves, the offer of divine healing that is understood in Pentecostal and charismatic traditions has great potential for flourishing autistic lives.

Trauma, liberation and the Pentecostal charism

> But we have this treasure in clay jars, so that it may be made clear that this extraordinary power belongs to God and does not come from us. We are afflicted in every way, but not crushed; perplexed, but not driven to despair; persecuted, but not forsaken; struck down, but not destroyed; always carrying in the body the death of Jesus, so that the life of Jesus

may also be made visible in our bodies. For while we live, we are always being given up to death for Jesus' sake, so that the life of Jesus may be made visible in our mortal flesh. (2 Corinthians 4.7–11)

This passage is a troubled and troubling one – it tells a distressing tale of persecution and difficulties. It is possible to read it as a passage that glorifies suffering, that says Christ is manifest in the suffering that Paul underwent. However, it is also one that implies a theology of remaining; that Paul is 'always carrying in the body the death of Jesus'. Christ's death, the Holy Saturday time, where all is dead and lost, is preserved in the suffering of Paul.

Trauma theologies confirm the need for remaining, for staying with, for rejecting the need for resolution and repair. In her groundbreaking work, Shelly Rambo writes of the need to remain in the time of Holy Saturday, the time between the death of Christ and the unknown of his resurrection.[35] The purpose of this remaining is to witness to trauma, not to resolve that which cannot be resolved straightforwardly. Rather than proclaiming healing, a theology of remaining requires us not to track the redemption story in a linear fashion. The difficulty with such tracking, of death to life, is that it can ignore the suffering and require the resolution of pain that can be impossible to find. I can live in the hope of the resurrection but I cannot say that the hope has changed my lived autistic experience now. I am still oppressed by the situation that I am in.

Trauma theology reminds us that theology is not necessarily a producer of neat theological solutions to problems. This is crucial when considering the messy difficulties of healing. There can be no clear pronouncement about the relationship between healing and autism.

So often, particularly in charismatic/Pentecostal communities, this is a foreign concept, impossible as a faith-filled response. It is better to travail in prayer, to anoint with oil, to declare freedom, and to access biblical (or perceived biblical) promises for life today. Macaskill reminds his readers that we are prone to read the biblical accounts of healing through modern, individualistic eyes that focus on health in medical and liberal democratic productive ways.[36] This, he warns, may not be the way in which flourishing is conceived of biblically. As such, it would be tempting to twin this troubled notion that is petitionary prayer for healing with a reluctance to remain *theologically* in suffering and say that there is no solution to autistic suffering that can be found in the charismatic and Pentecostal theological communities. However, it is the combination of liberation theology and Pentecostal *conscientization* that provides an avenue for reflection that works with that which is good in trauma theology – acknowledging suffering and eschewing resolving – with an active stance, one that works for a better future even if the present is not easily resolved. In this way I do perceive a troubled relationship between the two theological models; liberation theology seeks to act and change, whereas trauma theology resists such change as fundamentally at odds with the necessary theological work of remaining.

Therefore, I propose a two-stage process, where trauma theology acknowledges the existence of trauma and the impossibility of theodicies that seek to account for or acknowledge the role God takes in trauma. This stage is one that theologizes the existence of autism, the problematic relationship with disability and autism, and the complicated relationship with neurodiversity acceptance models and lived experience. Trauma theology allows for these things to be preserved as unresolved, sites of suffering and fracturing of selfhood. These things occur in the lives of autistic people frequently and the ability to return to the time before is lost. However, alongside this liberation theology can and should operate. For although there is an accounting of trauma there is a theological work to do that attempts to prevent trauma from occurring again, that seeks not to resolve that which has happened before or to reframe it as something that was in fact good (the so-called redemptive suffering model). Liberation theology does not necessarily whitewash the past but offers a model for change based on the gospel which allows us to frame this complex narrative of autism theologically and hopefully.

Liberation theology starts with human experience and seeks

to apply the values found in the gospel to those who are marginalized. It relates to this chapter on eschatology in surprising ways. Liberation theology is usually framed as this-worldly, focused on political and societal change rather than on future hope. However, this is insufficient in this chapter because autism theologies must engage with healing, ideas about normative human existence and disability. All of this has, of course, a future element. If a person is not healed now then perhaps they will be in the eschaton? What would be hoped for in the future? What is an autistic eschatology if it necessarily rejects notions of healing and perfection in the future? Can an autistic liberation theology answer this question? Does it have the tools required? To this the answer is yes, if taken alongside Pentecostal ideas of conscientization.

Earlier in this chapter I noted the two changes to early Pentecostalism that occurred during the twentieth century. The first, sometimes called health-and-wealth theology, was dismissed as damaging. However, the second has much more liberative potential. Pentecostalism's development into a this-worldly theology came about as the community moved away from the belief that the imminent return of Christ was signalled by their new understanding of the gifts of the Spirit. As this embedded into a more normative community behaviour, where the charism of the Spirit was experienced as a daily and lived reality, it became necessary to understand the Pentecostal worldview in light of the works of the Spirit. This is where Pentecostalism and liberation theology meet.

Cheryl J. Sanders notes that Pentecostalism has a history of social justice without a worked-through theology to accompany it.[37] This began with the belief that salvation is accompanied by liberation from all that oppresses people; this is achieved by the Holy Spirit's work in the lives of believers, and existed alongside the black theologies of liberation that were often found in the Pentecostal churches. A fluidic ecclesiology, says Sanders, understands that the sacred, via the church, transforms society. Right from the very beginning of the movement this is embedded in Pentecostalism, in its nascent form. William J. Seymour described some women who were baptized in the Spirit, and immediately the church became diverse. In that diversity of gender and race, social structures were dissolved in light of the equalizing gift of the Spirit. This is accounted for in the Pentecostal association with Acts and the giving of the Holy Spirit to many different tribes and tongues. This gift was given to a great diversity of people, illustrating that there was no differentiation between those who were willing to receive the Spirit. Of those who were touched by the Spirit there was no ongoing differentiation between them; they were all one in Christ through the Spirit. In the same way, at the very beginnings of American Pentecostalism in Azusa Street where the first American Pentecostal church began, there was a liberation from oppressions in society. This theme was perpetuated by Pentecostal ministers and members; for example, in the 1950s Bishop Smallwood Williams of Bible Way Church, Worldwide led a legal battle against segregated schools. The history of Pentecostalism is rife with liberative actions of believers and communities.

Archer and Waldrop recognize that liberal democratic values of success, such as those mentioned in earlier chapters as judging autistic lives, have no place in Pentecostal churches.[38] The early Pentecostal churches transformed the lives of the poor and the marginalized by offering them voice and belonging. Selina Stone finds this history to therefore be a political history, one that expects what happens in the life of the individual to permeate into the public sphere.[39] Stone calls this 'alternative citizenship', which corresponds to Archer and Waldrop:

> The early North American Pentecostal hermeneutical practice functioned as a means of liberation for those who were marginalized by modernistic culture and mainline Christianity.[40]

The suspicion of the alternative communities of Pentecostals was directed at those who did not live out a transformative, full gospel life in which the Spirit was understood to be poured out on to the marginalized.

Cheryl Bridges Johns describes Pentecostal formation as 'conscientization'.[41] This is where people are aware of the situations of oppression that are around them and their ability to effect some change in that. This is because of the revelatory and prophetic character of Pentecostalism: 'Pentecostalism had a dual prophetic role: denouncing the dominant patterns of that status quo and announcing the patterns of God's kingdom.'[42] As such, this prophetic role, initiated by the Holy Spirit, was subversive to the culture around it. Rather than describing the world according to the standards of modern thinking, Pentecostalism has a 'prophetic imagination' (after Walter Brueggemann) which describes the reality of God in the world and reveals the oppressions. The Holy Spirit's presence in the lives of the believers allows Pentecostals to describe a 'sacramental reality'.[43]

The presence of God in the troubled and suffering lives of believers does not equal resolution and healing as the Word of Faith Pentecostals might imagine; instead, it is the enduring presence of God while the believers wrestle and become aware of the oppressions in their lives. The healing that is understood in this Pentecostalism is sociological, economic and political as well as bio-medical. The Holy Spirit is transformative of all spaces into which she is invited, but that transformation is not predicated by the uttering of 'magic' words of faith, of providing evidence of the correct way of being; and does not result in particular outcomes that can be predicted by human agents. That belief is 'health and wealth belief' and is not the Pentecostal liberative healing hermeneutic. Rather, the Holy Spirit is not 'tame' in the Pentecostal imagination and the promise of healing is not the caricatured one; instead, there is a hopeful and optimistic interpretation of healing that incorporates many facets – not just the healing of physical and medical conditions.

Pentecostal healing is a social healing, one that levels the playing field, a healing that equalizes those who are unequal. Pentecostalism was born in the margins, giving voice to the poor and the oppressed (primarily black people and women) who were not heard in any other way. Pentecostalism raised up the uneducated black woman and allowed her to preach, speak and be heard.

Will I be autistic in heaven?

Disability, autism and suffering all coalesce in one issue: eschatology. How will those who are disabled, autistic or in any way 'non-normative' be at the resurrection? Will those who have had an accident and lost a limb still be without that limb? Will those who were born with congenital defects still have those in their resurrection body? For an individual who has been able-bodied throughout their life but acquired a disability at one point, how will their body present in the age to come? What about neurodivergent individuals? How will different ways of thinking and presenting to the world be translated to resurrection bodies? What about speech – will non-speaking individuals be speakers?

The issue at hand revisits the questions of normativity. It troubles assumptions of what is not only 'normal' for humanity but applies to it a moral category – perfection. The assumption that 'in heaven' all will be made 'perfect' means that which is not perfect now will be fixed. If an autistic person is no longer autistic in heaven, they will have their autism removed, fixed, repaired or changed, and will – at long last – be the perfect human that they were previously unable to be. The difficulty that autism theology and disability theology have at this critical point is conflation. All forms of bodily and mental conditions are reduced to convergence. They are treated as if they are the same issue. The elderly person with diabetes who tragically has their foot amputated as the disease progresses may very well question the bodily resurrection that doesn't include their lost foot. They would wish in their imaginative wonderings about the life to come to picture themselves with their foot. They lost it late in their life; most of their life they had both feet and the disability that comes from their amputation has not formed their existence until more recently. However, a person born without a limb, who has always navigated the world without it, who adapted at every stage to exist in a world that assumes two arms and two legs, may argue they would not want a limb that is not theirs to appear all of a sudden in the world to come; after all, they know no such limb, it would not be theirs.

Then we might consider a person with dementia, will they have dementia in the resurrection? Would the verbose and outgoing woman who lost her ability to speak as her brain lost functions that it had always had want to be unable to speak for all eternity? Probably not. Yet, what about the autistic individual who never spoke? They have communicated instead by assisted communication technologies, their brain and their relationships constructed via this media of engaging the world, not through the spoken word. They are articulate, just like J (see pp. 13–14 for J's writing), in the written word and are known by others through that way of communicating. They might want to be able to speak in the future, but they might not be able to, and who would they be if they could speak when everything about them has been formed through the communication that they have now?

It does not need much explanation to trouble these ideas. The neurodivergent discourse tells us that autism, and other neurodivergences, are not necessarily faulty mechanisms in need of repair but part of the diversity of human existence. The question of normativity is not a new one and can be found in ancient Christian texts. In *The City of God*, Augustine writes:

> The man who cannot view the whole is offended by what he takes to be the deformity of a part; but this is because he does not know how it is to be adapted or related to the whole. We know of men who were born with more than five fingers or five toes. This is a trivial thing and not any great divergence from the norm. God forbid, however, that someone who does not know why the Creator has done what He has done should be foolish enough to suppose that God has in such cases erred in allotting the number of human fingers. So, then, even if a greater divergence should occur, He whose work no one may justly condemn knows what He has done.[44]

Augustine continues to describe a number of individuals with 'conditions' that would be recognized today: androgyny, unsurvivable congenital differences, children who look unlike their parents. Brian Brock comments that for Augustine all normativity is found in Christ, that a physical resurrection only occurs in Christ.[45] Thus, a resurrection of a 'perfect' human body is only one that is found *in Christ*. Augustine then concludes that there is no such normative human outside of the person of Christ, so Augustine's anthropology can perhaps be said to embrace autism. If this is so it is not because Augustine accepts the nature of autism as yet another unacceptable post-Fall impairment, but rather that all humans are post-Fall impaired. The universalizing that Augustine applies is liberatory here; it means that neurodivergent people are like all other people – subject to fallen, sinful conditions and in need of salvation. Neurodivergent people are sinful. They are in the same state in Augustine's theological anthropology as all others and in the same need of salvation; and we shall revisit this idea in the section on Christian practices. This applies to our understanding of heaven in a profound way; they are just as non-normative as all other people who are not Christ! However, despite all being resurrected in Christ and all being subject to the Fall, Augustine believes that those who are 'less than' perfect will be more changed:

> Concerning monsters [monstra] which are born and live, however quickly they die, neither is resurrection to be denied them, nor is it to be believed that they will rise again as they are, but rather with an amended and perfected body ... And so all other births which, as having some excess or some defect or because of some conspicuous deformity [deformitate], are called monsters, will be brought again at the resurrection to the true form of human nature [humanae naturae figuram].[46]

Brock takes this to mean that each individual is subject to the Christological normalization in their own particular way. It is troubling because, despite the universalizing of all resurrected in Christ, there are some who are – in the manner of *Animal Farm* – more equal to Christ than others. This is unsatisfactory. What eschatology should be able to do is account for the ending of pain and misery in the perfection of the world to come without enforcing universalizing normativity with ideas of perfect human bodies. Answering the idea of disability or of neurodivergence with 'we're all disabled anyway' is the same as the oft-cited maxim 'we're all on the spectrum somewhere'. This is, of course, not true. We may all be falling short and all sinners, but that is not enough for those who lived in a different way from the majority. What, then, can be done to tease apart eschatologically ideas of normativity from suffering that is attendant on disability and to autism?

I have described how I believe autistic lives to be traumatized because of their existence in an inhospitable world. Their identity as a person is fractured, uninhabitable and unwelcome. It is identity that becomes the differential between standards of human physical perfection imposed from without and eschatological healing promised with the coming again of Christ. Popular Christian eschatology suffers from the 'pie in the sky when I die' trope that assumes heaven, in the sky, will be populated by beautiful people who are all having a wonderful time enjoying themselves in a perfect manner.

When I was a child, before I knew anything about autism, I used to entertain an anxiety about heaven. I thought it sounded awful. I had a picture in my head of an overcrowded, over-populated market town in middle England (obviously a very middle-class childhood!) full of people living together, in community and talking to one another. It was, in my mind, like the tea and coffee bit at the end of church for all eternity. Then, I would read that it would be worship for ever and ever too. My image of the 'market-town heaven' became one that involved music all the time. Not just any music, but trumpets and loud brass instruments. Angels singing without stopping. Alongside this, hell I was told, was full of weeping and wailing and gnashing of teeth. As far as I could see, whichever afterlife one ended up with was going to be loud and full of people. Neither appealed. My childhood anxiety (and sometimes still a current one) suffers from the terror of normativity creeping into theology. We must all be be saved – I understood that – but being saved towards something that sounded horrible. I would later read Adrian Plass asking whether there would be cricket in heaven (I was *quite* an unusual ten-year-old) and it occurred to me that for as many people who would want cricket, there would be plenty who didn't. How could these things be accommodated? Would there be a section of the eternal city dedicated to test matches that went on for longer than four days plus an extra fifth? If your preference runs to Twenty20 games, would this be allowed? How do we understand the disappointment of your team losing the cricket game in a heaven that is supposed to be perfect? Heaven was a particularly concerning idea for my childhood self because very little of it made sense when taking into account the diversity of human life, preferences and behaviour. Although this is a humorous take on the problem, it didn't feel funny when I was a child and it raises an important question about the future.

I've made the case that the neurodiversity paradigm and critical autism studies both in their own manner trouble the idea that autism requires healing. I have proposed that despite the typical understanding of charismatic and Pentecostal healing, there is scope in the theology of that tradition to consider healing in profitable ways, with regard to liberation into the Spirit-filled community of faith. This, then, rejects the idea of praying for healing from a condition, but instead healing towards inclusivity and freedom. However, there is also the difficulty that suffering and trauma are familiar to most people with autism and that the neurodiversity paradigm must accommodate that and so should autism theology. Traditional understandings of heaven and the resurrection understand that suffering will cease. This has led theology to assume that disability and autism will no longer exist in heaven. As I have indicated, this is difficult to countenance in the cases where these factors are fundamental to the person's existence and to the way that they encounter and understand the world. The formative elements of both disability and autism are woven so tightly into the fabric of existence that to try to take these threads out would be to cause the whole material to disintegrate.

Amos Yong offers an interpretation of the healing motif in Luke that is useful.[47] The Gospel of Luke appears to promote the healing of all ailments and to propagate negative stereotypes about blindness and lameness. However, says Yong, Luke subverts the ideas of the time that believed that bodily ailments reflected inner spiritual states. Both Zacchaeus, who was noted to be short (Luke 19.9), and the Ethiopian eunuch (Acts 8.38), would have been excluded from worship by the contemporary Jewish law. In Luke, however, these individuals are moved from the margins into the centre by the actions of Jesus and the knowledge of the Spirit respectively.

This is in fulfilment of the promise in Isaiah 56.3–5 that the eunuch will be included in the worshipping community. In the parables of the wedding feast and the eschatological banquet (Luke 14.7–24) Jesus overturns the standard hospitality rules and invites those who are the socially excluded. Yong claims that it is not the healing of physical impairments that mean that people will flourish in the Day of the Lord, but the inclusion of those who are on the outside. This is made possible by the paradigmatic work of the Holy Spirit who allows those of different languages to speak to one another (Acts 2.6–8). One such reading of this event, says Yong, is that it is a miracle of inspired hearing rather than inspired speaking.

This change of emphasis is constructive for autism theology as it suggests that the onus is not on the 'speaker' to be effective but the hearer to be attentive. Non-speaking autistic people in the Spirit's plan are not required to be understood by learning speech or healing into speech but to be *heard* by those who until now are failing or unable to listen. The Day of the Lord is begun at Pentecost with the coming of the Spirit and is completed in the end of things with the free communication through hearing of those who were unable to be heard before. This is the heart of the liberation programme for autism. Voices that have long been silenced will be heard not because they are healed but because the listeners are healed. This is metaphoric in the manner in which this listening occurs. It is not the listening of able-bodied, hearing ears but it is the listening of attention. That attention must come in many different forms depending upon the individuals. A theology that required normative hearing would exclude autists who do not speak with their voices (as well as d/Deaf people who do not hear) but a theology that understood hearing as attention and the ability to understand as inclusive and hopeful.

IT'LL BE ALRIGHT IN THE END

Heaven, amid the troubling cacophony of people and noise that my ten-year-old self was worried about, will at least be one where communication is possible through imaginative ways in the power of the Spirit. This implies my conclusion: that those who do not speak will still not speak 'in heaven'. I suggest that these non-speaking autists and their speaking sisters and brothers will remain autistic in heaven. For Yong, the important element of the resurrection of disabilities (and neurodiversity) is what I have already hinted at: the conferring of identity. If identity is conferred in a disability then it is probable that this will persist in the resurrection. In Yong's understanding this case is made by the marks of the crucifixion that Jesus displays to the disciples. These marks could be described as conferring identity. They are demonstrative of the conquering of death, and to remove them would remove a sign or symbol of the triumph of the resurrection. This means, for Yong, that those with disabilities would have these identifying and personal features of their existence before the resurrection yet they would not be unhappy marks; for example, Yong suggests that a heart murmur for a person with Down's Syndrome would not threaten their life but would simply remain.

For an autistic person, perhaps, this would mean that their distinguishing traits would remain but would not be considered a deficit. It is hard for me to imagine what this would look like. For myself as I am now would not want to be in the overcrowded and noisy heaven of my childhood worries. Yet, looking at the future Day of the Lord from the perspective we have now, through a glass darkly, we must accept that we cannot know entirely what it will be like for those who love cricket and those who hate it to dwell alongside one another, or for those who are autistic and find their existence troubling and do not rejoice in its continuing after death. It is hard to imagine, but perhaps not impossible to conceive of. As with all theological notions of the world renewed, we cannot make claims with certainty.

This chapter has suggested that the resurrection existence will contain autistic people who are still autistic and that this will be good. It has suggested that autism, with the help of the neurodiversity paradigm and critical autism studies, is in some ways good even now, despite the difficulties that the neurotypical world creates for the neurodivergent. Yet I am realistic about my own existence and the existence of my siblings who are autistic. It is not every day that I rejoice in my lot and I cannot remove my difficulties entirely with regard to the social sphere, but in some intrinsic way they exist within me and cannot be easily untangled. I wish therefore for any future hope to allow for autistic identity to prevail but in a way that ends suffering. It is a hope, but it is not exactly a clear hope and perhaps that is, after all, entirely what hope is.

Notes

1 Virginia Bovell, 'Is There an Ethical Case for the Prevention and/or Cure of Autism?', in Hanna Bertilsdotter Rosqvist, Nick Chown and Anna Stenning, eds, *Neurodiversity Studies: A New Critical Paradigm* (London: Routledge, 2020).

2 Jim Sinclair, cited in Bertilsdotter Rosqvist, Chown and Stenning, p. 48.

3 For example, Steve Silberman, *NeuroTribes: The Legacy of Autism and the Future of Neurodiversity* (New York: Random House, 2016), p. 287.

4 Lindsay O'Dell et al., 'Critical Autism Studies: Exploring Epistemic Dialogues and Intersections, Challenging Dominant Understandings of Autism', *Disability & Society* 31, no. 2 (2016): 171.

5 O'Dell et al., 'Critical Autism Studies'.

6 Bovell, 'Is There an Ethical Case?', in Bertilsdotter Rosqvist, Chown and Stenning, *Neurodiversity Studies*.

7 O'Dell et al., 'Critical Autism Studies'.

8 Bertilsdotter Rosqvist, Chown and Stenning, *Neurodiversity Studies*.

9 Bertilsdotter Rosqvist, Chown, and Stenning, *Neurodiversity Studies*, Introduction.

10 Bovell, 'Is There an Ethical Case?', in Bertilsdotter Rosqvist, Chown and Stenning, *Neurodiversity Studies*.

11 O'Dell et al., 'Critical Autism Studies'.

12 O'Dell et al., 'Critical Autism Studies'. p. 169.

13 O'Dell et al., 'Critical Autism Studies'. p. 169.

14 O'Dell et al., 'Critical Autism Studies', p. 170.

15 O'Dell et al., 'Critical Autism Studies', p. 167.

16 Dan Goodley, *Dis/Ability Studies: Theorising Disablism and Ableism* (London: Routledge, 2014), https://www.taylorfrancis.com/books/e/9781134060832 (accessed 25.11.22).

17 Goodley, *Dis/Ability Studies*.

18 Used to explain autism by drawing similarities between the way in which information is processed differently in a variety of operating systems that exist in personal computers. The metaphor suggests that neurotypical brains are one type of operating system and autistic brains are another.

19 Richard Woods et al., 'Redefining Critical Autism Studies: A More Inclusive Interpretation', *Disability & Society* 33, no. 6 (3 July 2018): 974–9.

20 Joyce Davidson and Michael Orsini, eds, *Worlds of Autism: Across the Spectrum of Neurological Difference* (Minnesota, MN: University of Minnesota Press, 2013), p. 12.

21 Chloe Silverman, *Understanding Autism: Parents, Doctors, and the History of a Disorder* (Princeton, NJ/Oxford: Princeton University Press, 2012), p. 235.

22 Davidson and Orsini, *Worlds of Autism*, p. 76.

23 Frances Mackenney-Jeffs, *Reconceptualising Disability for the Contemporary Church* (London: SCM Press, 2021), pp. 79–80.

24 Karen O'Donnell, *Dark Womb: Re-Conceiving Theology through Reproductive Loss* (London: SCM Press, 2022).

25 Wolfgang Vondey, *Pentecostal Theology: Living the Full Gospel*, (London: T&T Clark, 2017), p. 21.

26 Kenneth J. Archer and Richard E. Waldrop, 'Liberating Hermeneutics: Toward a Holistic Pentecostal Mission of Peace and Justice', *Journal of the European Pentecostal Theological Association* 31, no. 1 (April 2011): 65–80.

27 Karen O'Donnell and Katie Cross, *Bearing Witness: Intersectional Perspectives on Trauma Theology* (London: SCM Press, 2022).

28 Vondey, *Pentecostal Theology*.

29 Vondey, *Pentecostal Theology*.

30 Allan Anderson, *An Introduction to Pentecostalism: Global Charismatic Christianity*, 2nd edn (New York: Cambridge University Press, 2014).

31 Nancy L. Eiesland, *The Disabled God: Toward a Liberatory Theology of Disability* (Nashville, TN: Abingdon Press, 1994).

32 Colin Cameron, *Disability Studies: A Student's Guide* (London: Sage, 2013).

33 O'Donnell and Cross, *Bearing Witness*.

34 Marcia Mount Shoop, 'Body-Wise: Re-Fleshing Christian Spiritual Practice in Trauma's Wake', in Eric Boynton, ed., *Trauma and Transcendence: Suffering and the Limits of Theory*, 1st edn (New York: Fordham University Press, 2018).

35 Shelly Rambo, *Spirit and Trauma: A Theology of Remaining*, 1st edn (Louisville, KT: Westminster John Knox Press, 2010).

36 Grant Macaskill, *Autism and the Church: Bible, Theology, and Community*, first issued in paperback (Waco, TX: Baylor University Press, 2021), p. 52.

37 Cheryl J. Sanders, 'Social Justice: Theology as Social Transformation', in Wolfgang Vondey, ed., *The Routledge Handbook of Pentecostal Theology* (London: Routledge, 2020).

38 Archer and Waldrop, 'Liberating Hermeneutics'.

39 Selina Stone, 'Pentecostal Power: Discipleship as Political Engagement', *Journal of the European Pentecostal Theological Association* 38, no. 1 (2 January 2018).

40 Archer and Waldrop, 'Liberating Hermeneutics', p. 74.

41 Cheryl Bridges Johns, *Pentecostal Formation: A Pedagogy among the Oppressed* (Eugene, OR: Wipf & Stock Publishers, 2010).

42 Johns, p. 69.

43 Vondey, *Pentecostal Theology*.

44 Cited in Brian Brock and John Swinton, eds, *Disability in the Christian Tradition: A Reader* (Grand Rapids, MI: William B. Eerdmans, 2012).

45 Cited in Brock and Swinton, *Disability in the Christian Tradition*, p. 69.

46 Cited in Brock and Swinton, *Disability in the Christian Tradition*, p. 69.

47 Amos Yong, 'Many Tongues, Many Senses: Pentecost, the Body Politic, and the Redemption of Dis/Ability', *Pneuma* 31, no. 2 (2009): 167–88.

4

Motherhood and Solidarity

Solidarity

'Solidarity' is a term that is much used in common parlance, meaning something approaching 'sympathy' or perhaps 'empathy'. Although 'solidarity' has value in terms of people expressing sympathy and empathy, for some people I fear this word 'solidarity' has lost its value, especially in its theological sense. Solidarity is fundamentally a Christian idea tied up with the love of God for all humanity and with the missio Dei. Solidarity requires us to fully understand the other, the one who does not seem like us, as a complete human, made and loved by God. It is an ethical demand that those with power to act, but alongside those who lack power rather than towards them. It is therefore political, as most of the issues in this book are.

The exercise of power in the solidarity with autistic people is to be carefully navigated, relentlessly reflected upon, and always adjusted in light of new understanding. This chapter is something of an experimental foray into ways in which notions of solidarity can be theologically constructive, especially in areas of dispute. Although it focuses on a very narrow and particular dispute – that between mothers of autistic children and other autistic people – I propose that using the theology of solidarity has much value within and without neurodiverse communities, particularly in the church. As such, this chapter is partnered with Chapter 5, which discusses notions of what constitutes 'autistic' in a theological frame, with a generous application of these terms. Solidarity allows us to be *with* one another and discussions about community allow us to open wide the gates of the church to incorporate ideas of 'being with' that are nuanced for a neurodiverse theology.

This chapter examines a number of features of motherhood that describe the nature of solidarity as I conceive it. First, I will show that mothers are *alongside* their children, next to them, experiencing the world *with* them; this requires mothers to accept their children and fully know them. Second, I will show that these mothers in knowing their children do not claim to be the same as them; rather, that they share some of the same experiences and some different experiences and that solidarity is formed *in* this similarity and difference. After presenting these themes and the voices of the mothers, I move on to theological reflection. The first step in this process is a summary of 'the common good' upon which solidarity stands; this is followed by examining solidarity with autistic people. This has two characteristics: that it 'loves in place' so does not require change on the part of the autistic person to be acceptable, and that it does not 'mimic' autistic suffering.

I make use of the particular in this chapter and examine the specific, not as a closed set of options but as metaphors for wider application. The particular here is motherhood as a lens to explore solidarity. I chose mothers rather than fathers or parents because I am a mother and because the debate has focused particularly upon mothers in history (for example, 'refrigerator mothers' as the cause of autism, so called because their apparent 'cold' affect was impairing their children's development).[1] This is not because it is the only situation in which solidarity is applicable but rather it is a worked example of solidarity for the use in the church imaginatively. In the same way, in the next chapter the examples I offer of community are particular but not limited. The polarity between communities of mothers of autistic children and autistic people are a symptom of a wider trend. This trend is because of the recalibration towards prioritizing those with lived experience. The mental health treatment policy of 'not about me without me' reflects this also. The days when interventions were done *to* people without their consent, when conversations excluded the very people who were the subject, are *slowly* coming to an end.

The motives of a liberation theology should be to prioritize the voices of those who have not been heard; this is part of the remedial work necessary in situations of oppression. However, this has the potential to become a fundamental fracture in the community of God unless theological interpretation is brought to bear to prevent this. This fracture between those whose voices have long been ignored and those who still wish to speak on behalf of others need not be polarized. The prioritizing of one group, autistic people, who should justly be heard would ideally not be at the exclusion of those who love and care for autistic people. It is likely that the autistic readers of this book may not agree with me on this – that they carry with them the wounds of being silenced and 'done to', of being rejected and othered. If this is the case, they never again wish to have anyone else speak on their behalf. Or perhaps they feel that they continue not to be heard, and that if other interested parties, other stakeholders, continue to have voice in the situation of autistic lives then they will never have their own opportunity.

To these objectors I do agree – to an extent. I promote here something of an idealized vision, one that I would like to work towards rather than one that I feel is possible now or in the immediate future. I do so because I have experienced the love and compassion of those who are not autistic; those who have advocated for me and have done so for my good. I believe, therefore, that many voices in the spirit of love with the guidance of the Spirit are possible and it is worthwhile attempting to lay the groundwork for this possibility even if we never live to see the reality.

History of a debate

Mothers of autistic children's relationship with autistic adults, in particular autism advocates, is a difficult relationship. The typical narratives that emerge from the debate are to do with the 'tragedy' of autism. This is found in a family struggling to adjust to life with a child who does not fit at school, has medical needs, and requires services that are hard to access.

This compares with adults who advocate for autistic people; those who are either diagnosed or self-diagnosed and are working towards a more just world for those who are autistic. In many ways a first reading of this situation indicates similar drives and goals for the communities involved; however, this is not always the case. Daena J. Goldsmith describes these competing narratives as tragedy versus difference:

> For parents who are not themselves autistic and whose understanding of autism comes from the dominant autism-as-tragedy narrative, an autism diagnosis is often experienced as a disruption of who they are as parents and how their life will unfold.[2]

Feelings of uncertainty about the future and difficulties accessing help, alongside the pressures of not experiencing parenting as they expected it to be, result in the mothers in Goldsmith's research to describe their experience of autism negatively. She goes on to explain that many mothers may give up work, or work in reduced conditions, in order to function as carers and will experience the stigma that accompanies having a disabled child. Léon Van Omen writes of parents who cannot find suitable churches that will accommodate their children – churches that will allow for behaviour that does not suit the church's normative requirements.[3] Goldsmith reflects that, 'Even within a social disability model that sees strength associated with autism, there is acknowledgement that many parents must come to grips with a change in their expectations.'[4]

The experience of this polarity focuses on mothers because mothers disproportionately take on the role of carers and the daily work of raising an autistic child. They are more likely to give up their career and therefore experience a grief in their own hopes that is translated (perhaps wrongly) as tragedy that is fundamentally linked with autism. For a long time it was the parenting of mothers, the so-called 'refrigerator mothers', that was considered the cause of autism.[5] Mothers, says Goldsmith, are more likely to cite poor mental health as a consequence of their situation as the mother of an autistic child:

Much of the research on mothering autistic children focuses on how hard it is ... The dominant discourses of autism suggest that mothering an autistic child is worse than other experiences of mothering, without its own rewards, and meriting sympathy.[6]

Research into the differences between these two communities says that mothers are more likely to be interested in a cure for autism versus self-advocates who are not.[7] This is a high-stakes difference, indicating the very different outcomes and opinions that the two stakeholder communities hold. Parents of autistic children have historically been active in advocacy for research into treatment and cures for autism – such as the founding of Autism Speaks as well as the Cure Autism Now Foundation (founded in 2003).[8] The difficulty with groups that seek to research cures for autism is the operative belief that autistic people should not exist. Where autistic individuals find their autism as a core part of their identity (hence 'identity first' language), the conflict with parental groups that seek the elimination of autism is apparent.

The critical ideas at play in the differences between mothers of autistic children and autistic adults are part of the wider language difficulties that pervade autism dialogue. Chloe Silverman describes the differences as to do with 'kinship'.[9] This, she claims, is to do with neurological and genetic association versus nurture and familial ties. Self-advocacy movements 'demand that genetic likeness, which is presumed to unite the population that shares a diagnosis of autism, trumps familial relations in the contest over who gets to speak for children with autism'.[10] Whether this description is quite accurate or not, it is indicative of the strength of feeling and the depth of the argument; it relates to the nature and ties of children – an emotive and powerful rhetorical stance. Whereas autistic people might lay claim to be the voice of other people's children by dint of a medical diagnosis, parents lay equal claim to their children through the motivator of love. What a profound rendition of a child – this is akin to King Solomon's judgement over the baby in 1 Kings 3.16–28!

Alongside the debates about person-first language or identity-first language the issue here is to do with the ontological origins of autism and the formative and fundamental nature of it in the lives of autistic people. Once again, is autism something separate from the person or is it constitutive of them? What place does a person who is not autistic have in the conversation about autism? Is it secondary in order to prevent the silencing of autistic people, which has always been the case under the privileged gaze of the medicalized model of autism? Jessica Hughes uses the language of 'fracture' within the community to describe the difficulties that belie the community. However, she notes that these are formulated as types, whereas the borders are a reality likely to be permeable.[11] There is little space in online communities who constitute the majority of ways both groups interact with the world for those that fall into the gaps between, for example, mothers who are autistic or autistic people who would readily seek a cure.

The difficulty of discordant understandings about autism constitute a metaphor for the relationship between the church and the autistic community. The lack of shared horizons, or a mutual telos or dialogue, means that the church inhabits a similar space to the two parties in the mothers versus autistic adults debate that troubles much autism dialogue. It is my hope to offer some theological moves that allow for the wider conversation to be informed.

Mothering alongside

The polarized debate between autism mothers and autistic advocates is reductionistic. Mothers have potential for being their children's biggest advocates, seeking justice for them because of their utter devotion to their child and their intimate knowledge of them. Mothers, instead of being a lightning rod for a debate about who gets to speak on behalf of whom and whose needs come first, can serve as a heuristic metaphor for togetherness that has a long history in the Christian tradition: solidarity. Alongside my analysis of this process I will present the voices of mothers who write about their children, in part to show that they have employed this idea of solidarity naturally in their role as mothers, and also in part to show their understanding of where the oppression lies for their children. This is instructive for the church – how can we liberate that which we do not understand? How can we reveal oppression and seek justice if the oppression is not known? It is the voices of those who are autistic, or who are fundamentally standing in solidarity with those who are autistic, that can reveal it.

Mothers of autistic children are living their lives intimately in the presence of their children's experience; as they travel with their child their knowledge of them grows and this resources their understanding and ability to act for and with them. It is this shared existence of mother and child that allows them not to speak for their child, but to act alongside them for a better and just outcome from oppression:

> How can I speak of liberation without speaking of oppression? I think first of how long it took us to get an autism diagnosis for our daughter, partly because she was a girl, and partly because of my own fear and misunderstanding of autism. I thought an autism diagnosis would put us on a different path than the one I had imagined. But, looking back now, I can see we were already on that path from the moment my daughter was born. No diagnosis would change who she inherently is.
>
> I often think about how much suffering we could have avoided if I hadn't been so afraid to acknowledge her as autistic. Life got infinitely better after her autism diagnosis at age eight. Knowing that her brain was wired differently relieved the pressure for her to fit in with other kids. I began to understand how she viewed the world and rather than try to force her into a neurotypical set of behaviors, together we built an environment around her where she could thrive.
>
> We had tried both public and private schools. Both left her feeling burnt out, even as young as kindergarten. After the diagnosis, instead of expecting her to observe and learn from me, I started observing her. I noticed she was calmest and most able to learn when she had access to the outdoors, copious

time for transition, clear and consistent expectations, limited social interactions and a quiet working space. I always had an inkling she would do best home-schooled, but it took the four years of failed school experiences and the autism diagnosis for me to get the gumption to make home schooling a reality.

Home schooling has been a liberation for her. Being able to learn as she best learns with plenty of time to hyperfocus on her fixations has returned to us the bright inquisitive kid that was once hidden behind meltdowns and self-critical negativity.

Louise

Louise's honest account of her parenting experience demonstrates this fundamental alignment with her child that comes from a commitment to remain with her and to know her. She describes a process of 'learning her child', of removing her own assumptions, and of getting down in the mud (of her own back garden) in order to witness to her daughter's life. This process of witnessing, of being alongside, allowed her to enter her daughter's world rather than impose her own world on to her. As she attests, this is not a straightforward process, a romanticized view of parenting a disabled child where the commitment of the parent 'solves' the problems. Rather, she repeatedly attempts to help her daughter and it does not immediately work. Louise knows her daughter; she knows how well she is learning and is proud of her in the same way that any parent is proud of their child's achievements. She has adapted her own life to meet the needs of her daughter by educating her at home, rather than requiring her to persist in an education setting that does not suit. Louise is not, however, portraying herself as a hero; she is not the redeemer and her daughter the grateful recipient. Rather, Louise acknowledges that she didn't always get it right and that her daughter has served to redeem *her*, by them working together to find the best situation for her. Louise rejects the 'sacrificial' narrative imposed on her from outside, and by so doing illustrates the 'alongsiding' that she and her daughter share and the mutuality that comes from it.

Another mother, Emily, writes about her experience as the mother of twins diagnosed as autistic:

> When our twin sons were diagnosed as autistic, aged about two and a half, I had very little knowledge of autism, and had had no reason to question societal attitudes that are fearful of disability, threatened by difference and that cling to convention as a place of safety. Already exhausted by the challenge of mothering toddlers, facing up to this new reality in the context of my ignorance completely shattered my expectations and assumptions about our family life. My hopes for my sons were dismantled and replaced by uncertainty and fear for their future.
>
> In accessing health, educational and financial support we were immediately engulfed in the language of deficit and disorder. Our sons were measured against the development and milestones of other children and found wanting. Educators and health professionals offered interventions and treatments with the goal of making them more like the other kids, and we were glad to have a way forward – we wanted so much to help our boys to communicate their needs and to alleviate their distress, which was at times intense. We wanted them to flourish or at the very least to be safe in our unforgiving society. In my desperation I was sucked into trawling the internet for information on therapies, diets and treatments.
>
> Fortunately, at that very significant moment we encountered, through Mencap and the Portage home-visiting scheme, people who understood autism differently. We learned to play alongside our sons and immediately got better at appreciating their ways of having fun and we began to communicate more easily. We learned about the comforts of stimming and the pain of sensory overload, and it became easier to empathize with the difficulties they were experiencing. I read accounts written by autistic adults of the damage caused by inappropriate and cruel therapies, and we began to understand that much of the support on offer was oppressive to our sons – asking them to change, to be something that they are not and,

at worst, asking them to endure pain and distress so that the rest of us can keep our vision of normality.

Now, 15 years later, I think of that process – the painful dismantling of my expectations – as a gift. The realization that I did not have the power to arrange a happy future for my children, that I couldn't protect my family from unexpected life events, freed me to think differently about the conventions and attitudes that had given me a false sense of security. This experience of questioning and doubt has paradoxically empowered me in the difficult task of resisting societal pressures, pressures that I have internalized, to somehow teach my children to fit in, to be neurotypical, to pass as a 'normal' person. It has freed me instead to support them and appreciate them as the ever-interesting, unconventional, wonderful young men that they are.

Emily

Emily receives her changed understanding as 'gift', that which – although unexpected – is beneficial to her. The changed understandings allowed her to position herself not as one who judges according to society's standards, but to be *with* her children, an act of hospitality that they share between them. Her children are hospitable to her in that they welcome her into their world and she is hospitable to them by not changing them or judging them. This mutuality in hospitality is togetherness; although they are different (Emily's description of her process of learning illustrates this), they are with one another. By changing herself rather than her children she accepts them as they are. Sometimes this 'with-ness' is against a world that prevents their flourishing; Emily can see this oppression and works to alleviate it where she can, by seeking their flourishing and working to prevent their suffering.

Alongside supporting their autistic children, parents who are in solidarity with their children recognize them as fully human rather than as children who are trapped or imprisoned by autism. By knowing a child completely, one also knows their frailties and fallenness. Full humanity includes the very real potential for sinfulness. Rebecca is a mother of an autistic teenager who met with me to talk about her son. She rejects the notion of the saintly mother who sacrificially parents a child with additional needs; rather, she has also committed to knowing her son as he is. She does not seek to fix him nor to romanticize him. He is not a project for her to cast herself as his saviour. Rather, she understands his interests and has found herself taught by him things that she did not previously understand. She has learnt from her son rather than solely teaching him. She has investigated his interests and joined in with them where she is able to access them. She lives alongside him and with him in a way that treats him as fully human. Rebecca appreciates that her son is sometimes behaving badly, that sometimes he is in the wrong; for example, he frequently calls her 'a dickhead' and she laughingly told me she would rather he didn't. He knows he shouldn't but chooses to anyway.

To appreciate that an autistic child can be sinful is to allow for them to be fully human in the way that humanity is described after the Fall. It is an issue of theological anthropology. By recognizing her son as behaving badly, Rebecca understands that her son is fully human rather than a project for her own self-understanding, one whose sole purpose is cast in the light of making her a mother who cares for a child with a disability.

Theological anthropology, understanding the nature of the person in light of the revelation of God, is instructive for the inclusion of autistic people. It says in Romans:

> For there is no distinction, since all have sinned and fall short of the glory of God; they are now justified by his grace as a gift, through the redemption that is in Christ Jesus. (Romans 3.22–24)

Rebecca argued that so often disabled children are cast in this romanticized light: they are grateful, quiet and obedient; they are tragedies that other people can save. They are not children who get into fights at school and call their mums 'dickheads'. When children don't fit the narrative of a grateful disabled child they are actually revealing to themselves and those around them something profoundly theologically important: that they are human. The mothers who, alongside their children, stand next to them are witnessing to their humanity also. The understanding of the liberative potential of autistic sinfulness is further examined in Chapter 6, for now it is significant that solidarity includes the recognition of ethical agency in the autistic child – the ability to get it wrong and sometimes on purpose.

Solidarity as similarity and difference

There is no requirement for same-ness for a fully outworked belief in solidarity. The commitment to being an 'ally' does not require the experience of the same situations in the same way. It is the case that no two autistic people are the same, therefore those who are autistic when among other autistic people will have to enact a solidarity that is founded upon similarity and difference because there is no homogeneity in autistic people. For example, intersections of race, gender and sexuality significantly alter the experience of autism in the world.[12] Rather, solidarity is a commitment of love. The love of a mother for her child is a profound metaphor for solidarity. If we, the church, recognize that we are called to love, then the act of solidarity between people who are different or people who are the same is the natural outcome.

One way that mothers are in solidarity with their autistic children is through also being autistic. I am in this situation. I find myself standing as an interpreter for my autistic child; and, occasionally, as interpreter to his neurotypical father. I appreciate when I do this that this is never translation, that all speech on his behalf comes with interpretation – that there is a process in this communication that involves me and my own beliefs and experiences. I, therefore, with the benefit of some methodological training in Practical Theology, attempt to reflexively interpret for my son, holding as contingent all that I try to negotiate on his behalf – but always doing so with the privileged knowledge I have from two directions: as a person who has lived experience and as the person who knows him best in the whole world. I see this as my gift from him rather than my gift to him. He allows me to know him.[13] Our mutual autism does not offer solidarity through sameness, but through common experiences.

One mother, Penny, also encounters solidarity differently through neurodivergent mothering; in her account she illustrates that although being an autistic mother gives her levels of insight that she finds useful, it also reveals that everyone on the autistic spectrum encounters the world as an individual and therefore no person can claim a standpoint other than their own:

> I live in London with my partner and primary-age child – all of us are autistic although all three of us have different strengths and weaknesses; we are no more identical in our neurology than a neurotypical family would be!
>
> What needs to be liberated? Expectations. There are so many stereotypes around what autism should look like, and it doesn't usually include me. As a woman and as a mother I am 'not autistic enough' when I try to keep my differences hidden, and potentially incapable of parenting my child if I don't. I do not disclose my diagnosis at work beyond a confidential discussion with HR, so my experience of sharing this has been with friends and with other parents. I find that some of the neurotypical parents in groups for ASD children find me alarming – they don't want to think that their child might grow into me.
>
> Having said that, my daughter is at a church school which is strongly celebratory of difference and equality, and the staff and many of the parents there have managed to be accommodating without being patronizing, which is such a rare combination. I treasure that. My church is similarly welcoming and has a strong disability-inclusive stance.
>
> Mothering neurodivergently does have its advantages. I can explain to my child what challenges we share and what I have found helps. When she first started to show signs of autism such as meltdowns, stimming, screaming at noise and so on, my first thought was that it was probably autism and I could support her whereas I think many NT parents unfamiliar with autism would assume it was misbehaviour. I hope that I will

also be able to model to her that you can be happy and autistic – I am extremely content and I hope she will be too.

Penny

Penny illustrates that she encounters the world in ways that are similar, that are familiar, to her child but that are not identical. The key issue to highlight in her account, beyond her insightful words about the needs of the church to act, is that she cannot claim to be the same as her child despite also being autistic. To argue that the church should stand in solidarity with autistic people is not to argue that somehow all parties have the same point of view, that we can claim full mutual understanding. Rather, solidarity is, as these mothers demonstrate, to do with knowing and loving and can be argued for as not equal with respect to each particular situation. Even among autistic people no one perspective is the same as another. One does not, in church tradition, have to be in the identical situation as the other to show solidarity with them.

The differences between neurotypical and neurodiverse individuals does not negate the possibility of solidarity. This can occur when a mother feels the same rejection that her children encounter. By encountering her situation in a similar way to her children, Jenny experiences the same form of crippling expectations that cause her children misery:

> I am a mother to two autistic children. The thing that we as a family need liberating from is the crippling weight of neurotypical expectations. And this comes from both external forces and internalized ableism we carry ourselves.
>
> People who don't have autistic people in their families or close experience of it, cannot begin to fathom how much low-level trauma is just a baseline for every day. A mum friend referring to her autistic child recently said, 'The world is a violent shock to him every morning.'
>
> Neurodivergent people struggle to differing levels with many things that neurotypicals barely register – executive functioning, or the ability to organize oneself with correct levels of urgency for priority, to keep track of personal be-

longings, time management, etc. Then there are the sensory processing issues that usually accompany autism – the ability to understand the body and what it is telling you, and how that relates to action needed from you. Put simply, the struggle to understand hunger, to recognize thirst, to register pain before urgent levels. Then there is the ability to incorporate different textures in food and clothing, tolerance for loud noises, or the need for extra-sensory stimulation as the body doesn't receive these signals the way neurotypicals do. Dyslexia, dyspraxia, dyscalculia. The list goes on. Now I could spend time explaining the value of hyper-focus, the delight of literal thinking, but I demonstrate these difficulties as they are often invisible, and therefore overlooked by others who, not seeing the intense disadvantage autistic people are given, expect them to behave in the same ways and have the same social stamina as themselves.

Families are viewed as difficult, odd or dysfunctional purely because their children have less tolerance for chaos, for loud noises, ability to cope with lack of routine. Notably all these things that commonly make up 'a party' or social gathering. Families need to be given compassion and understanding that they may need to navigate the same things as others differently. A different pace, more breaks, more thought. This isn't awkward or rude. It's about keeping things accessible and manageable.

However, awkward or rude is exactly how we are made to feel when we ask for the slightest of alterations.

We see the odd looks, the pitying glances, and we also see when you ignore us as it just doesn't fit in with your ideas of how families socialize. We see it all. And the worst thing? We internalize it and bring it home. Thoughts like 'Why can't my family just cope?' 'Why is EVERYTHING so hard for us?' 'Why are we not able to manage?' creep in.

The result is shaming your children who feel the weight of expectation upon them. Next is self-recrimination as you analyse your parenting methods. Strain in relationships occurs as yet another event has ended in meltdown and stress, leading to arguments between caregivers.

Liberation from this weight is needed. Letting go of societal expectations. And being able to answer the above questions with 'Things are hard for autistic people in a neurotypical-designed world, but if we see what you struggle with and how you cope daily we would praise you for showing up again and again with fresh hope. You manage exactly as an autistic person should in this strange world. And we don't need you to cosplay as a neurotypical to be worthy of love and attention.'

Jenny

Jenny explains that by identifying with her child she feels the wait of 'neurotypical expectation' despite not being neurodivergent herself. She experiences similarly, although not identically, the value judgements of others. She also finds that she expects her children to behave differently to avoid the condemnation of others. This demonstrates the same-ness and different-ness of mothering. The correspondence of experience is mirrored by the differences of power (parent to child) and Jenny's response to external and internal criticism. This is illustrative of solidarity's purpose. To argue for solidarity between the church and the autistic community is not to argue for the homogenization of experience. The mothers who recount their stories do not claim to have the same stories as their children but ones that are mutual, that are coherent with one another, that are difficult to tease apart but rather weave in and out of one another's lives vividly different colours of warp and weft, but still together in the woven pattern.

'Alongsiding' with autistic children and living life together is the culmination of *being with* in both similiarity and in differences. Imagine a mother and a child stooped over a patch of mud. They are both carefully examining the mud, the child pokes at it with a stick, the mother watches the child as much as the child observes the mud. In the mud a worm wriggles, the object of fascination that has particularly captured the child's attention. She moves to poke it with the stick but the mother stays her hand, *gently*, and the child withdraws. Both the mother and the child are watching the same worm; they are together in the same patch of autumnal sun, bending over the same patch of mud. They see the same things but they interpret them differently. They have similar sensory input but their bodies respond differently. They are together in the same place but they experience it uniquely. What they experience is not so other from one another that there is no correlation; they can discuss it together and share meaning. There is a familiarity with the way that they experience the event. They are together in the same place, hold between them the same memory, and toss it back and forth as they grow older – *do you remember the time in the muddy patch?*

Ruth Part 1 – Biblical alongsiding

> Do not press me to leave you
>   or to turn back from following you!
> Where you go, I will go;
>   where you lodge, I will lodge;
> your people shall be my people,
>   and your God my God.
> Where you die, I will die—
>   there will I be buried. (Ruth 1.16–17)

The book of Ruth captures something of the alongsiding that the mothers suggest they already do. It demonstrates commitment in the face of uncertainty, as a result of the unexpected turns in a person's life. Ruth, in the same way as the mothers above, did not expect her life to turn out the way that it has. Ruth has experienced tragedy, and although the mothers and I do not conceive of autism as a tragedy, at the same time it is not expected – it is unplanned and has consequences that cannot be foreseen. The journey that the mothers take to understand their children is a journey towards understanding with commitment. Ruth does not understand Naomi's world, not fully. She has never been to Naomi's country; she has only experienced Naomi's storytelling and the customs that Naomi, and Ruth's husband presumably, brought with them to Moab. Yet she sees in this prospect of an unfamiliar world a route towards family with Naomi and a God whom she only partially knows. Ruth, like the mothers who have shared their stories, commits to going along with Naomi, to being with her despite differences in culture and religion. She doesn't promise to fully understand Naomi, or to cognitively explore their differences – she simply holds fast and promises to journey with her. There is no certainty in this journey but there is commitment and love. This is alongsiding and it is the precursor to solidarity as it is borne out of love and commitment to that which is strange and unfamiliar, that which is unknown.

Towards theological solidarity by way of the common good

Solidarity is the feature of liberation that determines the rest of this book. It is the ground upon which all else that I propose for the liberation of autistic people is built. It is generous enough to allow for varieties of belief about the ontological nature of autism; it does not require battle lines to be drawn between medical models of autism and social models. It allows for the murky and complex experience of autism as a disability or as a difference – or as a combination of both. It requires much of all participants, which is liberative in itself, as solidarity poses an ethical challenge for both those with power to act according to their powerful status, but also those without power; in this instance, the autistic who is oppressed by whichever situation they find to be oppressive, to be actors in their own liberation. This allows for the fully realized humanity of autistic people to be acknowledged. From there, other acts of liberation, such as I suggest in this book and anticipate that others will also suggest, can follow.

Solidarity is a Christian stance founded upon the belief that all humans are made in the image of God and all who believe and follow Jesus are one with one another and Christ in his body. This does not necessitate a dual type of solidarity, one that exists in one way for all humanity and in a special and different way for Christians. Rather, it is one that respects all humans as equal and created as good and fallen as a result of sinful human choices. Solidarity is required under the umbrella of the common good, a theological anthropology that says all humanity is deserving of that which is deemed good and suitable for flourishing.

Solidarity as a theological idea is often linked to Catholic Social Teaching on the common good. This, importantly for the task of this chapter, has linked to it notions of collective struggle.[14] The negotiation of those with and those without power, the struggle for the possibility of justice, are key ideas in the notions of autistic good. As the mothers earlier in this chapter show, common-good ideas of education do not currently reach their children. Four of these mothers mention schooling, and only one has found a school that is satisfactory; another, Rebecca, took her son out of his first secondary school after instances of degrading abuse and has since paid substantial sums to place him in a private school that is more suitable. The common-good idea of education – that it is for the benefit of the individual and the world to educate children – does not currently accommodate autistic children acceptably. Yet to seek the good of all people is to accept that there are theological ideas at play that describe all people as the same, connected to God by their nature as humans and by all good things stemming from God.

Daniella C. Augustine makes clear the links that I have sketched above between theological anthropologies and quests for the common good.[15] She argues that we fear that which is unfamiliar, which is evident with the shame and stigma of autism, and that we fail to understand that all of our flourishing is linked to one another, that 'relationality is the hallmark of creation'.[16] She states that we are only secure in all the ways that we would wish when this is true of the other also. This she casts in a trinitarian vision, one that we all participate in. The call of the Christian is to participate in Christ's kenosis (self-emptying, Philippians 2.7) for the benefit of others.[17] In this participation we are 'Seeing through the eyes of the suffering, self-emptying Christ – the icon of love's kenosis for the life of the world – enables the saints to discern his face in that of the suffering other (Matthew 25:31–46).'[18] This suffering other in autistic liberation theology is the autistic person but it is not limited to the autistic person. It is possible, and probable, that the autistic person can also identify the suffering other and discern Christ's face. It is no longer universally believed that autistic people are unable to notice the emotions of others. It is certainly my experience that I feel deep empathy for others who suffer and anecdotally this is noted to be a strength of autistic individuals, that they have a wealth of compassion for those around them.

It is patronizing to see the direction of Augustine's description of kenosis as only towards the autistic person. Of course, it must be towards them because of autistic people's need for liberation, but in their process of discipleship they also should seek to peruse Christ's pattern of kenosis for their own life. There is then mutuality in the pursuit of biblically informed beliefs about the common good: all who seek to mimic and participate in the life of Christ in the world do so for the benefit of the other. This dual motion between autistic people and non-autistic people speaks to a true mutuality – that they are indeed together, able to identify Christ in one another and act accordingly.

The Spirit, says Augustine, allows for the identification of the face of God in the other. All who pursue the common good are empowered by the Spirit to identify God and be so identified themselves.[19] This is called *sobornost* in Orthodox theology and refers to the church's life as 'living an organic unity which reconciles the conflicting claims of freedom and obedience', says Bishop Kallistos Ware.[20] The theological symbolism of the divine face, the icon of the divine face, is significant for Augustine. Humanity recollects the vision of the face of the divine, lost in the 'primordial memory of Eden'; the result of fallen humanity is the loss of this vision of the face of the divine.[21] However, the nature of humanity is also this memory, the imprint of the divine face and the ability to recognize it in the face of the other. Flourishing, says Augustine, is the ability to see this face and to recognize it as an icon of God in the other. Humanity has a social nature; we are required to, in the same way that God does, turn our face towards the other and be vulnerable in the communion with one another.²² Augustine's theological articulation of theosis and the communality of creation is doubly significant in an autistic theology.

First, it articulates by explaining human relationality as groaning with creation for their original relationship with God – the profound fracture of interaction. We are fundamentally other to one another. Any autistic person will likely understand this in a deeply personal way. The very description of the word 'autism' comes from the Greek *autos*. This refers to the self, and fundamentally suggests that the original naming of autism spoke of individuals trapped within themselves, unable to reach into the outside world. Indeed, the origins of the term began with Eugen Bleuler who believed that the individuals he was describing had unsatisfactory engagements with reality, and that they retreated to fantasy to resolve this.²³ Although the study of autism has changed almost beyond all recognition from such descriptions, there is still the belief that the autistic person is somehow separate, inaccessible, other. In Joanne Limburg's fascinating book, *Letters To My Weird Sisters*, she examines the lives of women who might now be considered autistic and acknowledges the autistic reality of being understood only as 'uncanny':

> I unsettle people. I'm uncanny. Being around me doesn't always feel like being around a fellow human being, and that discomfort rarely brings out the best in people.²⁴

This otherness that Limburg describes illustrates the importance of a doctrine of solidarity founded on theological anthropology and the idea of the common good that stems from it. No other theological response will highlight the demand upon the church to recognize the humanity and the divine image of autistic people everywhere. Without this theological articulation all claims for solidarity become expressions of well wishes, and ineffective ones at that. Autistic lives are in need of liberation because of the belief that they in some way lack a key essence of humanity, that those affected are like robots, that they cannot understand another person because they lack empathy – and thus because of this they are not human. If humans are relational, as they are made in the image of God, then this empathy issue, this alone-ness that autistic people are portrayed as having, removes something of the divine image from them. Autistic people are perceived as lacking humanity, lacking divine input, and sit somewhere outside of the view that God has made them just as he is. Yet this cannot be so, be it because autistics do not in fact lack empathy (see Damien Milton's 'Double Empathy Problem'[25]) or any other theory of the status of autism. Rather, we turn to scripture and see that in fact the first thing that is true of humanity is not a feature of one's own personality or behaviour, but instead is a feature of God's.

> So God created humankind in his image, in the image of God he created them; male and female he created them. (Genesis 1.27)

The action that makes the person in the image of God does not correlate to their own behaviour but to God's first action towards humanity. The divine likeness comes from God, not from the behaviour of humans. Thus there is the divine face in all because of the gift of God, not the work of humanity. To find the source of theology of the common good is a turning to the face of God that necessarily rests in all people rather than to look for symptoms of divine behaviour constructed as relational skills or particular social actions. The common good is theologically necessary because of the creative work of God in humans.

Rowan Williams argues for the necessity of a theological imagination regarding the common welfare of all humanity; this is because of the necessity for the divine view – the ability to understand that the other is always known and loved by God. In his discussion about the failures of secularism, he states:

> ... secularism fails by bidding for an ultimately exclusive, even anti-humanist closure; it looks to a situation in which we are not able to see the world and each other as always and already

'seen', in the sense that we acknowledge our particular perspective to be shadowed by others that are inaccessible to us.[26]

This failure to recognize that the other is seen by God in a way that is inaccessible to us is causative in the dehumanizing of autistic people. To reconcile the uncanny to oneself requires not just an adjustment emotionally – to accept that 'everyone's different' – but to admit to a failure of imagination, an imagination that God has a view of humanity that correctly places them as primarily in relationship with him before one another. This is Augustine's argument – that we must face the divine face before we face one another.[27]

In so recognizing that every human face is in fact an icon of creation – of the dependence of the human self on their createdness by God – only then can a fully rounded notion of common good be described that has any potential to inform the solidarity that I argue is necessary for the liberation of autistic people, but also the unity rather than division of autistic and non-autistic humans.

Solidarity: loving in place

Gustavo Gutiérrez is my primary conversation partner in my proposal for solidarity with autistic lives. Gutiérrez presents solidarity as a thoroughgoing Christian act, founded upon the love of Christ.[28] He claims that it cannot be simply social action; it is not a theological explanation for the sort of social work that governmental agencies conduct in the UK, but rather a conversion of life sitting comfortably in the Christian tradition all the way back to St Benedict and beyond, who required that the Christian must 'convert' to the Christian path – have an absolute about-change.[29] The Christian character of this form of solidarity is crucial; it is not solidarity of an emotional stance but one that is ontologically situated because of the new life in Christ that a Christian has, and the ongoing call to convert their life into one that mimics Christ and represents him to the world in the power of the Holy Spirit. Solidarity, based upon the divine image found in all humans and the common good that is required for flourishing, is a Christian response to the saving action of God in our own lives. It is the requirement of us to transform our lives so that the face of God, the icon of creation in all other people, is visible to them.

Gutiérrez says that to reject another person is to reject God. This is because of the image of God in the other. To reject the other is to limit oneself to the possibility of seeing the face of God in the other; it damages us as well as damaging the other before us. But if we accept the other, then the possibilities for the flourishing of all are vast and this is where the acts of solidarity permit, allow and open up these divine encounters in the other. So, then, what does solidarity look like theologically and what suggestions, moving beyond the somewhat abstract theology I've presented to the concrete, are possible?

Solidarity is the opposite of this sin of rejection for it is *actively* rejecting the sins of silence. For Gutiérrez the sins of omission that relate specifically to the act of solidarity are to do with keeping silence. In the case of autism this is the church's lack of acknowledgement of autism. The openness to the presence of autistic people in the church is missing; there are very few public church figures who are autistic or are open about being autistic. The routes into church leadership require demonstrations of social skills that are not always fitting for autistic people. To be active in solidarity requires conversion. Conversion, framed by Gutiérrez, is a break from the personal and social forms of sin; in other words, it is not simply interior. Autistic solidarity is active not passive, active not emotional. It is more than an intention to good will, but a movement, a change and an about-turn based on the conversion of life necessary for a Christian.

Gutiérrez identified this active stance as in line with Christ's identification with the poor. As all Christians follow Christ, we follow him to such an identification. It is my contention that the poor and the maligned in society today include autistic people. Not only because their chances of employment are so poor that they are likely to be financially poor, but because they are poor of the connections and love of the church and society necessary for their flourishing. They are the poor of both Luke's Gospel and of Matthew's Gospel – the poor and the poor in Spirit. Gutiérrez's instruction to attend to the poor applies to attending to autistic people and drawing them out of the world's imposed silence.

I will develop this next line of thinking in the following chapter; however, it is pertinent here also to state that solidarity according to Gutiérrez means not removing a person from their social situation, but loving them in their social context. My interpretation of this for autistic people is in the form of a radical hospitality that does not necessitate them undertaking the bulk of this social change. The mothers in this chapter demonstrate this by joining in with the children in their world; by removing them from situations that caused them distress and by acting on their behalf for their good. They did not describe the requirements of the child to change to meet the world's neurotypical standards.[30] By loving poor people in their place, Gutiérrez is not suggesting that they are not helped or allowed to help themselves out of poverty, but is instead suggesting that the activity of help does not change their own social choices and culture. Autistic people, who are fully part of the community and who all Christians stand in solidarity with, are not required to change. The onus is not on the autistic person to behave in a different way socially, but for the church to accept them as they are in solidarity with them. It is not solidarity if they have to reject themselves in order to be welcome. This aspect of solidarity is therefore radical hospitality and I will address it more in the subsequent discussion on community.

Solidarity without mimicry

The risk with solidarity is that it valorizes situations that need improving or causes people to falsify their own situation in a mistaken act of sympathy. It cannot be with solidarity that poverty, for example, is viewed as an essential state for the Christian, a closer route to God. It cannot be that people's real and troubled experiences of poverty are passed over for a romanticized version of poverty that is entirely the choice of the impoverished and could be stopped at any time. In the same way, autistic solidarity is not valorizing the real difficulties with autism, though it is conceivable that choices to live apart from others within the Christian tradition – such as monasticism or the solitary life – could be conflated with autistic otherness and loneliness. However, one involves a choice and a vocation, and the other involves a lack of choice and misery. It is not solidarity to confuse the two. Gutiérrez appreciates this difficulty:

> Material poverty is a subhuman situation ... concretely, to be poor means to die of hunger, to be illiterate, to be exploited by others, not to know that you are being exploited, not to know that you are a person.[31]

This is not the sort of situation that people who choose to live alongside the poor usually pick. If this were mapped on to autism, it would be to reject employment, to accept a shortened life expectancy, to imitate the physical and sensory pain that comes alongside autism and to attempt to rewire thinking to mimic autism. Not only is this not really possible, it is unlikely to help and still remains the problem of it being a choice that one person has and another doesn't. What, then, is solidarity if it doesn't accept this mimicry?

Gutiérrez notes that the traditional route is to adopt a 'spiritual poverty' that is typically thought of as an unattachment to goods; but that even if you do own lots of things, you aren't emotionally beholden to them. You tread lightly in the world, not using much and not needing much. This has much in common with the Franciscan way and is commendable. It isn't solidarity, though; it is a choice to depend upon God rather than material circumstances and is not the choice that the poor can freely make. Nor can the autistic person choose to have society accept them or not. They do not freely choose. Spiritual poverty, aesthetic practice as useful and as worthy as it is, should not be conflated with solidarity as if the outcomes are the same.

Indeed, Gutiérrez sees it as risking being a 'vague' form of 'sentimentalism'.[32] Such a sentimentalism risks doing the opposite of what it sets out to do – maintain the political status quo. It does so by pursuing a 'righteous poor' narrative. If autism is treated in the same way by misguided acts of solidarity then social situations will not improve; and the social model of disability will become something imbued with a theological potency rather than being a tool to highlight inequality and injustice. If the mothers quoted in this chapter were to remove themselves from education, to limit their healthcare choices, to reject employment and to abandon communities in a bid to act in solidarity with typical autistic experience, what would they achieve? This mimicry is not a true form of solidarity.

What then can be done? What is solidarity? For Gutiérrez, it is twofold: it is the recognition that poverty is scandalous, and that poverty is a spiritual childhood. Gutiérrez says that poverty in the Bible is against the will of God and against human dignity (Job 24.2–12, 14; Amos 2.6–7; and Isaiah 10.1–2). We should therefore understand that solidarity with those who are poor involves not valorizing poverty but illustrating that it is an injustice. Second, poverty is to be seen as a form of 'spiritual childhood'. This is a willingness to be used by God or to be open to God. He cites Zephaniah 3:

> For I will leave in the midst of you
>   a people humble and lowly.
> They shall seek refuge in the name of the LORD—
>   the remnant of Israel;
> they shall do no wrong
>   and utter no lies,
> nor shall a deceitful tongue
>   be found in their mouths. (Zephaniah 3.12–13)

This is the opposite of pride; it is in the image of the theosis of Christ to be less than, not in a way that humiliates but in a way that throws the self on to the God who loves them. Poverty that is spiritual childhood acknowledges the inability for anyone to be self-sufficient and, as such, for all to seek the welfare of others. The Lord commands that those in Israel seek justice and speak the truth, so spiritual childhood is the pursuit of the good of those who are oppressed. In the Psalms the opposite of the poor are the proud (10.2, 18.28, 37.10, 86.14) indicating that poverty is not necessarily the material type but the way in which the individual relates to God.

Finally, says Gutiérrez, the most obvious form of this is the Beatitudes. Matthew's version is more obviously related to this idea of spiritual poverty whereas Luke can be read as a valorizing of poverty. Luke appears to celebrate material poverty in a way that Matthew changes or rejects. However, when we read Luke alongside Acts, we see that the sort of poverty that correlates to this is the poverty of holding all goods in common. Gutiérrez also argues for a somewhat niche reading that says this is to do with realized eschatology: that the poor are blessed because the kingdom of God has come. While this is possible, it is not the necessary reading of Luke in this instance; and that it should rather be noted that Luke is complicated on this issue but appears to show in Acts that nobody should have need that speaks against the absolute poverty that many live in today and then. Gutiérrez therefore presents a reading of poverty that is instructive for acts of solidarity. It is to view poverty as scandalous and to accept the practice of poverty as spiritual childhood.

Autistic solidarity correlates to this form of solidarity. Those who are in solidarity with autistic people should view the oppression of neurodivergent bodyminds as scandalous. Injustice and oppression is against the will of God:

> Ah, you who make iniquitous decrees,
>   who write oppressive statutes,
> to turn aside the needy from justice
>   and to rob the poor of my people of their right,
> that widows may be your spoil,
>   and that you may make the orphans your prey!
>   (Isaiah 10.1–2)

Isaiah shows that God is against those who oppress the poor, who steal from those without power. It is the work of the church to understand how autistic people are robbed of their rights, how they are written out of flourishing by the law and by society. It is the role of the church to understand these things because it is the role of the church to act according to God's will, and God's will is to protect the poor. The mothers quoted earlier in this chapter, as their children's advocates, attempt to restore to their children their rights, to understand fully their children's situation and to enact the will of God for their good in their children's situation. Gutiérrez says the poor should not be exploited, yet autistic people are frequently exploited. They do not have good access to care; they are locked up in mental health units without hope of release and poorly cared for.[33] Autistic people are more vulnerable to sexual exploitation.[34] They are more likely to die prematurely than non-autistic people: 'Premature mortality is estimated to be three to ten times higher for individuals with ASD.'[35]

Solidarity with autistic people is achieved by witnessing to their oppression, to revealing it both to the world and to the autistic people themselves:

> The commitment is to witness to the evil which has resulted from sin and is a breach of communion. It is not a question of idealizing poverty, but rather taking it on as it is – an evil – to protest against it and to struggle to abolish it.[36]

We return to where we began in this chapter to articulate the solidarity with autistic people, the lived example of motherhood. The question in hand is whether there is a fracture in the communities of stakeholders that cannot be bridged. Whether the language of identity combined with the nature of caring for children, the issue of right to speech combined with an oppressed people group, makes it impossible for those who are invested in the issues surrounding autism to speak to one another. What role can the church have as the body of Christ in these issues?

Theological anthropology can describe all humanity as an icon of creation. Icons serve to point to something beyond themselves. An icon writer will create an icon that will be used by people for prayer, they will mix their paints, their egg tempera or their oils, they will prepare their boards and set up their brushes. They might enter a period of fasting and prayer before they begin. They then create a likeness that is deliberately an unlikeness. It is not a realistic representation of a saint or of Mary, or perhaps even Christ.

Icons are deliberately unlike the thing they represent. This is so the worshipper is constantly recalled in their prayer back to their primary object of devotion – not the icon, but God in Christ through the Holy Spirit. Icons have a particular style; you might even describe them as uncanny. They are a bit odd, they don't look quite right. If you are unfamiliar with icons then you would think them old-fashioned, or a strange style of painting. However, through the iconography of the divine face in every human being we are brought before God by the other. The other is not us, it is different to us, separate; no matter what we might try to do we cannot view the other as if 'from above', the way that God does. When we remember this then we can recognize that something fundamental about our creatureliness not only draws us towards God by the appreciation of the other; the other as *not us* but something fundamentally joins each of us to one another. We are all the same because we are created creatures before God. Any other claim upon ourselves or our identity can come after this.

The unity of being creatures before the gaze of God, the creatures that see the icon of creation in the gaze of one another, means that we have theological reason to be united and to stand in solidarity with one another. Not only that, but we have theological reason, based not on behaviour of any type or relationality or lack of it, to recognize God's image in us as put there by the action of God. We are drawn to solidarity as a Christian vocation because of these things.

Solidarity can so easily look like a form of, at best, patronizing, meaningless sympathy or, at worst, pretence. The mothers who shared their stories of parenting earlier do not pretend to be autistic if they are not, nor do they lay claim to have the same experience of their child. Rather, they demonstrate the solidarity of utter love and commitment to their children walking alongside them companionably. They share their lives with them and accept the hospitality their children offer. Solidarity does not equal identical claims to lived experience or require some voices to be silenced in pursuit of others. Instead, it requires theosis; a self-emptying in order to pursue God as a form of spiritual childhood that is not a humiliation but is a surrender of self to God, and as a consequence, to the other.

Pragmatically speaking, what does solidarity look like for the church today? I believe, based on my own lived experience and the testimony of the mothers we heard from earlier, and of other autistic people, that there are many places where need can be addressed. Churches need to check themselves and their hospitality to difference. Churches have long had an interest in education and it is education where autistic children face the most difficulties. Christians have long been involved in the delivery of healthcare and services, but now is the time to help autistic people access that which is denied to them. Christians, in solidarity with autistic people, have to listen to the needs of the community as a liberative spiritual act; each autistic person will experience the world differently and to stand in solidarity one must first incline one's head and hear.

Notes

1 Bonnie Evans, *The Metamorphosis of Autism: A History of Child Development in Britain*, Social Histories of Medicine (Manchester: Manchester University Press, 2017), p. 92.

2 Daena J. Goldsmith, 'Mothers as Stakeholders and Storytellers in Autism Discourse', *Daena J. Goldsmith* (blog), 11 April 2017, https://daenagoldsmith.com/2017/04/11/mothers-as-stakeholders-and-story tellers/ (accessed 31.01.23).

3 Armand Léon van Ommen (2022) 'Re-imagining church through autism: a Singaporean case study', *Practical Theology*, 15:6, 508–19, https://doi.org/10.1080/1756073X.2022.2080630. p. 514.

4 Goldsmith, 'Mothers as Stakeholders'.

5 Chloe Silverman, *Understanding Autism: Parents, Doctors, and the History of a Disorder* (Princeton, NJ/Oxford: Princeton University Press, 2012), p. 61.

6 Goldsmith, 'Mothers as Stakeholders'.

7 Jessica M. F. Hughes, 'Changing Conversations about Autism: A Critical, Action Implicative Discourse Analysis of U.S. Neurodiversity Advocacy Online' (Boulder, CO: University Press of Colorado, 2015).

8 Evans, *The Metamorphosis of Autism*.
9 Silverman, *Understanding Autism*.
10 Silverman, *Understanding Autism*, pp. 162–3.
11 Hughes, 'Changing Conversations'.

12 For example, see Amanda Saxe, 'The Theory of Intersectionality: A New Lens for Understanding the Barriers Faced by Autistic Women', *Canadian Journal of Disability Studies* 6, no. 4 (24 November 2017): 153–78.

13 For some good examples of reflexivity see Pete Ward, *Participation and Mediation: A Practical Theology for the Liquid Church. Introduction* (London: SCM Press, 2008); Helen Morris and Helen Cameron, *Evangelicals Engaging in Practical Theology: Theology that Impacts Church and World. Introduction* (London: Routledge, 2022).

14 Anna Rowlands, *Towards a Politics of Communion: Catholic Social Teaching in Dark Times* (London/New York: T&T Clark, 2022), p. 113.

15 Daniela C. Augustine, *The Spirit and the Common Good: Shared Flourishing in the Image of God* (Grand Rapids, MI: William B. Eerdmans, 2019).

16 Augustine, *The Spirit*, p. 14.
17 Augustine, *The Spirit*, p. 19.
18 Augustine, *The Spirit*, p. 22.
19 Augustine, *The Spirit*, p. 23.
20 Cited in Augustine, *The Spirit*, pp. 23–4.
21 Augustine, *The Spirit*, p. 25.
22 Augustine, *The Spirit*, p. 27.
23 Evans, *The Metamorphosis of Autism*, p. 41.

24 Joanne Limburg, *Letters To My Weird Sisters: On Autism and Feminism* (London: Atlantic Books, 2022), p. 4.

25 Damian E. M. Milton, 'On the Ontological Status of Autism: The "Double Empathy Problem"', *Disability & Society* 27, no. 6 (October 2012): 883–7.

26 Rowan Williams, *Faith in the Public Square* (London: Bloomsbury Continuum, 2015), p. 15.

27 Augustine, *The Spirit*, p. 27.

28 Gustavo Gutiérrez, *We Drink From Our Own Wells: The Spiritual Journey of a People*, trans. M. J. O'Connell (London: SCM Press 1983), p. 96.

29 Benedict et al., *RB 1980: The Rule of St. Benedict in Latin and English with Notes* (Collegeville, MN: Liturgical Press, 1981), chapter 58.17; Cyprian Smith, *The Path of Life: Benedictine Spirituality for Monks & Lay People* (Ampleforth: Ampleforth Abbey Press, 1996), p. 27.

30 This does not mean that the mothers, as I mentioned above, do

not hope and expect their children not to sin. This is a different quality of change from the change that solidarity with the oppressed requires.

31 Gustavo Gutiérrez et al., *A Theology of Liberation: History, Politics, and Salvation*, rev. version of the orig. English-language trans., SCM Classics (London: SCM Press, 2010), p. 255.

32 Gutiérrez et al., *A Theology*, p. 256.

33 BBC, '"My Boy's Autism Was a Difference, Not a Deficit"', https://www.bbc.co.uk/news/uk-scotland-south-scotland-61411824 (accessed 23.06.22). Nicola Dowling and Gail Champion, 'Father "Devastated" at Lack of Progress on Autism Care', https://www.bbc.co.uk/news/uk-60877292 (accessed 23.06.22).

34 Vide Ohlsson Gotby et al., 'Childhood Neurodevelopmental Disorders and Risk of Coercive Sexual Victimization in Childhood and Adolescence – a Population-based Prospective Twin Study', *Journal of Child Psychology and Psychiatry* 59, no. 9 (September 2018): 957–65.

35 Regina Sala et al., 'Bridging the Gap Between Physical Health and Autism Spectrum Disorder', *Neuropsychiatric Disease and Treatment* 16 (June 2020): 1605–18.

36 Gutiérrez et al., *A Theology*, pp. 266–7.

5

Community

Community, mutuality and creation

It is commonly believed that autistic people are isolated and inaccessible. The image is that they are loners, who wish to be without other people and are incapable of human relationships. They are odd, difficult, uncanny. This is a theologically problematic assumption to make if all humans are made in the image of God and are of equal worth. If community is the appropriate mechanism for the church to be expressed, as the ecclesia, then autistic people should be part of it. This participation in the church is complete when we are full members of the body of Christ.

This chapter proceeds from the argument of the previous chapter. I have argued for the imagination of autistic solidarity and now I wish to describe what a community formed on such principles might look like. In the same manner that solidarity is formed through an understanding of being made in the image of God, so also has Christian thought formulated ideas about hospitality upon which my arguments for liberating communities are based. I will chart a course through ideas of welcome that range from the failures of the liberation project so far, through to the unacceptability of hospitality based on inclusion and accommodation, to a Christian vision of belonging. I will then suggest that an autistic community might include non-humans, and that if this is the case then it is acceptable in light of the goodness of creation and the mandate in scripture that we are all creatures before God. Finally, I will describe the correspondence between the agenda of liberation theology and ecotheology and the place of autistic theology within it.

Failures of universalizing liberation: 'missionaries from the margins'[1]

Liberation theology has not fully achieved the liberation of all people because it has forgotten some of the most significantly marginalized populations. Marcella Althaus-Reid writes of the need for liberation beyond the bounds of liberation theology. She shares the need for the poetry written on the walls of Buenos Aires to be considered the archaeological resource of the theology of people on the streets. This theology of the people is prepared to say 'priests are shit' and 'the government is full of thieves' because their lived experience does not correspond to the church, theology or beliefs about what is decent.[2] The church, she claims, has appropriated the liberation movement and Westernized it.[3] Grand narratives, the way in which society explains and accounts for itself, necessarily homogenizes and smooths over the bumps of alternativity.

In the case of Latin America these acts of explanation involved mutilation, the 'cutting off of the breasts of truth, the reductionism into a new bodily order, that is humanity reduced to one formula, one law of union and compulsion'.[4] Althaus-Reid writes of the lemon vendors on the streets of Argentina, who sell their wares without wearing underwear. They subvert the acceptable discourse of behaviour and morality, by boldly intermingling social expectation, religious discourse and economics in their lives in the streets of the city. Such lemon vendors, and their theologians, are indecent because they challenge the assumed order of things: that Christian religious and Latin American social/economic/ethical boundaries are immutable and accepted, inherently truthful and obvious. They are the assumptions of normalization. In the same way, assumptions of normalization result in autistic lives being whitewashed or condemned as indecent. Correlated to this is the complicity of Christianity in the economic systems that pervade, both in Latin America and elsewhere; this lends religious authority to systems of abuse and exploitation and continues to create 'decency' in socio-political structures that tell individuals, groups and communities what is acceptable and what is not. The church, and theology, continue to label that which is decent and that which is not in its correspondences with systematic theologies. Althaus-Reid states that it is connected intimately with 'Western Grand Narratives'. These narratives explain and control and discursively exclude the other. It is not difficult to see that where this applies to sexual behaviour and excluded bodies in Althaus-Reid's work, it can similarly apply to excluded bodyminds in autistic lives – those who trouble the Grand Narrative of human behaviour, who disrupt the understanding of theological anthropology.

Althaus-Reid finds that liberation theological thought fails to undress itself, to join the street vendors who refuse to wear underwear. Liberation theology is 'decent' theology, concerned with 'discourses of authority in Latin America', but fails to reject oppressive influences and acknowledge that always theology is a sexual theology because of the categories of 'heterosexual binary systems' that order behaviour and tell others what is acceptable and unacceptable – in other words, what is 'decent'.[5] Liberation theology, Althaus Reid claims, has not become *indecent* because it has failed to reject the sexual imaginary of Western theology. Liberation theology accepts that which is considered given, the received and uncriticized prepositional faith that is founded in Western, heterosexual systematic theology. As a woman who has been fully educated and formed in Western theology, whose very warp and weft is constructed as Western, British, white and heterosexual, this does not immediately make sense. Althaus-Reid writes of something different and foreign – the sexualized other of the lemon vendors who do not wear underwear is a challenge to my own understandings of decency until I notice the point of correlation: the affective resonance with my own experience of being indecent. Of being branded as behaving indecently, of disrupting the ideals of neurotypical womanhood with expectations of behaviour, of evangelical womanhood's socialization demands, of the expectations of academic theology to conform to certain values of production and intellect. This is when Marcella Althaus-Reid speaks to the neuro nonconformity of autistic lives of all types and shapes. My experience of nonconformity will be different to others' nonconformity in autistic lives, but this is indeed entirely the point of Althaus-Reid's 'indecent' contribution – that liberation fails at the starting point when it conforms mid-air (in her flipping pancake analogy) to idealized notions that undercut the liberative aims.

Liberation theology has conspired with certain notions of normativity that must be repeatedly railed against for its full potential to be realized in this project. As black theologians, feminist theologians and queer theologians push the boundaries of what a true liberation can be, imaginatively and experienced, so also must autistic and neurodiverse theologians push the discourse of liberation to accept the peculiar and the diverse in theological communities and faith communities. Anything less is the failure of the liberation project.

Liberation theology truly is liberative when it accepts that liberation must understand boundaries with clear sight. Boundaries relate to this chapter's current concern when we accept that they are necessarily descriptive and participatory for communities of faith but are also blurry and complex, especially when we consider those who are 'in' and those who are 'out'. Even more complex are the difficulties of community boundaries for those who wish to be 'in' – but are unallowed, or allowed only partially or conditionally. Such conditional membership of faith communities is noticeable in practices of accommodation – for example, autistic people who must mask their own behaviour to be accepted, or who are placed in special groups that exist on the margins of the main community. These autists become like the lemon vendors who say, 'Fine, I'll promise then never to leave my house again without my pants on.'[6] They cover up the indecent aspects of their self in order to be included. This inclusion is not adequate or acceptable; it is not decent because of the moral imperative to behave decently according to a confusion of religious, economic and social demands that bear no relation to the faith founded upon Jesus Christ. Indeed, the notion of inclusion itself is indecent.

John Swinton critiques 'inclusion'.[7] Inclusion, he says, is a political rhetoric that is not especially well understood or defined. Autistic liberation theology, as I hope to have already conveyed, is deeply suspicious of neurotypical political rhetoric that is too closely correlated to economic value and production. Inclusion can be 'thin' in application, Swinton says, in that it maintains the person who is 'included' as other. Such 'others' are seen as not human in their own self, but only in the way they reflect kindness and accept the practices of others. The autistic person who is included by being placed in a special programme for disabled people within a church, but simultaneously without, is not particularly included. They are partitioned from the main church, and treated as subject to the vision of a hospitable church community rather than subject to their own story of faith and salvation. They are a 'project' that the church is engaged with, chronically 'doing good' without recognizing that this community's attempts at inclusion are exclusionary.[8] This might appear to be unduly harsh on church programmes that have no sense of this, that attempt only to do that which is good to the best of their ability. However, the work of the liberation theologian in whatever guise is to call out oppression even when those who are oppressed do not recognize it.

The members of community groups for disabled people may not see it as oppressive, and may wholeheartedly enjoy their time in programmes designed to meet their needs. Indeed, I have spoken to individuals who prefer to sit in a separate room from the main congregation so that they do not disturb them with their exclamations and tics, their verbal disturbances that are unpredictable and embarrassing. However, this is not actually community; it is mitigation. The autistic person in their own room, separate from the congregation, is included but is not welcome, is not embraced, for they always remain a stranger in the midst of the congregation. 'Indecent' in their exclamations and tics – disruptive presences that restrict the worship of the community that performs 'decently' in the presence of God. They are geographically, surprisingly, unapologetically marginalized by the church. They aren't in the sanctuary with the rest of the congregation! How this can be considered to include them defies my imagination; this is exclusion and it is the failure of 'inclusion' to achieve anything other than mitigation of strangeness.

Miroslav Volf indicates this crucial point in his work describing the theological work required for acceptance of identity and otherness.[9] Liberation runs a risk of excluding those whom it seeks to liberate by maintaining their status as victims of oppression. Narratives of liberation can 'imprison them within the narrative of their own victimization'.[10] Inclusion requires boundaries; it necessarily defines who fits into a community and who does not. In the same way that we encounter through E. P. Sanders's work on Paul's understanding of salvation – something that initially troubled many – it is seemingly the way in which we define acceptability.[11] I believe that the reason the evangelical church found this such a difficult perspective to digest was not the result of the rationality or theological/biblical accuracy, but because it revealed something about the nature of church and the salvation community that we were not prepared to look in the eye. Evangelicals, I think, did not like the idea that Paul was concerned in any way with those who were in the community and those who were not because it appeared to emphasize not a logical, emotionless acceptance of prepositional truth such as the Luther/righteousness by faith narrative did, but something akin to the playground cliques or partisan political groups that exist by enforcing the walls of their community, by showing what it means to be insiders and outsiders. Whether or not this reflects what Sanders was trying to say or not is irrelevant; the emotional response to his proposition was that it couldn't be true – Christian communities are inclusive, welcoming and open to anyone. It cannot be that we have boundaries in any way. Community, in the Christian sense, is infinitely complex when we consider that it is by its nature formed by – in whichever way we deign it, Reformation salvation views or not – accepting and including those who are acceptable and rejecting and excluding those who are not.

On this journey from Argentinian street vendors, to a young autistic man alone in a side room at church, to Palestinian Paul trying to understand where the community was and was not, I chart a path that relates to autism because the core issue that many autistic people feel is that they do not belong, that they are different. Sometimes that comes, as for me, as something that slowly dawns over many years: that no matter how much effort I put in there was not a place that I could truly fit in. In contrast, it can be felt violently from the earliest pre-school years when language fails to arrive as expected and gross motor function looks and sounds unacceptable; such otherness is perhaps the single identifying feature of autistic lives. Liberation theology, theology at large, bears a responsibility to address this peculiarity that autistic people feel both in and out of the church if it is to correspond to the aims it has to set people on their path to God without impediment and with lives that are – now, not in the future – lived to their fullest.

The neurotypical church is guilty of more sins than the appropriation of liberation theology. When the church cannot accommodate those who approach God in ways that are counter-normative then the church has failed in its most basic mission to those who seek it. Before we even attempt to reach those who have not made it within the walls of the church, we must look to those who are valiantly trying to stay within and failing because of the behaviour of the church that contains them. Is it not better that a millstone be around their neck than such a response? And yet, it is so unobvious to many that this is a sin that it requires a lengthy explanation to describe it.

Radical hospitality, radical mutuality

The church tradition has called the practice of welcoming the other 'hospitality'. Using similar ideas to those I explored as foundations for solidarity, hospitality is a principle recognized as based on a theological anthropology. Christine Pohl describes this as 'recognition'. It is the tradition of the church to understand difference in these terms:

> Recognition involves respecting the dignity and equal worth of every person and valuing their contributions, or at least their potential contributions, to the larger community.[12]

To recognize someone as the same as you is a subversive practice, says Pohl. It is more than simply dinner parties and tea and biscuits but the intentional act of welcome to someone who is unfamiliar. This has challenged the church since its inception. Peter did not know how to welcome the Gentiles – the church did not know how to understand different cultures, races, genders. It is important to bring this conversation into the sphere of neurodivergence too. Throughout this history of welcome (or lack thereof) theological ideas have been entertained to understand the urge to draw others in, which is a spiritual act. John Calvin, says Pohl, argued that the stranger was the same as us because they are 'marked' with the image of God. In the same way, John Wesley believed that all humans had been made for God and for relationship through Christ.[13] The identification with God primarily in the question of recognition becomes the great leveller; all humans are of equal value and worth before God. This is the fundamental basis for acts of hospitality. I will describe the theological foundations of such hospitality. It is radical because it is the subversive community of Christ that reallocates all other categories of personhood to being secondary to the primary identifier: being baptized in the Holy Spirit. I will then propose that the most fitting way to understand this reallocation of identifiers is to make use of the Benedictine practice of hospitality founded in humility before the other.

This kind of levelling that I suggest is counter to the universalizing plurality of liberal democracy that Daniella Augustine critiques. She argues that pluralism and multiculturalism remove the voice of the other as they are always and continually among the many voices that are governed by Western multicultural acceptance.[14] This is a failure of acceptance because it flattens difference, effectively muting the distinct notes of individuals into a monotone of everyone together. There becomes then an inability and an unwillingness to learn the language of the other and that dialogue becomes impossible. However, if we recast this deliberate ignoring of difference and instead place theological anthropology as created difference we can learn the language of those differences deliberately. We hold in tension the unity of equal value with the diversity of created difference.

We are all one in Christ Jesus: mutuality

Hospitality is located in our shared human nature, that we are made in the image of God. That which links all people and makes a way for us to share solidarity also links us in a theologically constructed understanding of community. We have seen that solidarity is a fundamental theological category of togetherness. Gustavo Gutiérrez argued that true solidarity does not require the individual to be removed from their social circumstances.[15] For Gutiérrez, this referred to the situation of poverty; for the purposes of my argument, though, it refers to the autistic community. The self-understood autistic community is in its infancy; growing out of the neurodiversity movement notions of autism as a social group are new. However, the notion of remaining is pertinent. It is the case that solidarity has a drive to sustain the individual in their own social circumstances – not the circumstances of oppression, but their own self in community. For the autistic individual this has radical and practical outworking. It resists the demand for an autistic person to change their own social being-in-the-world. They are not required to be removed from their own social situation and they should not have to act or behave contrary to their own nature. Typically referred to as 'masking', autistic people are often pressured to behave in accordance with normative social values and practices. Behaviour that is deemed unacceptable is 'trained out' of the individual, either deliberately by the other (such as a parent or a therapist) or reflexively by the autistic person in a bid to fit in. This is the equivalent of changing the social circumstances of the poor in Gutiérrez's description.

In an almost equal and opposite situation autistic individuals, alongside other disabled people, are often placed in 'disability' groups within churches; the groups are focused on the autistic person's needs and are separate from the rest of the congregation. This is more frequently the case with those whose support needs are more visible to the congregation. The disadvantages of this are the exclusion from mainstream congregational practices and community and the theological fracturing of identity.

As my friend J comments, 'We are set aside in special groups and are not connected to our peers.' Indeed, it is the case that these special groups forcibly create peers for the individual from among other disabled people, and thus remove from them choice and participation. I propose that this is not only socially unacceptable – because of the removal of freedom and choice – but also theologically unacceptable because of the belief that all Christians are one in Christ and all humans are made in the image of God.

This twofold problem of force in communities, seemingly at opposing ends of a scale – removal from social communities of choice, and being forced into communities without choice – are based on flawed theology. We are required by our theological anthropology to understand everyone as made in the image of God. Even more, within churches we should understand that all Christians are one in the body of Christ.

I strongly reject specialist church communities for autistic people, however well-intentioned they are. I reject the situation that causes them to be safe places for families and children while acknowledging that for many this is sadly the case. For those individuals or families that find safety in church communities that are separate from the main body of believers who come together at a particular time and place to worship, I grieve. I appreciate that many autistic children and their parents prefer such church environments, but I cannot accept that this is theologically valid. The body of Christ is not divided into partitions of acceptability. The reasons that individuals might prefer specialist groups for autism in churches amount to condemnation of the church itself, the worldwide church, which has made itself inaccessible to those who seek it and has made it necessary for people to seek alternative provision.

This is not the message that Christ gave to the church in John 17 and it is not acceptable to promote it. The church is the kingdom of God represented on earth; it should strive to be the most inclusive and welcoming place it can be, and alternative provision accepts failure, accepts the narrative that the not-yet of the kingdom trumps the now. It says that fallen communities of fallen humanity cannot hope to represent the body of Christ as a unified whole but must accept division, partiality, hidden groups. I do not write this for those who facilitate these groups, those who heard a call from God to welcome people who are unwelcome; in fact, they are saints in the midst of the church. Rather, I write this to the church as a whole that has designed itself to be a community that cannot include all by its nature and is unrepentant. The church should move from a position of accommodation and alternative arrangements to a place where autistic people can truly say 'I belong'.

Hospitality: belonging and embrace

Miroslav Volf notes that 'us and them' creates a polarity, a separation of types and intrenchment of difference. In some ways, as helpful and constructive as the neurodiversity paradigm is to deconstruct medical and prejudicial judgements, it must be prohibited from making theological demands that are unsubstantiated. By this I mean the pervasive divide between autistic and other neurodivergent people and those who do not have these labels. There must be a defining characteristic that transcends these categories in order for true hospitality and welcome to exist. Volf's main point about embrace is that 'God's reception of hostile humanity into divine communion is a model for how human beings should relate to one another.'[16] This challenges the distinctions between oppressors and oppressed, between those who are in need of liberation and those who maintain the conditions that discriminate and cause suffering. This is partly because the modern Western thinker, and the postmodern Western thinker, will prioritize 'freedom' as the ultimate end of liberation. This freedom is usually described in individualized terms about individual destiny and choice. Everyone is free because everyone is equal and human dignity means that this equality is fundamentally related to self-determination.

As I have suggested with my engagement with indecent theology, liberation theology has not always answered the needs of neurodiverse people straightforwardly.

In this way, the quest for freedom found in liberation agendas may fail to account for the autistic experience. What is freedom if I cannot feed myself or gain employment? The liberal economic agenda, to which many accounts of freedom are tied, does not allow for diverse requirements of freedom. Freedom that is defined entirely as individual agency and lack of external interference may not be the best way to describe autistic freedom. Autistic freedom may indeed have elements of ability to choose for oneself but also the ability to receive help.

This, perhaps, is the socialist agenda versus the liberal one. The socialist agenda, politically, would expect more cooperation among individuals and for decisions to be made that do not always prioritize individual agency. However, both social and liberal political forms still maintain divisions of us and them. They seek to highlight those who oppress and those who are oppressed – however these terms may be parsed. This is unhelpful to an extent because of the maintenance of these binaries. Although Volf is quick to maintain that there are still oppressions and instances of injustice and those should not be ignored (quite the opposite, in fact), however, it is the oppression/liberation schema that he questions: the pervasive us and them. Neurodiversity and neurotypicality are useful tools to question and critique the medicalized model of neurodiversity but they should be kept in their place and should not dictate terms to theology. They are not the ultimate reality, the final word about an individual or about a community. There is a word after that, this word is the Word of God, who radically accepts all people and does not just include them.

If we are able to question these individualized accounts of freedom we are called to look beyond our own articulation of freedom in these terms. If we no longer understand liberation as a tool that is wielded against others who are oppressors, we can begin to understand that liberation is a challenge to our sense of prioritizing self or individuals. As Swinton claims:

> *In order to find ourselves we need to look away from ourselves.* Looking at ourselves through the politics of modernity keeps our perspective on inclusion thin and narrow. Looking

to Jesus offers us a thick description of who God is and what it means to be a human being.[17]

A primary characteristic of Benedictine spirituality is humility. In chapter seven of the Rule of St Benedict the monk encourages his followers to practise the biblically saturated attitude of humility. With perhaps only the merest trace of irony, Benedict advises those who wish to speedily ascend to the highest steps of humility and thus have exaltation in heaven to follow his advice; we must always have the fear of God 'before our eyes'.[18] This keeps the follower of Christ fixed on the source of all things and their relative role within creation; the fear of God puts us in our place. It also acts as a guard upon our actions; we are seen by God always and all our steps our noted by him. Similarly, we must not love our own will but prefer the will of God.[19]

The third and fourth steps of humility are perhaps the most alien to postmodern ears: that we must obey those in authority over us.[20] Combined with the sixth step of humility, that of satisfaction with the most humble tasks (perhaps cleaning the toilets or making the tea after church), the rule suggests humility to be something that appears at first glance to be unpalatable.[21] Despite this, I would suggest that it is this practice of humility, as advised historically by Benedict but when it is translated into current understanding is the practice that makes community possible, that is radically inclusive and embracing of those who are other.

What, then, to say of Benedict's advice to obey and to take on menial and unsatisfying tasks? Benedict does not advocate humiliation of a damaging type. We are not publicly to shame ourselves as a route to humility. Rather, it is founded on an understanding of truth. We are, says Michael Casey (after Bernard of Clairvaux), not divine but creatures – all that we have comes from God and we are in a situation of complete dependence on him for all life.[22] We are also all sinners; none can do right before him but all rely upon the grace through Christ Jesus for our justification:

Part of the truth of human existence is that we are called to live for God. Humility, oddly enough, leads us to recognize our human dignity. It reminds us that we were created for God and that we will be profoundly miserable until we devote the substance of our energies to the realization of this innate potential.[23]

The practice of humility is a great leveller. All are before God, no matter what bodymind that they live in. No matter if they are of great value in society – maybe a doctor, a famous actor, a politician – or the least in the eyes of society: which in our case is those who are cast out of society because of autism. Humility primarily resists the instrumentalization of the other for purposes that are self-serving. No other is an instrument because the self is rejected as the object of actions. It is of course necessary also to do this with open eyes and sensible moderation lest I be understood to be promoting choosing the subjugation of self. Rejecting the other as an instrument in our own ends does not require us to make ourselves instruments. Christian humility is the worship of God and the remembering of our own place in the worship of God, not the positioning of ourselves in places of vulnerability. This may be something that cannot be achieved without the help of the Holy Spirit.

Kathryn Tanner describes all human relationships as competitive; not in the sense of a competition for resources or power (although it can be these things), but the necessity of the person who is one thing means that another cannot be. This is in contrast to relationships with God which are non-competitive.[24] This is an important point to recall in this theological construction of humility: that it has limits and boundaries that – if pushed – will become power exchanges that simply change who suffers. Resisting instrumentalization is crucial to the belonging in community of autistic people because it is the way in which a fully humble and hospitable church welcomes the other without keeping them as *other*.

Humility prevents us from managing to include people at the expense of them belonging. This is a distinction that John Swinton draws, between inclusion as an inadequate act and belonging as the ultimate concern of the church.[25] In the same way as I have already indicated, inclusion seeks to find a suitable space in which to accommodate people perceived as different and difficult. It attempts to take structures that already exist and make minor adjustments so that people can access them who would otherwise be prevented from so doing. It places in the primary place the structures as they stand and seeks to maintain the status quo. Those who are seeking to be included are the agents of change; they must adapt in order to move from the outside to the inside of a community.

The inside of the community is the sphere of people who are committed to the community as it stands and as it exists. To be considered part of this community, behaviours, practices and attitudes must conform to the majority and 'inclusion' is the process by which this conformation occurs. Inclusion at its least successful mitigates for situations that do not suit the person who is to be included. A working example of this is headphones worn to protect a person with auditory sensitivity from loud music or conversation noise. This purportedly includes the person by causing them to adapt their own preferences to the preferences of the majority. This does not maintain difference but homogenizes to the majority choice.

Daniella Augustine writes of the Pentecostal event as paradigmatic for the understanding of diversity and plurality.[26] There is a longstanding belief that Pentecost reversed the events of Babel in Genesis, where the hubris of humanity in seeking to build a tower that accessed the divine was diverted by making people unable to understand one another. However, Augustine finds that there is continuity in the accounts; it is the imperial homogenization, the quest for the universal majority, that is scattered at Babel. In neurodiverse terms, Babel was the metaphor for neurotypical power dominance which suppresses diverse minds and forces them to the majority way of being in the world. This is an act of violence, following Augustine, because it wilfully suppresses uniqueness. Autistic exclusion is the exclusion of novel thought patterns, novel creativity, and interaction with the physical environment. These unique behaviours are found to be different, and then understood to challenge majority thinking and existing; they are peculiar and therefore other. They provoke questions about the way that people exist in their worlds and this in turn provokes fear.

No tower can be built at Babel if diverse minds do not conform to the imperial architectural plans for tower building. If instructions cannot be followed or will not be understood, then the homogenizing necessity for tower building is lost – the communal will to self that the imperial agenda expresses cannot be achieved when divergent individuals disrupt the best-laid plans. Babel is, following Augustine, not the punishment for all humanity but the preservation of difference, the continuation of diversity, and the divine judgement on majority rule at the expense of the marginal and particular. In this way Pentecost is not a step change in the divine plan; it is not a reversal of core principles about difference, but a continuation.

The core metaphor at the heart of both Babel and Pentecost is language. The diversity of ethnicity is represented by the way in which people communicate, through their different languages. When the Spirit descends at Pentecost with tongues of fire the individuals in the crowds all understood in their own language. They do not all regain some common tongue that allows them to communicate with one another; rather, the Spirit communicates to them as they are, in their own speech. Communication is fundamental to autism; it is considered deficit in many situations, or unique and particular in others but it is the metaphor and reality to which the autistic community circle around time and again.

Damien Milton's double empathy problem, which is to do with mutual incoherence between neurotypical and neurodiverse people, is fundamentally about communication.[27] Moreover, autistic people might communicate in ways that are different to the majority – they might spell to communicate or use other assisted technology; they may never speak or only speak sometimes; they may speak with an unusual affect that becomes an obstacle because it is striking in its difference. The difficulty with communication in the autistic life is directly related to the biblical narrative of Babel and Pentecost.

Augustine argues that human community post-Babel is only

possible if the languages are learnt. Language functions to construct thought as well as express it; it is the way in which we think, know and create ideas. It is profoundly more complex than mere expression but captures something of the fundamental self when we use it, however that may be. Therefore, the mutuality required to translate languages and the profound act of hospitality that this involves is significant for neurodiversity:

> The translation of language is not a mere tool for transforming an obscure sound into a coherent thought. It is a path of convergence of contents and identities into a dialogical whole which takes a life of its own.[28]

Community is formed in such identities and their sharing, adapting and co-creating. Any given group of people will have shared languages, terms and idioms that express their history and their ideologies. In a family it might be the re-telling of stories; the repeating of one single word that evokes a longstanding joke; the shorthand between long-married people which reduces the number of words spoken to a mere scattering. These are communities of speech that are more than the words, but never less than them. Autistic people who do not use spoken language, or autistic people who have 'social communication difficulties', exist on the outside of these communities of speech. The only way in which access is granted is if they learn the language, or fake it, in order to enter the community. There is no reciprocal language learning, where the neuromajority learn the language of autism positively, rather than to correct it. Being on the outside of these speech communities is paradigmatic for the homogenizing effect of inclusion. Inclusion allows for entrance to a speech community with adaptations so that the common tongue is preserved. This does not allow for diversity of languages but flattens them.

This section has attempted to show the ways in which universalizing behaviour and normativity does allow for difference that is celebrated in scripture. Attendant to that celebration of difference is the requirement to enact hospitality that rejects homogenizing but welcomes difference on its own terms.

Augustine says that scriptural mandates of hospitality, welcoming the widow and the orphan, the stranger and the foreigner, do not demand that they change their status to receive their welcome. There are no conditions to the welcome of the other. In autistic lives these conditions are regularly placed on us, whether through treatments to make autistics more 'normal' behaviourally; employment conditions that restrict or upset us; social rules that are obscure and unexpressed. To fit into neurotypical society and to thrive means that conditions must be met.

Yet at Pentecost these conditions do not exist; the Holy Spirit does not meet individuals who have conformed to predetermined rules of engagement. Rather, each individual hears in their own language God's glorious revelation of himself. God meets the autistic person in their own language, with their own communication. This has great personal resonance for me. In charismatic churches, such as the one I attend, there is much language. There are the common expressions used to describe Christian experience; there are many 'scripts' rehearsed for mutual encouragement in worship and in prayer. It is informal and spontaneous. It depends heavily on emotional experience. I have found this to be an obstacle at times, when I can't find the words to improvise in prayer or access my emotions in a moment of spiritual encounter. This is not simply a charismatic problem – all corners of the church experience this – yet we learn from the account at Pentecost that God speaks all languages, even when nobody else nearby can understand it – God can understand it. God does not universalize but instead particularizes. Community is formed through this particular rather than eradicating it.

Augustine says that the biblical mandate for the newly formed, post-Pentecost community is to love the stranger as they are. The autistic stranger should not be treated with fear but with welcome. This is because of the new 'Christ-like communal consciousness' that comes from Pentecost.[29] It is Christ-like because it mimics the self-giving of Christ which has selfishness as anathema; the priority of the wellbeing of the other is central. This is directly in contradiction to homogeneity in community.

Benedictine stability

I have long been impressed with the sisters at my local abbey, St Mary's Abbey in West Malling. They are, both in themselves and in what they represent, a source of hope and peace in a world that seems rarely to offer much of either. When the sisters lead their guests in worship, when they raise their voices in their beautiful chapel, they open a gate to heaven; the presence of God is among them, and through their own hospitable welcome this transfers to their guests. It is very different from Pentecostal and charismatic worship; the sisters know God quietly and with dedication. The abbess once welcomed some students from nearby St Augustine's College of Theology to stand in the chapel and consider the architecture. I was trying very hard to do just that but mostly I watched the abbess herself. She had something that I still cannot describe about her, something that appeared to be an utter stillness, a steadiness.

I know that, having spoken to the sisters, they do not claim a saintliness for themselves. The sisters understand themselves to be fellow pilgrims in the walk towards God. Yet I fully expect that they occasionally fall out with one another and fall into such mundane sins as failing to wash up their coffee mug or whistling in the corridor despite their vows to keep relatively quiet. I do not do them the dishonour of failing to recognize their humanity.

However, the abbess did say something that was about the architecture of the chapel but has remained with me for a different reason. The chapel at West Malling Abbey is a brutalist design; I (as you may be beginning to realize) can tell you nothing further about why that is interesting – but what I found significant then is that the windows are quite high up near the ceiling. You can't really see from the chapel the truly beautiful gardens that the sisters keep. But you can see the light glancing through, in beams that pool on the floor like touches of divine revelation; and of course this changes throughout the year. The light is higher or brighter in the summer, dappled in the autumn, harsh and cold or nearly absent in the winter; obviously, at many points in the day when the sisters pray the hours at night, the light is completely absent. The abbess described how she would notice these changes of light as she went in and out of the chapel seven times a day, every day for years and years. As ecclesial architects are both wise and artistically brilliant, I am sure that this was the intention; however, the days upon days of the presence of the mother abbess is also brilliant. The abbey, being Benedictine, is committed to stability.

Stability in Benedictine communities is to that individual community rather than to the movement or monastic tradition particularly. Movement of individuals between Benedictine communities is rare. Rather, once one enters that community you remain there. You see in and out the seasons of your life with the others who are also in the community. If you are ill they care for you; if you are annoying they put up with you; if you are unhappy they sit with you. Always and for your whole life you are the community and the community is you. The lines between the individual and the group are blurry in an inarticulate way. Yet you are a fundamental part of the Benedictine community; nothing can change it.

Benedictine stability appeals to me and always has. I think this is because of my autistic dislike of change. It is also because it takes me a long time to get to know people and, to some extent, to trust them. I wish for the people I know to remain; for friendships and community to be based upon something other than my own social skills. For there to be something that causes us, a bit like being in a family, to be there always no matter the fluctuating ability of both neurodivergent and neurotypical people to be socially present. In real terms this means that the church community becomes like a family that worships together. It means that the community bonds count for something that is not casual, not temporary or provisional. It also means that church leaders remain where they are placed rather than take on new jobs and leave or stay for predetermined short periods. This is because to go beyond inclusion and hospitality to something that is deeper, thicker and more fundamental requires a commitment that is not based on ephemeral things such as socializing, Sunday attendance alone, community groups or any other temporary or unstable church strategy.

When the sisters enter the chapel they bow at the cross and walk past the baptism font. They cannot come to worship without remembering the death of the Lord Jesus or their baptism into the community of faith. By making the death and resurrection of Christ and the baptism through which we participate in that death and resurrection the fundamental element of community worship, the sisters deliberately identify themselves as belonging to something permanent and unchanging. This identity transcends all other identities that we may choose or have thrust upon us. By remembering our baptism we remember that the community of faith is one that remains throughout all other changes and transitions, one that is the core of who we are and our primary focus for community.

Church communities should be places of encounter with God and with one another. They should identify all within them as glorious examples of God's creative and loving hand. To do this fully for the autistic person is to do so with warm embrace and radical hospitality, not with accommodation and inclusion. The ever-still and present love of God should model to us, like the sisters at the abbey, the ability to remain with our fellow human beings out of love of God and the other; not out of our ephemeral social graces or fragile human connections, but instead held by the loving gaze of God on his ordained community of faith.

On animals

Ivy is ten months old, brown with golden red highlights and full of traditional cocker spaniel energy and mischief. She is also socially much more adept than her owner. She meets many people with such vigorous tail wagging that the whole back half of her body bends in the middle as if governed by a pivoting mechanism. Ivy is internationally loved; she has been spoken to in Finnish, Welsh and, recently, Ukrainian. As I write, the war in Ukraine is devastating the country and many refugees are living in the UK, including a few who have taken up residence near my home. When I walk Ivy along with my two youngest children to the primary school, we regularly meet the Ukrainian children. They arrive at school and look for Ivy; they come over to her and stroke her and cuddle her and whisper to her. They shyly look at me for permission and continue to let Ivy abundantly love and adore them while demanding that her tummy is rubbed. One of the children has begun to learn English and sidled up to me and said, 'Your dog is beautiful.' I see this as a demonstration of a beautiful thing; my ridiculous spaniel has done what hardly anyone else had managed to do and communicate with these children, who were no doubt traumatized and troubled by their wrench from their homeland. And what she had communicated was love.

My reflection upon animals is because of this love that is expressed by Ivy and, to some extent, my cat.[30] Ivy loves her family unconditionally and uniquely. She shows her affection for each of us in slightly different ways – she always licks my son's face; she without fail jumps right on my head in the morning with very little warning; she stands and waits for the older children to arrive home from school. She loves us all. She is my most easy relationship; I am able to be much myself without any pretence or complication and I rarely misunderstand what she wants me to know. We exist in a dynamic based on things other than words (although she has a good grasp on 'biscuit') and largely a gentle rhythm of companionship. I am aware that many autistic people would attest to similar relationships with animals.

This part of my argument for autistic community makes the claim that community is best understood as one that incorporates the whole of creation. This notion is given an autistic theological hue because the autistic community casts far and wide for relationships beyond only human ones – understanding community outside of a neurotypical formulation that is anthropocentric. Liberation theologians have made the link between the need for liberation of humans who are oppressed by other humans and animals who are oppressed by humans. Thus kinship is found both in individual relationships between animals and humans, in relationships of mutuality as created beings, and in solidarity with those who are in need of liberation.

The relationship with animals for autistic people is demonstrated both in academic literature and in the popular imagination. Recently the television personality Chris Packham recollected the role that his miniature poodles have had in his life, making the link between the common use of autism assistance dogs and his own experience and expressing a hope that other autistic people would know the relational value of animals.[31] Therapies directed at autistic people make use of animal relationships to further the bonds between individual and therapist as well as to make therapy more 'effective', with improvements in social behaviour noted.[32] It is not only dogs but other animals, such as horses, that are considered to 'improve' autistic symptoms.[33] The relationship between humans and animals extends beyond autism therapies to the broader psychological research themes:

> Most researchers have, when examining the roots of animal assisted therapy (AAT), made a point of acknowledging a uniquely intermingled and inherent relationship between humans and animals that manifests a rather mystical guiding quality (Fine, 2006; Pavlides, 2008).[34]

Despite a negative view of autism and a desire for a cure to be eventually found, Merope Pavlides makes some important points about the relationship with animals that autistic people may have. She reminds us that not all autistic people, much like any other person, will enjoy the company of animals. This reality is why this section of my thinking is found among the broader section on autistic theological visions of community. I appreciate that autistic people are diverse and although some value the companionship of animals, many do not. It is one theological reflection that is possible among many. Pavlides also reminds us that the link between animals and autistic humans is not 'magical'. It does not represent a special ability on the part of autistic people that neurotypical people do not have to relate to animals.[35]

In the same way that the superpower mythos that surrounds autistic people is profoundly unhelpful, to propagate a view that autistic people cannot relate to other people but can relate to animals would be unhelpfully simplistic. Rather, what I hope to demonstrate in this section is the potential for the companionship, therapeutic and emotional value that animals offer to some autistic people can be conceived of theologically. It does not need to be unsaid or embarrassing in the church community, much like the view that many have of the traditional village-green pet blessing service; rather it is theologically rich and in keeping with scripture and tradition to place a high value on animals and their co-inheritance with humans.

David Clough cautions about understanding theologically animal lives solely in their relationship to humans. It would be a straightforward analysis that claimed autistic lives have often found the companionship of animals to be both comforting and structuring for their lives, and therefore construct a theological reflection upon said relationship that values the instrumental element of support and assistance only. It is my casual observance of others, and my own belief concerning my own relationship with animals, that disabuses me of this. When animals are described as 'part of the family' this is not a metaphor but a statement of a relationship. Animals, companion or wild, are often in the autistic world (although not universally) a true form of community that deserves a theological account.

I no longer call you servants: towards kinship creation

Traditionally the human relationship with the world has been understood in two primary ways. The earliest accounts described the relationship as one of dominion; humanity was to tame the earth and subdue it based on the interpretation in Genesis 1:

> God said to them, 'Be fruitful and multiply, and fill the earth and subdue it; and have dominion over the fish of the sea and over the birds of the air and over every living thing that moves upon the earth.' (Genesis 1.28)

This verse in Genesis seems to imply something of a separation of humanity from the rest of creation. In particular, following on from the previous verse that demarcates humanity as made in the image of God, a complex and peculiar description that has lent itself to the argument that humans are fundamentally different from the rest of the created order. David Clough reminds us that such biblical passages as Psalm 8, that humanity is 'a little lower than God', and Luke 12.7 that we, humans, are of more value than the sparrows, has added weight to the notion that we are distinct and special above all other created beings.[36]

Daniel Horan argues that this viewpoint developed under the influence of Hellenistic thought to become a question of anthropology not directed towards the rest of creation but towards God; in what ways, asked patristic and medieval theologians, are we like God?[37] The conclusion, he tells us, was based on Aristotle's view that humans have a rationality that is not present in animals. Once again we are reacquainted with a view, this time an ancient one, that human worth is found in our abilities to think and produce via rational, mind- and thought-based productivity. This was a view of the human–divine–animal relationship that was not based upon scriptural exegesis, says Horan, but on prevailing thought in the culture of the time. This thinking gained traction in the Italian renaissance when humanity was considered to be well above the rest of creation because of its God-like status as controllers of the rest of creation – in other words, a sovereign right that is bestowed upon humanity as distinct from the rest of creation. Autistic theology should question such an emphasis on value forged in the ability to think; and compounding the devaluing of the created order on such an ability should further question this presumption.

Time has adjusted this view of anthropology that forgets the created world.[38] Richard Bauckham notes the change represented in the 1991 statement by the Board for Social Responsibility of the General Synod of the Church of England. This emphasizes sharing the same world as the rest of creation, that God has trusted us to care for creation as those who are made in God's image and that we should therefore not exploit creation.[39] This is the stewardship model of humanity's relationship with creation. Creation is under the care of humans who still maintain a semi-divine status in between the created world and God. There are a number of ways in which theologians and biblical scholars have dismantled the stewardship argument, not least that it does not do justice to the Genesis texts that it requires for authority.[40]

The ways in which stewardship understandings of humanity and creation do the most harm for autistic theology is in the anthropological model it promotes. Humans are required to have a special role in the created order because they are made in the image of God; the imago Dei sets us apart and gives humanity a divine spark that cannot be found elsewhere. Horan finds that the imago Dei concept has been associated with rationality for a long period of Christian history. It has required over time this rationality to be the thing that distinguishes humans from non-human creatures.[41] Alongside this is the ability to construct relationships and make moral decisions that are markers of the specialness that humans are gifted with, and that animals and the created world are not. This, says Horan, is a 'sense of superiority' which of course not only finds animals in need of rational thought, but also those humans who do not fit the mould. As I suggested in Chapter 1, autistic individuals think and act differently, in a different key. I am not making a claim that some autistic people are not rational, but I am questioning the valorizing of rationality, which is often construed as academic ability, as the greatest good and the thing that divinity is defined by. In the same way autistic relationships, that characteristic of relationality that is suggestive of the imago Dei, is something that autistic people are often thought to lack. I contest that autism per se does not make an individual lack relationality but that it presents very differently in autistic people. Notwithstanding this, the promotion of relationality and rationality as a characteristic of the imago Dei that lends credence to the stewardship model is damaging – not only to creation but to theological anthropology.

The relationship between some autistic people and animal

companions is instructive of a theological anthropology that disavows understandings of ability and disability. The ability (or lack of) for any individual person is very much reduced to irrelevance with this anthropology. Miguel J. Romero indicates this when he argues that much scope is placed on a kind of perfection that is found in 'normate' humanity, and which is lost in those deemed disabled. He calls this an 'idealized, anthropological caricature' that theologians are prone to reach for.[42] This anthropology presupposes someone who is neither vulnerable nor dependent, and who expresses no need for others in their self-sufficient existence. Beliefs that account for anything less than this idealized perfection account for flaws in humanity through the theological description of sin and the Fall. These flaws, the image of the less-than human who is not perfect, are not the human's natural state. The human being was designed to be perfect and by being imperfect – through illness, injury, disability or neurodiversity (so construed as lack) – they are indications of the consequences of sin entering the world. The requirement for people to be the best of all creation in the stewardship model requires certain types of human characteristics to become necessary for full humanity.

Community of creation

Community with animals becomes possible once we override the argument that being made in the image of God makes us fundamentally different from animals; in other words, ontologically distant. A more recent contribution from ecotheologians and theologians who have taken an interest in the environment envisages creation differently and the relationship with humanity also. This is called 'community of creation theology' and has become increasingly understood as a viable and significant move in theology for the benefit of all creation and also for humans. It is in this community of creation that I wish to suggest autistic theology can benefit. I will briefly overview some theologians' contributions from a diverse spectrum of the church, but first I will look at some examples from scripture of community with animals.

Community with animals in scripture

The scriptural witness places value on the created order in its entirety. Humanity is placed within the glorious breadth of the created order, in full and harmonious interrelationship. Richard Baukham argues that the creation narratives of Genesis place humans in solidarity with the created order (a theme returned to later) rather than set above it:

> All of God's creatures are first and foremost creatures, ourselves included. All earthly creatures share the same earth; and all participate in an interrelated and interdependent community, orientated above all to God our common creator.[43]

For example, Psalm 104, says Bauckham, indicates humanity sharing the earth with all creation. Throughout the psalm the author puts all agency and all praise to the God who has formed the great and the minutiae of creation. In the taxonomy of all created works humanity is but one feature among many, all of which are worthy of acclaim and praise because of the wondrous acts of the creator. The birds and animals are cared for (verses 10–12), the grass is watered for animals (v. 14), as well as supplying food for humanity. Creation is a great leveller – it requires the work of God who sustains it. As Bauckham tells us, humans have little of an exceptional role but are co-inhabitants of a creation that is loved by God. This idea is incorporated into Jesus' words in Matthew 6.25–33. Bauckham argues against reading this passage as evidence for the relative importance of humanity; instead, that birds have value and God cares for them. In the same way, Psalm 148 illustrates that all creation is involved in the worship of God – this most fundamental of callings.

The worship of God is the great goal of creation, and not only by humans. Not only that, but the role of creation in Psalm 148 is to 'praise the name of the Lord' (v. 5), usually understood as part of the process of recognizing the divine through naming (e.g. Matthew 16.15–17). Humanity is not the only thing that the Lord receives worship from nor is it the only thing that is cared for. So also in Job humanity is firmly put in its place. God's ways are indeed not the ways of humanity – to the extent that humanity's understanding is poor and incomplete. This is illustrated in the detail of knowledge that God has about the rest of the world – the mountain goat that gives birth in a remote place (Job 39.1–4); the ostrich's questionable maternal instincts (39.14); the mighty ways of the Leviathan (41.1). Not only do these verses demonstrate the might and power of God but also the intimate knowledge and care of creation. Vividly rendered in the writing we can appreciate the secret places that the goats rear their young, or the eagles who nest high in the mountains (39.27). The focus on the rearing of young in these passages indicates not only this secret knowledge, but also the attentiveness to the primary concerns of animals.

Scripture indicates the importance of creation and the relative unimportance of anthropocentric theology. All of creation is cared for by God, loved and valued and involved in the worship of the creator. As a community of creation the world and its inhabitants are oriented towards God.

Community of creation theologies

Rowan Williams, perhaps not readily identified as a community of creation theologian per se, argues for the renewal of the understanding of creatureliness in theology.[44] His main argument is that we are fundamentally creatures in relationship with a God who is not created. The doctrine of creation ex nihilo illustrates that God is separate from his creation; God is not contained within it or conditioned by it and this places humanity in a position of reverence and awe with regard to God's difference from us. We neither create ourselves as humans nor regulate ourselves.[45]

Rowan Williams calls this solidarity in creatureliness, a theme that I will take up shortly in relation to liberation. We position ourselves as no longer masters over creation but woven into it. Indeed, it is the rejection of our creatureliness, as I suggested above, that is found in our tendency towards seeking unjustified power, of valuing people via the measure of that power, of the quest for absolute control and maintaining that control as individual subjects or as nation states.[46] God is the ultimate controller of power of which we must all bow and imitate. We are, as humans, distinct from creation but with it – not in any way subsumed within it lest we be discussing pantheism and our relationship to that structure. However, we are creatures, created and alongside the rest of creation, which gives a good position from which to address the way we can relate to that creation.

Laudato Si' is the 2015 Papal Encyclical from Pope Francis. In this letter he writes to the Catholic Church and the world about the pressing concern that he has for the environment through a focus on Saint Francis of Assisi. The opening lines of the letter connect worship of God with the created world in a doxological move that understands creation as part of the glory of God's gift and power. In writing the letter he made sure that the destruction of the environment as a central topic for Catholic thought was established. The subtitle of *Laudato Si'* is 'care for our common home', and in making use of Francis of Assisi's spirituality he notes that we can worship God inspired by the world around us. Indeed, not only that but Francis of Assisi was reported to preach to the flowers and the birds and refer to the other created beings as brother and sister.

Among the compelling arguments for the need to preserve the environment from the destruction wrought upon it by humanity, it is possible to detect a notion of community of creation in Pope Francis's writing. The fall of humanity into sin damaged three relationships, he says: between humans and God; humans and one another; and humans and creation.[47] What should have been a 'harmonious relationship' was distorted and the result of that distortion was dominion theology. Saint Bonaventure believed, he notes, that reconciliation was between all creatures, a touch of eschatology in the Pope's writing here that is suggestive of a telos that understands relationships with animals as significant. The letter has a materialist tone reminding the reader that all humans are intimately linked to the created order, not only as created ourselves but formed by the creation around us. We cannot be removed from creation:

> Our insistence that each human being is an image of God should not make us overlook the fact that each creature has its own purpose. None is superfluous. The entire material universe speaks of God's love, his boundless affection for us. Soil, water, mountains: everything is, as it were, a caress of God. The history of our friendship with God is always linked to particular places which take on an intensely personal meaning; we all remember places, and revisiting those memories does us much good. Anyone who has grown up in the hills or used to sit by the spring to drink, or played outdoors in the neighbourhood square; going back to these places is a chance to recover something of their true selves.[48]

Very firmly, humanity is put in its place; the imago Dei does not remove our createdness or our intimate connection with the rest of creation. Celia Deane-Drummond highlights the liberationist vision of Pope Francis, something that we can come back to in the final section of this chapter. Francis is a liberationist holistically, she says, one who cannot see the liberation of people divorced from the liberation of the earth.[49] This is in keeping with his two principles significant for this constructive theology: that parts of humanity are oppressed by other parts, and that creation's damage affects the marginalized humans most.

Remaining with Catholic theology, Daniel P. Horan OFM presents an articulate and well-resourced vision of community of creation, much of which interacts and takes permission from *Laudato Si'* and the changes of emphasis in Catholic theology. He understands the community of creation as having a 'familial' basis.[50] He believes that creatures and creation are 'companions'. This is insightful for an autistic theology that may fundamentally assume something that has only recently been theologically articulated: that relationships are not simply between distinct, individual humans as isolated units that interact. Relationships are broader, less defined, more fluid and less anthropocentric.

Autistic theology would maintain that the natural inclination towards friendship with animals is in fact the way in which humanity is designed to be. Continuing my all too brief references to scripture, he notes that in Hosea 4.1–3 the animals and the land are connected to the sinful behaviour of humanity. Other than human creatures have agency; they are depicted as 'mourning' for the impact of humans. In the same way, the land 'mourns' in Jeremiah 12.4. The result of this in-depth scriptural and theological analysis is a proposal for a Franciscan theology of creation that understands St Francis's contribution, sometimes called 'nature mysticism'.

'Nature mysticism' is a provocative term, certainly in the evangelical and charismatic theological worlds I inhabit. It is difficult because it implies a link to religious practices outside of Christianity, new age religions and others that seek spiritual connections with nature rather than with God. While I acknowledge these fears, I do not wish them to prevent a proper (and biblical) relationship with creation that in particular aids the autistic community. The autistic community requires reworked understandings of Christian community, ones that are less reliant on interpersonal, individualized, socially constructed faith development. Rather, this community should be broadened and understood to be found within the greater created world, in order to recognize what many autistic people already know: that God is known in a truly Christian way outside of the boundaries of human relationships.[51]

Kinship in liberation

I wish to describe an autistic theology of creation with the aid of liberationist views as a fecund move for a constructive theology of autism and creation. This is because there is solidarity with the oppressed in creation from those humans who have been oppressed. Feminist theologians were quick to make this link, alongside some liberation theologians of the original school; Rowan Williams describes it:

> ... pressure has come from certain feminist quarters: has not a redemption-orientated Christian theology functioned as an expression of the male urge to shake off the threatening and humiliating ties that bind spirit to body, to the earth, the cycle of reproduction, woman imaged as the sign of fallenness, of unspiritual nature?[52]

What may have started in feminist spheres in this manner has developed into a nuanced account of oppressions. These narratives developed from looking at human oppression to seeing it as something that involved the whole of the created order; as something that could not be separated and has mutual causes and consequences. Feminist theologians recognized this oppression, with the consequences more likely falling on women than men, says Deane-Drummond.[53] The natural correspondence goes beyond the embracing of the physical nature of being a creature but also draws towards recognition of similarity in feminist theologies. Autistic theology similarly can recognize such overlapping or intersecting oppressions. When the climate crisis impacts humans it impacts those who are most vulnerable. For many autistic people with precarious or limited employment this is where the poverty associated with climate change is particularly pressing.

In the interest of brevity I will engage with Clair Linzey's views on Leonardo Boff and draw some conclusions on the nature of liberation and animal community.[54] Linzey notes the link between theologies of liberation and animal ethics. In so doing she articulates the connectedness that exists between those who are oppressed by other humans and the oppression of animals by humans. Her critique of Boff as one of the first liberation theologians was that his liberative programme did not achieve the full cosmological breadth that it was capable of. Boff, she claims, attempted to divert from anthropocentrism but did not achieve it. Despite highlighting the cosmological significance of the Christ event in history, he fails, she claims, to truly engage with the scope of liberation beyond humans. Linzey suggests that the Word becoming flesh and dwelling among us achieves more than simply the individual salvation of humans but incorporates all that has *flesh*. This includes animals. If we restrict to humans alone, we commit the 'scandal of particularity' which forgets that Christ came to redeem all, not just those who can be mapped perfectly on to his 'type'.

Feminists have questioned how Christ can save women if he came as a man, and the same question could be asked by autistics – can Christ save the neurodivergent if he happened to be neurotypical? To avoid trying to read back into ancient texts modern descriptions of neurodevelopment it is better to highlight that when Gregory of Nazianzus wrote 'that which is not assumed is not redeemed' he did not mean that only men in their early thirties of Palestinian descent were included in the kingdom of God. Linzey's reminder that all flesh could include animals achieves two goals. First, it draws into the kingdom of God the creation that aches and groans to see itself free from bondage and decay (Romans 8.20–24) – thereby allowing for this expansion of community that I suggest for autistic theology. It also – as something of a by-product – reminds us that reading into the text neurodiversity in order to seek reassurance that it can be found in scripture forgets the significance of Christ's coming to redeem all creation.

Nature mysticism: Finding God in alternative spaces

Autistic people describe feeling different, that they move through time and space in a way that is discordant with the majority. It is possible that the spirituality of autistic people is expressed in a similar way. Nature mysticism as a broad category is suggestive of a possibility of alternatives. It does not require the abandonment of the ecclesia as proscribed and understood by Jesus in the Gospels, nor does it empower nature writ large with a pantheistic power *not* found in scripture. Rather, nature mysticism draws the spiritual outcomings of an understanding of God's created community as something whose boundaries are fluid and open to change. Throughout this chapter I have suggested two different types of community that interact. First, the community of faith that must acknowledge belonging as a key feature formed by faith and centred on Christ, and, second, the community of creation that has imbued within it a knowledge of God and the status of creatureliness that humans are part of. For autistic people these broader and more flexible boundaries of community do not undermine gospel messages of what is needed when approaching God – that is, in Christ with the power of the Holy Spirit – but it does mean that we can join creation in worship; seek solace with creatures that are non-human; understand family and worship as being with non-humans; and that this has a place in theology and the life of the church that is fruitful and authentic. Next time Ivy the dog greets someone on a walk with passion and enthusiasm perhaps I will see this as the welcome of God from one creature to another.

Notes

1 Marcella Althaus-Reid, Lisa Isherwood and Hugo Córdova Quero, eds, *The Indecent Theologies of Marcella Althaus-Reid: Voices from Asia and Latin America* (Abingdon/New York: Routledge, 2021), https://ereader.perlego.com/1/book/2095911/7?element_originalid=intro1 (accessed 05.09.22).

2 Marcella Althaus-Reid, *Indecent Theology: Theological Perversions in Sex, Gender and Politics*, reprint (London: Routledge, 2010), https://ereader.perlego.com/1/book/1617716/7 (accessed 29.09.22).

3 Althaus-Reid, https://ereader.perlego.com/1/book/1617716/8 (accessed 29.02.22).

4 Althaus-Reid, https://ereader.perlego.com/1/book/1617716/8 (accessed 05.09.22).

5 Althaus-Reid, https://ereader.perlego.com/1/book/1617716/8 (accessed 05.09.22).

6 Althaus-Reid, https://ereader.perlego.com/1/book/1617716/7 (accessed 05.09.22).

7 John Swinton, 'From Inclusion to Belonging: A Practical Theology of Community, Disability and Humanness', *Journal of Religion, Disability & Health* 16, no. 2 (April 2012): 172–90.

8 For more on the autistic experience of exclusion in worship services, see A. L. Van Ommen and T. Endress, 'Reframing Liturgical Theology Through the Lens of Autism: A Qualitative Study of Autistic Experiences of Worship', *Studia Liturgica* 52, no. 2 (September 2022): 219–34.

9 Miroslav Volf, *Exclusion and Embrace: A Theological Exploration of Identity, Otherness, and Reconciliation*, rev. and updated (Nashville, TN: Abingdon Press, 2019).

10 Volf, *Exclusion and Embrace*, p. 101.

11 E. P. Sanders, *Paul and Palestinian Judaism: 40th Anniversary Edition* (Minneapolis, MN: Fortress Press, 2017).

12 Christine Pohl, *Making Room*, reprint (William B. Eerdmans, 1999), https://www.perlego.com/book/2985999/making-room-pdf.

13 Pohl, *Making Room*, https://www.perlego.com/book/2985999/making-room-pdf (accessed 29.02.22).

14 Daniela Augustine, 'Pentecost Communal Economics and the Household of God', *Journal of Pentecostal Theology* 19, no. 2 (2010): 219–42.

15 Gustavo Gutiérrez, *We Drink from Our Own Wells: The Spiritual Journey of a People* (Maryknoll, NY: Orbis Books, 2003), p. 101.

16 Volf, *Exclusion and Embrace*, p. 98.

17 Swinton, 'From Inclusion to Belonging', p. 185 (italics in the original).

18 Benedict, *The Rule of St. Benedict in English: RB 1980*, ed. Timothy Fry (Collegeville, MN: The Liturgical Press, 1982), 7.10.

19 Benedict, *The Rule*, 7.31.

20 Benedict, *The Rule*, 7.34–35.

21 Benedict, *The Rule*, 7.49.

22 Michael Casey, *Truthful Living: St Benedict's Teaching on Humility* (Chicago, IL: Gracewing, 2013), chapter 2.

23 Casey, *Truthful Living*, p. 41.

24 Kathryn Tanner, *Jesus, Humanity and the Trinity: A Brief Systematic Theology* (Minneapolis, MN: Fortress Press, 2001), p. 4.

25 Swinton, 'From Inclusion to Belonging'.

26 Augustine, 'Pentecost Communal Economics and the Household of God'.

27 Damian E. M. Milton, 'On the Ontological Status of Autism: "The Double Empathy Problem"', *Disability & Society* 27, no. 6 (October 2012): 883–7.

28 Augustine, 'Pentecost Communal Economics', p. 34.

29 Augustine, 'Pentecost Communal Economics', p. 45.

30 For those who are interested, my cat is called Gertie after St Gertrude the patron saint of cats. She continues to resist any other similarities to her namesake.

31 'Chris Packham: The Walk That Made Me' (BBC), https://www.bbc.co.uk/iplayer/episode/moooxqgp/chris-packham-the-walk-that-made-me (accessed 21.06.22).

32 François Martin and Jennifer Farnum, 'Animal-Assisted Therapy for Children with Pervasive Developmental Disorders', *Western Journal of Nursing Research* 24, no. 6 (October 2002): 657–70.

33 Tomasz Trzmiel et al., 'Equine Assisted Activities and Therapies in Children with Autism Spectrum Disorder: A Systematic Review and a Meta-Analysis', *Complementary Therapies in Medicine* 42 (February 2019): 104–13. 'A total of 15 studies with 390 participants (aged: 3–16 years) were included. The interaction between psychosocial functioning and EAAT was investigated in most studies. Improvement was reported in the following domains: socialization, engagement, maladaptive behaviors, and shorter reaction time in problem-solving situations after EAAT. The meta-analysis revealed no statistically significant differences for the investigated effects. Conclusions: Despite the need for further, more standardized research, the results of the studies included in this review allow us to conclude that EAAT may be a useful form of therapy in children with ASD.'

34 Turner Jocelyn, 'Animal Assisted Therapy and Autism Intervention: A Synthesis of the Literature' (Carbondale, CO: Southern Illinois University, 2011), https://opensiuc.lib.siu.edu/gs_rp/119, p. 5.

35 Merope Pavlides, *Animal-Assisted Interventions for Individuals with Autism* (London/Philadelphia, PA: Jessica Kingsley Publishers, 2008), https://www.123library.org/book_details/?id=2504 (accessed 14.09.22).

36 David L. Clough, *On Animals* (London: T&T Clark, 2012), p. 5.

37 Daniel P. Horan, *All God's Creatures: A Theology of Creation*. (Minneapolis, MN: Fortress Academic, 2020), p. 5.

38 Horan, *All God's Creatures*, p. 23.

39 Richard Bauckham, *Bible and Ecology: Rediscovering the Community of Creation* (London, 2010), p. 2.

40 Bauckham, *Bible and Ecology*, pp. 12–20, and Horan, *All God's Creatures*, pp. 24–6.

41 Horan, *All God's Creatures*, p. 37.

42 Miguel J. Romero and Mary Jo Iozzio, *Journal of Moral Theology, Volume 6, Special Issue 2 Engaging Disability* (Eugene, OR: Wipf and Stock Publishers, 2017), p. 244.

43 Bauckham, *Bible and Ecology*, p. 64.

44 Rowan Williams, *On Christian Theology*, Challenges in Contemporary Theology (Oxford/Malden, MA: Blackwell Publishers, 2000), p. 64.

45 Williams, *On Christian Theology*, p. 76.

46 Williams, *On Christian Theology*, p. 77.

47 Pope Francis, *Laudato Si'*, https://www.vatican.va/content/francesco/en/encyclicals/documents/papa-francesco_20150524_enciclica-laudato-si.html. § 66 (accessed 14.09.22).

48 Pope Francis, *Laudato Si'*, § 84.

49 Celia Deane-Drummond, *A Primer in Ecotheology: Theology for a Fragile Earth* (Eugene, OR: Wipf and Stock Publishers, 2017), p. 61.

50 Horan, *All God's Creatures*, p. 85.

51 This is not a soteriological claim; God is not known salvifically through any other way than Jesus Christ. Rather, the formative elements of discipleship and of worship are often considered found in the ecclesia. I wish to argue that the ecclesia is found outside of the boundaries of the church building.

52 Williams, *On Christian Theology*, p. 64.

53 Deane-Drummond, *A Primer in Ecotheology*, p. 44.

54 Clair Linzey, *Developing Animal Theology: An Engagement with Leonardo Boff* (Abingdon: Routledge, 2022).

6

Practices

Liberation and belonging: Christian practice

The practices of a radically hospitable community are themselves radical. Practices and community, theology and expression cannot be separated. Pete Ward suggests that theology is the lived, outworked behaviour of the Christian community, 'When we pray, sing hymns, make decisions about life, preach and teach, and so on, we inhabit our theology.'[1] The behaviour and practices of the church cannot be separated from the theology that it articulates. It is perhaps unfortunate therefore that this chapter is the last in the book, when maybe it should be the first – arguing for things that we should do and then reflecting upon the theology in those things.

However, it is necessary that the things we should do are in fact woven through the preceding work and here in this chapter are the final moves. I have already suggested there are practices and beliefs that are liberative for autistic lives. There are also practices and beliefs that are excluding and do not aid in the flourishing of autistic people. The outcome of a radical hospitality, in itself a practice recognized through Christian spiritual tradition, is other reframed practices. These practices are understood in the light of the hospitable practice of Christ. I will examine such practices that exclude both inside and outside of the church, making comment on the notion of behaviour and sin. From there I will consider practices that are liberative for autistic people and then some practices that I think are suggestive of belonging for autistic people.

Practices of exclusion

Exclusionary practices are those behaviours and habits that create isolation, rejection or inhospitality. For autistic people such practices are legion. These repeated, embodied behaviours serve to make autistic people feel deficient and unacceptable. My first encounter with this was during the Anglican sharing of the peace. I watched as people spun around and shook hands with one another, greeted one another with much enthusiasm and left their seats to find their friends. I didn't have any particular friends. I felt too shy to interrupt these reunions and couldn't quite make out what social dynamics were at play. The spiritual and theological import of this praxis was lost on me. The swirling of other people as they confirmed friendships and greeted new people felt like the repeat of every school lunchtime and classroom instruction to 'get into groups of three' – I was left standing on the sidelines.

Practices of exclusion are these minor interruptions that signify difference alongside the bigger, more extensive practices that damage irreparably. I would like to suggest that there are two types of exclusion that a liberation theology for autism should examine – exclusions in the church and exclusions in society. The church should take care of its own community, exhibiting the love and care that Christ did to those on the margins of society, but the church should also – in the spirit of public theological endeavour – seek to change the wider society for the better; it should stand as an advocate for those who cannot, on their own, make enough noise and garner enough attention to bring about change.

The two types of exclusions that I wish to raise are located in the church's praxis, laden with meaning and attempting to locate God in the midst of the worshipping community, and the behaviour modifications that autistic people are subject to both intentionally and unintentionally through prejudice. The naming of prejudice and the revealing of that which stigmatizes is part of the task of the liberation theologians. Alongside this, suggestions for improvements can be made, yet consciousness is key. The liberation theologians first sought to raise awareness, even among those who were poor and oblivious to their subjugation. Practices of exclusion need to be called out for what they are – described and demonstrated to raise awareness and to change the unconscious behaviour into conscious behaviour and, by so doing, show those who design and implement the worship life of the church – and attempt to influence the behaviour of society – that more can be done to prevent this treatment of autistic people.

When I describe the church as having practices of othering I need to give concrete examples, to provide a rich and thick description. As I have attempted to show throughout this book, autistic and neurodivergent people are systematically placed on the outside of a society that prioritizes and valorizes ways of being in the world that are different to autistic bodyminds. Nancy Eiesland describes 'bodily reactions' to people with disabilities. Eiesland deliberately focuses on physical disability, in a way that I find troubling; however, I do appreciate her point when she shows how these reactions are damaging. She uses Erving Goffman's label of 'rituals of degradation'.[2]

Rituals of degradation, when they are located within the church, have the doubly damaging effect of taking the othering that an autistic person might find in their lived experience and incorporating into that experience the powerful theological weight of praxis. That which draws the individual towards God, with those around them, in community by the power of the Holy Spirit, is turned on its head; it takes that person and situates them outside via praxis that shows they are insufficient to enter the presence of God.

What are such practices? They are found in all avenues of the community of faith, whichever expression or denomination that autistic people belong to. I cannot find a type of church that does not exclude the autistic person. Armand L. van Ommen and Topher Endress find in their research with autistic people's experience and worship that many tell of practices that exclude them from worship in churches.[3] The results of this qualitative study are suggestive of the fact that autistic people's worship methods are not allowed for in congregations. They note the studies that suggest autistic people are less likely than others to attend a place of worship.[4] The participants in the research noted times when they felt unwelcome or unacceptable, or found the experience of church uncomfortable or dysregulating. Despite this, the participants did attend a church and persisted, with some positive reflections, in being members of worshipping communities. This suggests that churches are both capable of the radical hospitality that I proposed in the previous chapter, and are places where autistic people wish to be because of their own faith commitments and the potential for welcoming community. None the less, the obstacles that are experienced by autistic people are often related to the behaviours of the church that are experienced as exclusionary or disruptive for the autistic bodymind.

In my own church expression, the charismatic church, much is made of encountering God in emotional, expressive ways. Underpinned by theological readings of the Pentecost experience and the continued gifts of the Holy Spirit, this has become a sociologically conditioned way of encountering God through particular forms of music and expression that can be prohibitive for the autistic person. When I engage with what is commonly called a 'worship service', if my emotions do not tally with those in the room, if I do not weep with those who weep, or experience joy at the same time as those who are joyful, my route to God via the community of faith is interrupted. Similarly, my particular church expression is heavily founded upon friendships; faith is constructed in small, intimate and dedicated friendships that journey together over many years expressing faith and nurturing one another.

In many ways this is a beautiful thing and I have focused much of my PhD research on this very facet of church life as a community of love and care for one another. However, what happens when the autistic person is not included in these friendships? When their behaviour over time, being able to be consistent in a friendship, being able to communicate constantly and commit the emotional energy to sustain work, life, health, family alongside an intense mutual friendship, cannot occur? Their route to spiritual growth is inhibited. Their access to God, formed in this church community via friends, is prevented. I do not believe, however, that this is only found in the charismatic church communities. In liturgical churches – where worship is formed by gentle rhythms of rising together and speaking; sitting together and keeping silence; of saying the creed, moving and bowing and adoring; and receiving the Eucharist – similar problems exist. These churches require people to move at the will of the one who is instructing it, who are able to be silent and speak at specific moments, who can launch from one stage of expression to another. These are not necessarily any more accessible to autistic people, despite being predictable.

Any autistic person who cannot access the church because of the worship practices of the community is also subjected to that community's treatment of them outside of the formal, in the realm of the informal and the daily. These behaviours of rejection, those that Eiesland describes as 'deep-seated unconscious aversion to people with disabilities', compound the effects of the church's worship. Jesus Christ condemned those who rejected others; he called them whitewashed tombs and said that the 'heirs of the kingdom will be thrown into the outer darkness' (Matthew 8.12). Those who have little faith, who cannot accept difference because it challenges their own security, are like the Pharisees who could not understand the message of radical love and inclusion that Jesus brought as he ushered in the kingdom of God on earth.

This kingdom recognizes faith when it comes from someone who appears to behave and know God differently. The centurion who approached Jesus with compassion for his servant who was paralysed and suffering did not know the ways of the religious leaders. He did not exist in the world in the same way; his was the Roman world, where knowing and being were formed differently. He may or may not have been autistic – this is not such a reading; rather, it is a reading that shows Christ being recognized for who he was on earth, by someone who was thought of as too different to belong in the religion. Christ turned it around: rather, the one who was different was able to recognize the one who walked among them, whereas those who rejected that which was different could not see what was before them. In the same way, the Caananite woman of Matthew

15.21–28, rejected because of her nationality, which was political and emotional; this is just like autism – a difference. Her faith was recognized. Her voice has been written into the Bible as one that echoes through the ages, a voice of difference that is a voice of faith. Despite her rejection – 'send her away, for she is crying out after us' – because of her difference and her behaviour, it is those who reject her that are shown as lacking in understanding and faith; those who display their rituals of degradation.

The other side of this rejection of the interpretation of autistic behaviour is a wide acceptance of all autistic behaviours as part of the church. This is, on the surface, something to be warmly welcomed. To appreciate the diversity of God's creation and to welcome all expressions of it is profoundly inclusive. However, as highlighted in the previous chapter, inclusivity has a dark side and it does not always equal belonging. Recognizing autistic practices with an inclusive mindset can accidentally result in instrumentalizing autistic people as sources of inspiration – and thereby stripping them of their agency and permission. A particular example of this comes to mind.

At one conference I recently attended a presenter suggested it is prophetic to witness to autistic behaviours in church. The example this person referred to in their own experience was a child standing in front of the altar removing their clothes. I appreciated their point, but felt a profound unease. It is true that the Bible is littered with examples of people enacting with their bodies the revelation of God: David danced undignified; Hannah wept for a pregnancy; Elijah was fed by angels; the prophets spoke of body metaphors (dry bones, unclean lips); and Jesus went to the cross. God speaks and these people interpret it as a body metaphor, their actions communicating something of the truth that God wishes to be conveyed. Nevertheless, these individuals had agency and revelation. They were the people who interpreted their own actions; they did something and they explained it, and it was recorded in scripture for us all to learn from. When an autistic person walks to the front of the church and removes their clothes, and this is interpreted as prophetic by an academic at an academic conference we remove the agency of the autistic individual. Here is a reflection from a mother of an autistic son at the very same conference:

> I had a few ponderings about stims /odd behaviors – based on my conversations with spellers with autism ... I was struck, though, by one speaker telling a story about his son sitting by the pulpit and taking off his shoes and socks, how that might be a prophetic statement to the too-concerned-with-perfect-appearances church. Yes, it could be. But from what I am hearing from my non-speaking friends, when they are doing something very unusual they often DO NOT want to be doing it and are deeply embarrassed. Was that young shoeless person dying on the inside, wishing that someone would help him NOT to do those things with his body? As I write, I realize both things could be true: a challenge to the church brought by socially 'inappropriate' actions AND a person who wants to be restrained or redirected from those actions. As a parent/helper, I am thankful that now I can communicate with [her son] about these things so I am not simply imposing my desires on him. What are parents to do who don't have that option? Is it dishonouring to intervene, or dishonouring NOT to intervene? Where are we asking the autistic person to 'mask' and where are we helping them actually feel more comfortable socially?

This mother comes to the heart of my concern about these ways of interpreting. Once, my son, in a church service, got hold of a flag that is occasionally used in worship. It was quite large and he was wielding it like a weapon, swinging it about and causing no small amount of stress to his parents about potential injuries to the church congregation. After the service a member of the congregation approached me in raptures. My son, she thought, was prophetically engaging in spiritual warfare. He was enacting a spiritual battle during the worship with this flag. I was sceptical. He looked to me as if he was enjoying himself tremendously, but I wasn't sure that he had spiritual warfare in mind. Who gets to make such calls? My son was behaving like any other child might do when given a bit of space, a long stick and otherwise occupied parents. Is it prophetic if he doesn't think it is? Is it worship if he was intent on whacking his brother on the head when we were not watching? Does it stop being prophetic if he achieves the goal of injuring a sibling? How about when this is an autistic person? Are their visible acts of autistic behaviour for the good of the church if we make use of it at their expense?

In the same way that people with physical disabilities reject being 'inspiration porn' when their achievements are scripted as overcoming great obstacles – *look at what even they can achieve, that means I can do ANYTHING* – I see that we run the risk in churches of embracing autistic behaviour as inspirational and challenging without the permission of those whose behaviour it is. I strongly question whether a child who is taking off any item of their clothing at the front of the church is consciously addressing notions of perfection in their actions. If they aren't, then we should consider our own interpretations of their actions as removing their choices and making assumptions about the relative value of their embodied actions.

The mother we have just heard from raises the challenging question of intervention: how can we know when to step in, as part of the family of co-worshippers, and help a person who is in a situation they do not wish to be in? When do we assist in their remaining with their behaviours and allow them to express themselves in it? As a community of believers we are called to 'bear one another's burdens' (Galatians 6.2) and by so doing help one another to avoid sin and live according to the ways of the Spirit. The community of faith is called to mutually help one another in their journey of faith. This naturally leads me to my next and final issue in the oppression of autistic people through the lens of praxis – that of autistic sin.

Liberation theologians have an obligation to speak to the wider society, to reflect the will of God whose orientation is towards those who are on the margins of society. With regard to the theme of this chapter, it is important to highlight the societal emphasis on modifying autistic behaviour to make it acceptable and to 'treat' the deficits so perceived by medical models of autism. The focus of this issue has been on applied behavioural analysis (ABA), which is an autism 'intervention' that attempts to promote better skills for living in a neurotypical world and help autistic people:

> ABA uses learning progression and stimulus fade in to adjust the sensory reactivity, communication and behavioural presentation of participants, approaching autism as a condition to be influenced or changed through the application of ABA. The aim to change or 'cure' autistic participants demonstrates a reductive understanding of autism in its attempts to reduce and remove anxiety reducing self-soothing techniques ...[5]

Owen McGill describes ABA as a way in which the worst excesses of autism are reduced; in other words, the visible behaviours – or indeed, practices – of autistic people are suppressed in order to conform them to the world around them. However, as he notes, this understands autism as something that is additional to a person and can be removed, changed or dampened. It does not acknowledge that the visible practices of the autistic person – for example, stimming – are not separate from the whole person. The stimming is the warp, and the anxious mind that the stimming soothes is the weft of the fabric of an autistic life. To remove the visible sign does not cure the person; it simply internalizes and separates that person from their own self.

As practical theologians are increasingly noticing, the embodiment of the person is key to their spiritual flourishing. We cannot speak of a mind and a body that are separate, but rather of a whole, created being who is loved by God and made in a particular way. The church must highlight this dualism and charge the 'therapies' aimed at autistic people to love the whole person rather than change them.

Autistic sin is something that humanizes autistic people. This is because without the possibility of sin there is no possibility of full humanity; of being in the same situation as all other humans: fallen and in need of the mercy of Jesus. Denying the possibility of autistic people choosing to behave wrongly, of making bad ethical decisions or acting out of selfishness or pride, diminishes them as moral agents in need of redemption. Practices of repentance, conversion, baptism and communion acknowledge this fully human need for the mercy of God. Grant Macaskill writes of a theological interpretation of behaviour modification:

> In fact, recent research has demonstrated greater potential for adaptation based on educational intervention than was previously believed possible. Individuals with ASD can learn appropriate behaviour and can learn to read appropriate and inappropriate behaviour in ways that allow them to manage or move beyond their neurophysiological limits.[6]

Autistic people are predisposed to learning behaviours, 'training instincts, or adapting appetites', and this is a challenge to the church to integrate formation into the life and thinking of the faith community.[7] This, he argues, makes for a habitus of inclusion as well as an account of virtue in the church. However, this is a challenging notion that resorts to behaviour-modifying techniques that are widely criticized within the autism community. ABA seeks to train autistic children to stop displaying signs of their autism. Designed as an early intervention, it seeks to teach children how to conform to society's expectations.

The success of these interventions is contested.[8] However, this is not the important point. Designing individuals to conform to external norms of behaviour is pragmatically unavoidable. Neurotypical children are taught the manners of their society. But it is a different type of liberation work to argue whether that is valid or not. Neurodivergent children have potentially a much harder time in learning these behaviours because they have to be taught more deliberately and some of their particular self-soothing and comforting behaviours will resist elimination. The question that is critical is whether it is fair to eliminate and demand change? Many in the autism community would say that it is not.[9]

The common claim is that 'higher functioning' autism is correlated with better adaptation, that there is less difficulty for certain autistic individuals who 'cope' better. This is also challenged among the autism community and is beginning to be questioned by psychologists.[10] High functioning correlates to a view of autism as a disability. It says that autism is only disabling if it impacts others negatively. It fails to account for the functional disabling existence of individuals who might have to work especially hard to adapt to the neurotypical world that surrounds them.

'High functioning' refers to a quantifiable and externally value-driven measure of the worth of an individual based on their intellectual ability and their ability to adapt. It does not benefit anyone on the autism spectrum to be so designated. For those who are considered 'high functioning' – a term that I myself have been labelled with – it minimizes a very real, daily struggle to survive and flourish, to manage myself, and to take into account the amount of largely unseen 'care work' that others provide for me. It can effectively silence me and says that I do not suffer. At the other end of this miserable scale are those labelled 'low functioning'. These individuals are commodified in a different way, they require care and intervention, do not contribute, and are regarded negatively. They do suffer, but mostly so does everyone else. They are the tragedy that requires curing, or at least managing.[11] The functioning labels are damaging for everyone on the autistic spectrum and the attendant autism training narrative requires liberating. In fact, autistic individuals are, claims Macaskill, more likely to learn formative practices of Christian faith deliberately and consciously than their neurotypical peers because they are without a 'potentially limiting intuitive framework'.[12] Perhaps they are a blank slate for the church to impose its ideas of behaviour modification on instead.

It is important to understand the role of an autistic notion of sin. Liberation theology has highlighted that sin is societal, and that it is the sin of society against the lives of the poor and the oppressed that should be repented of and changed:

> But in the liberation approach sin is not considered as an individual, private or merely interior reality – asserted just enough to necessitate 'spiritual' redemption which does not

challenge the order in which we live. Sin is regarded as a social, historical fact, the absence of fellowship and love in relationships among persons, the breach of friendship and love in relationships among persons, the breach of friendship with God and with other persons, and, therefore, an interior, personal fracture. When it is considered this way the collective dimensions of sin are rediscovered.[13]

Gustavo Gutiérrez understood that the emphasis upon individual sin was merely a theological note in the story of personal salvation, a necessity for those who were saved to acknowledge their need for redemption. Cast widely, sin understood as located in society – for, after all, it is the existence of the first society that drew it out initially between Adam, Eve and the deceiver – acknowledges the social reality of those who are marginalized and the social obligation of all to rectify this wrong. It becomes located in the here and the now, the kingdom as it is realized on earth, not at the expense of the telos of God's liberation in eternity but in the reality of the kingdom which is being realized, which is breaking into human society with liberating power. The practice of sin, the practice of exclusions, is a societal sin that must be recognized and understood in the flavour of autistic othering. To understand it as anything other than sin misses the depth of the wrong that is rendered unto autistic people when they are treated as less-than in the world they were created for by God. Sin, however, is not just for the society-level behaviours and practices. Sin is also found in individuals, and in following the liberation theories I do not wish to minimize this grounded and specific element of human practices. It is necessary to have it as a both-and situation where sin is still found in the individual before God; and God, through the death and resurrection of Christ, saves the individual as well as the restoration of a good and faithful society.

Practices of exclusion such as behaviour modification and churches response to autistic behaviour do not acknowledge that all humans act according to their sinful nature and all need to be 'modified'. This modification is merciful by way of the salvation of Christ and the transformation of the Spirit, and it should be 'gentle' (Galatians 6.1) when it is encouraged in the community of faith.

Practices of liberation

Keshgegian states that the reorientation of hope towards present-centred and cyclical understandings of time (see Chapter 2) can be reinforced, and our experience changed with practices of habitation.[14] Similarly, so also does Nancy L. Eiesland advocate for practices that are emancipatory and transformative.[15] These practices serve to re-symbolize the frameworks that are being liberated, the understandings and beliefs that are challenged and reformed as no longer shaped by dominant groups but open to the diverse experiences from the margins. In Chapters 2 and 3 the case was made for renewed understandings of hope and time in conversation with ideas of future, production, neo-liberalism, eschatology and disability. I theologized an autistic concept of time and of hope with a view to making familiar the notion of autistic experience and expectation. This theologizing about time naturally leads to theologizing about practices. The discrete moments of existence in and through time, those that Keshgegian argues narrates stories, particularly more suitable stories, are concretely expressed and liberatively performed in faith-filled habits, or habitus.

Practices, as I hinted at in the beginning of this, are embodied behaviours that are deeply meaningful and expressive as well as constructive. Practices are constructive in the way that their repetition or their significance forms our very selves; our ways of being in the world; our interaction with those around us; and our relationship with God. Practices can be better understood as 'orthopraxy'. Orthopraxy is an embodied way of knowing that is part of a cohesive view of faith that describes its nature as to do with knowing, acting and affectivity.[16] The knowing part of faith has traditionally, especially in evangelical circles, taken the predominant role. This looks like an assent to statements of faith, a cognitive acceptance of the 'truth' of a gospel message, an ability to verbally agree and understand a commitment made publicly and a willingness to increase knowledge through biblical studying and listening to sermons.

All of this is problematic for people who access knowledge differently and, argues David Trementozzi, not necessary for a full and complete faith. Alongside knowledge of the tenets of faith should be added orthopraxy, which is embodied knowing. This embodied knowing draws alongside the affective response to right knowledge and right action to complete the rich possibilities of faith. For the purposes of autistic theology it is important to highlight this right practice and the reasons are twofold. First, right practice, properly understood, allows for the autistic person whose intellectual and cognitive approach to faith is hard for others (such as church ministers) to know to access to the full breadth of church membership in any given congregation. It also provides scope for particular autistic practices – perhaps 'stimming' – to be described as orthopraxis. 'Stimming', of course, is the name for the 'stereotyped or repetitive motor movements' that is common in autistic people.[17]

First, a working definition of orthopraxis that is constructive for these two aims. In keeping with this version of autistic theology I will attempt to locate orthopraxis in an evangelical and charismatic theology.[18] Trementozzi notes that orthopraxy relates to soteriology when the experience of salvation is highlighted alongside any intellectual acceptance or knowledge. This corresponds to a charismatic belief in the experience of the Holy Spirit at the time of conversion (or soon after) that confirms the believer's entrance into the community of faith via the mercy of God. By way of William J. Abraham's Canonical Theism, Trementozzi highlights that the early church practised catechetical schools that taught students the way of the Christian faith and emphasized the soteriological value of practices such as baptism and the Eucharist.[19]

Abrahams variously highlights this process in his written works – for example, his *Logic of Evangelism* – and points out that mere intellectual assent does not fully allow for the breadth of the soteriological *process* so described in scripture and in the early church.[20] The rites and practices of the church were significant in the embodied knowing of God in salvation that constructs the believer's journey of faith. Alongside this he notes that orthopraxis has potential for social transformation.

Ultimately, says Trementozzi, practices that participate in soteriology or practices for social change are focused on transformation. For Trementozzi, these practices are limited to baptism, the Eucharist and reading scripture for his discussion but he sees potential for this to be extended beyond these.[21] This potential is indicated when he speaks of practices as a 'means of grace' because they heal and transform the believer via the Holy Spirit. This transformation is because believers are not only saved by grace but participate in the life of God. This is called theosis or deification and is the sanctifying work of the Spirit in the lives of believers.

These practices are communal, ritualized and sacramental in nature. They are communal as they exist in and as part of the church. All members of the faith community, sharing the common life together, participate in the acts of worship that form the church. They are ritualized because they are regularly practised, repetitively, and are formative in this repetition. Trementozzi notes fasting, prayer and contemplation in this category. These acts, importantly done in the name of Christ, form the believer and facilitate that work of the Spirit in her life. This forms an 'attentiveness' to the Spirit and helps focus. A broad understanding of the nature of a sacrament is the final element. Broad in that it incorporates the traditional church sacraments – baptism and the Eucharist (as well as other sacraments, depending upon the tradition) – but can be considered expansively when described as sacramental because these sacraments 'mediate the grace of God in a way that is not abstract or intangible but physically and materially embodied'.[22]

Autistic behaviour, when directed towards Christ, can be formative for the autistic person. This allows for behaviour that is unwanted, that is unpleasant, or cannot be stopped, to not be interpreted by the church as somehow holy but also allows for sacramental stimming. Sacramental stimming is repetitive in the ritualized way, oriented towards God, and can be communal if the church is open-minded, and is therefore transformative. Stimming is a self-soothing action when under stress – for example, an autistic person might rock or twirl or fiddle with something to help calm them. If this is transformed into a positive act, one that is oriented towards God and chosen by the autistic individual, then it has the potential to mediate grace. Rocking becomes a worshipful activity done within an accepting community which does not make observers anxious or feel the need to change it, but is understood as the natural and neurodiverse way of worship that is fitting.

A theology that seeks to be liberative for autistic individuals should have two aims. It should aim to accept the neurodiverse paradigm and not train individuals to artificially be neurotypical, and it should seek to welcome, draw and witness autistic individuals into (and in) the realm of the sacred. God is present in and with autistic people. Practices that reflect either the theory or the affective dimensions of behaviour modification are unsuitable to meet these aims. However, neurodiverse and autistic people in particular can draw upon their own resources to facilitate these divine encounters. Theology has the traditions to create depth and liberation for those individuals without denying their personhood or requiring them to change into neurotypical behaviours.

However, I write this with a caveat. All those who walk with Christ into the kingdom of God are required to change; we are to 'pick up our cross and follow him' (Matthew 16.24); we are to be those who are lights in the darkness (Matthew 5.14); a people of God who witness to the relentlessly pursuing God. It would be derogatory, reductionist and limiting were I to suggest that autistic people do not have the potential to change to become more Christ-like – that they should be left as they are while other neurotypical people 'run the race set before them' (Hebrews 12.1), effectively leaving others behind. I consider myself able, and sometimes willing, to take the narrow road of discipleship. Therefore the remainder of this chapter will attempt to do two things. It will seek to demonstrate the resources within the Christian tradition for autism, and it will demonstrate how a pneumatology for autism, with assistance from Pentecostal theology, will aid in a corrected and liberative formation for autistic people.

Autistic sin moves towards a liberative understanding of autistic practices. This is because it humanizes the autistic person. The humanizing of the autistic person is to do with expectation. If the autistic person is considered unable to change or improve for the better, if their potential is never realized, then they are fully immersed in the tragedy narrative of autism. They can never be other than they are; they cannot change and grow and be sanctified; they cannot be 'being saved' as Paul believed, but are interrupted. This interruption because of the 'curse' of autism means that they cannot enter into the life of Christian growth, of drawing ever nearer to God through a daily walk made up of big and small, macro and micro behaviours and practices that shape and form them as disciples of Jesus Christ. For too long the narrative about autism has been to make use of it as a metaphor for being shut off from God. Not long ago I noted a well-known theologian who used a description of autism to describe a failure of a church service, and alongside this a favourite theologian of mine described 'spiritual autism' as an inability to reach God.[23] This is because autistic people are, both consciously and unconsciously, believed to have no ability to speak to God, to know God or to be changed by God. They are isolated islands, adrift from humanity and the blessed relationship deemed by God when he created humans and animalkind to be in community with one another and with him. The joyful recognition of the autistic ability to sin goes hand in hand with the recognition of our potential to be saved.

Autistic sin is crucial but should not be out of balance with the practices of sin that exist around it. Autistic sin as a liberative practice on the journey of salvation that God wills all should embark upon is good, understanding autistic sin as the same sin that all humanity is oppressed by, is good – but with certain cautions and caveats. Miroslav Volf rightly illustrates that all sin is not equal despite us all sharing solidarity in our sinfulness.

'Solidarity in sin' is disturbing because it seems to erase distinctions and unite precisely where the differences and disjunctions matter the most – where dignity is denied, justice is trampled underfoot, and blood is spilled. Solidarity in sin seems to imply *equality of sins*, and the equality of sins lets the perpetrators off the hook. The world of equal sins is a world designed by the perpetrators. The logic is simple: if all sins are equal, then the action of the perpetrator is no worse than the reaction of the victim; all are perpetrators and all are victims, all are equally evil.[24]

It is accurate to signify that the depth of our sin puts us all far below the goodness and righteousness of God. Volf argues that despite this we cannot find *equality* in sin. The hatred a woman feels towards the person who raped her is less of a sin than the violation of the rapist, who is guilty of a far greater sin. We do not dissolve sin 'into an ocean of undifferentiated sinfulness' says Volf, but follow Christ and the prophets in making distinctions. Christ turned his wrath most fully on the social sinners – those in power who oppressed those without power; however, he still understood the powerless as sinful: 'go and sin no more' Jesus said to the woman caught in adultery (John 8.11). This woman, a victim of a patriarchal society that condemned her to death while ignoring the male participant of the sinful practice, still was sinful according to Christ. She was instructed to go and live differently. However, this was a gentle instruction, filled with compassion as well as rebuke. Jesus did not minimize her sin, but he did contextualize it. He was full of rage when he turned the tables over in the temple, or rebuked the Pharisees, but none of this rage is displayed in this moment with the nameless woman whom he saved from brutal punishment. The autistic sinner, in a world that oppresses them, is much more likely to be the woman caught in adultery rather than the Pharisee.[25]

Practices of belonging: beyond hospitality towards reconciliation

In the previous chapter I argued for hospitality as a core feature of community for autistic people, and I want to develop this line of thinking beyond a limited view of hospitable welcome to belonging fully. Hospitable welcome maintains boundaries of otherness – the power is with the one who welcomes; the grateful receiver of that welcome is left powerless. True hospitality requires acts of belonging that remove the boundaries of otherness and incorporate ontological oneness through the reality of the Christocentric community baptized and renewed by the Spirit.

This section seeks to draw together the threads of solidarity and hospitality into a firm commitment to belonging for autistic people. Rather than being repetitive, I hope that these distinct ideas formed in persecution (solidarity) and Christoformed welcome (hospitality) interact to bring the autistic other inside the community of Christ. However, this is hopeful and requires acts that acknowledge the separateness and the disadvantage for autistic people that has thus far existed. Therefore, the acts that bring belonging must recognize these sins and work towards the belonging via the embodied actions of the worshipping community.

Strange words: speaking in tongues

> And suddenly from heaven there came a sound like the rush of a violent wind, and it filled the entire house where they were sitting. Divided tongues, as of fire, appeared among them, and a tongue rested on each of them. All of them were filled with the Holy Spirit and began to speak in other languages, as the Spirit gave them ability. Now there were devout Jews from every nation under heaven living in Jerusalem. And at this sound the crowd gathered and was bewildered, because each one heard them speaking in the native language of each. (Acts 2.2–6)

Many autistic people speak differently from neurotypical people. This may appear as speaking quietly or loudly, or with a different cadence or rhythm. It may involve echolalia. This is the practice of repeating words or sounds, often repeated from 'previously heard speech'.[26] On a first hearing, this type of speech may appear to be meaningless, without form or function. It is common enough in autistic people that it has been suggested to be a defining characteristic. It functions alongside other speech differences as part of the communication element of autism that can cause difficulty with non-autistic people. It is tempting to reflect theologically upon instances such as echolalia and other communication elements of autism in light of Acts 2. It is possible to think that the giving of the Spirit might be interpreted as a way in which the other languages of autism are made understandable to the majority of forms of speech. However, this type of interpretation may fall into the trap of externally spiritualizing an act without the autistic person's participation – much like the stimming interpretation noted earlier in this chapter. It may indeed be useful to understand the language of autism in light of the potential for translation; in other words, for those who can't understand the autistic person to be enlightened by the Spirit so that the autistic person can have their language uncovered or made knowable. However, to make this move persists in the autistic person being the 'other', the one on the outside who must be understood by the normative group. I think that the giving of the gift of tongues by the Spirit so described in the Pentecost episode can be more fruitful than this.

Speaking in tongues as a modern practice is hotly contested. What exactly is contested is whether speaking in tongues is legitimate or not: that is, whether it is a sign of emotional behaviour – even hysterics – or whether it is a sign of a special gift from God for the person concerned. Beginning in the origins of the Pentecostal movement – the dates and locations for which are equally contested – it has become something of an identity marker for those in the Pentecostal movement as well as for some in the charismatic church. It is pertinent to an autism theology to understand tongues speech as saying something significant both about God and about the community of God. Tongues speech is known in the language of theology as 'glossalalia' which means either speaking in a previously unknown language or in ecstatic words that are not structurally languages. For a long time the Pentecostal church insisted that the tongues were of human languages that were unknown to the speaker. This appears to be for a twofold reason: to rationalize it to the outside world when it appeared to be strange and odd; and to further explain it as having an evangelistic outcome – to speak to those people who couldn't understand the native tongue of the speaker. However, for an autistic theological reading of the Acts narratives of tongues speech this is not necessary nor helpful. In Acts 10.46 when Cornelius receives the Holy Spirit there is not an evangelistic outcome; there are no observers nearby who can hear the speech in their own tongue in the same way that it occurs in Acts 2.[27] However, what does occur is the exhalation of God. The scattering of the people after attempting to build their tower to the heavens and the multiplication of languages can be understood as an act of divine mercy says Frank D. Macchia.[28] As the Babylonians went about forcing uniformity to work towards the ultimate end of becoming like God, they applied social and political forces to evil ends. To this end, says Macchia, God spread about the people in order to let them find him again. No longer should they seek to serve themselves and to seek their self-aggrandisement but instead to worship him as created beings.

The grace of multiple languages is found not in the inability of people to communicate with one another (such as we might describe between autistic and non-autistic people), but in the glorious diversity that puts people into social relationships that are appropriate. The reversal that occurs at Pentecost is not one of translation. When the Spirit comes to dwell within us we do not expect, nor does the Bible indicate, that we will all speak in a common tongue. Rather, we expect to live in a diverse community where communication is possible in light of the love and mercy of God. The Spirit's gift of tongues speech indicates the preservation of difference rather than the homogenization of all people. An autistic reading of Pentecost would not seek, necessarily, for translation of autistic speech so that it can be understood. Instead, the spiritual practice of tongues speech indicates an open and welcoming community that preserves differences.

The practice of tongues speech in those churches that adopt it becomes a practice of resistance. James K. A. Smith described speaking in tongues as 'resistance discourse'.[29] For Smith, it is resistance discourse because it defies characterization as a type of human speech. The quest to explain or interpret autistic speech – even the desire of the authors of the research about echolalia, to say that it has meaning in contrast to the belief that it is nonsense – misses the resistance element of autistic dialogue that is so in keeping with the radical nature of Pentecost. Autistic speech should not necessarily be translated, nor should it be held to non-autistic speech standards. When understood theologically autistic speech is a practice of resistance to homogenization and in keeping with the glorious diversity that is illustrated both at Babel and at Pentecost.

Prayer directed at God need not conform to neurotypical language structures. Macchia notes that prayer can, and frequently does, transcend verbal dialogue.[30] Dancing, silence and art are all examples of acts of worship and prayer that do not require, and would be restricted by, language. Autistic communication, be it repetitive echolalia, gestures or stimming, should be allowed to be understood as practices of worship. This is not to say that external observers may offer their insight to the actions of an autistic person in order to make Christian that which is distressing, but that when an autistic person offers their speech and their body to God as worship then it should be acceptable to the church as surely as it is acceptable to God. In the same way that ecstatic mystical worship, repetitive glossolalia, dance and movement are described and find their origins in scripture so also can autistic communication – in light of the theology of Babel and Pentecost – be recognized as worshipful and acceptable within the broad church community.

Ruth Part 2: Practices from the outside

In my second visit to the book of Ruth I would like to consider how Ruth was hailed as a woman who was worthy of report because of her willingness to commit to a community that she did not know. I do not, as Macaskill reminds us, try to diagnose autism in the biblical person of Ruth; instead, in a non-historical critical way, I reimagine my own life experience as being familiar to Ruth, as someone who does not fit in socially, as someone who feels different. My intention here is to offer an autistic hermeneutic, although a very provisional one. This is the idea that specific practices should *not* be suggested, for all autistic people are different, but rather it highlights the way in which we join in with groups who have their own rules and way of doing things that we aren't familiar with because we are seeking after God.

In the book of Ruth we see an individual who makes a decision to join the faith community despite having no real purchase in the practices and lives of that community. Let's look again at Ruth's speech:

> Do not press me to leave you
>   or to turn back from following you!
> Where you go, I will go;
>   where you lodge, I will lodge;
> your people shall be my people,
>   and your God my God.
> Where you die, I will die –
>   there will I be buried. (Ruth 1.16–17)

Ruth decides, as an outsider, to confess the Lord (before she had even joined the faith community) and throw in her lot with strangers. I find this resonant. As a Christian I have often thought of the church as full of strangers, but my confession of faith meant that I was going to throw my lot in with them anyway. I suspect that many Christians, neurodiverse or not, may feel the same. Ruth even declares that she will adopt the practices of the community – she'll be buried next to Naomi, not in her home land or anywhere else. As a stranger with no financial means nor way in which to survive unmarried in a time and place where women had few resources outside their male family, Ruth adapts the practices of the community. She makes use of the Israelite law of gleaning not only to get food but also to catch the attention of Boaz. She behaves outrageously by finding Boaz on the threshing floor and uncovering his feet, and eventually via the exchange of a sandal she is accepted into Boaz's family. She adopts social practices that are imbued with religious overtones in order to join the worship of God and the community of faith.

For many autistic people this is also necessary; we enter this land full of strangers and we adopt their peculiar customs in order to enter the presence of God in church. As a spiritual discipline, it has a degree of cost associated with it, but adopting strange practices as an outsider can be valuable. It *does* cost me to attend church, and I don't always want to go. I dislike the loud music and the practice of speaking to other people in informal and unstructured ways. Sometimes it costs me so much that I cannot attend. When I and other autistic people can attend *and* bear with the practices that are not familiar and make us feel like strangers in foreign lands, I would suggest that they are received by God in a similar way to the story of Ruth. They are a profound 'sacrifice of praise' (Hebrews 13.15), one that God receives, I believe, as acceptable.

Towards practices of justice for autistic people

Alongside the autistic theological reading of Pentecost there should also be an autistic theology of transforming practices. There is nothing liberative about a theology that only requires those in need of liberation to adapt; the reading of Ruth that I suggest is a fragment of the theological work that should be done for autistic liberation. It should be understood as rewriting past practices, as doing something for the memories of adapting to church that many autistic people have to do; it is not the future-oriented theological work of liberation. For a liberation theology of autism, practices of the church should be recognized as insufficient to meet the needs of autistic people at this time. In order to make the necessary changes to church environments, the liberative practices of autistic people should be recognized as sacramental acts; acts that resist homogeneity and embrace justice.

Nancy Eiesland wrote that the struggle for justice begins in the worshipping practices of the church. The practices of the church are the body language that is 'the physical discourse of inclusion and exclusion'.[31] How, then, can the worshipping practices be the language of justice for autistic people? To fully answer this question requires the time and patience to listen and hear. The first worshipful practice should be *attention*. Attending to the needs and wants of individual autistic people in the congregation is an act of honour and justice. The most inclusive and comprehensive empirical research on autistic worship behaviour cannot replace individual attention to members of a congregation. This is an act of worship because it recognizes the elements of theological anthropology that have been described throughout this book.

Worshipful attention to the other is an act directed towards God because of the value that it places on God's creation. It is attending to the 'least of these', those who are marginalized, and prioritizing their needs. When Jesus rejected intentions of his disciples and offered the children to come to him (Matthew 19.14) this was not a sentimental act but a radical inclusive act. Children, then as now, have relatively little social capital, power or influence. Christ required that the disciples gave the children access. The disciples had to act to honour that requirement; they were previously a proactive obstacle, offering their rebuke to the children and those who brought them to Jesus. This was turned on its head and Jesus asked of them that they make room, make space and allow the children to enter the presence of the Son of God – so even this should be the case for autistic children and adults. This is not to draw a comparison between autistic adults and the children in the Matthean text; rather, it is to say that those who are ostracized by the people with power are those who Christ time and again demands are given time and attention. The worshipful act of giving autistic people attention is one that is demanded by Christ who overturns the social order and prioritizes those who are rejected or excluded from coming into the presence of God.

The second worshipful act therefore is *access*. In keeping with the practice of attention to autistic people, so also should the church give access to autistic people. They should allow for the practices of the church to be within reach of autistic people. This means that there should not be separate services, special rooms, adaptations that emphasize difference. Rather, the belief that all are one in Christ Jesus requires the church to make the worship of the church available. Eiesland suggests that the practice of the Eucharist is more often a 'ritual of exclusion'.[32] This is because for the physically disabled to be treated differently, to have the elements brought to them rather than being able to go to the altar, or to be unable to kneel in the way that the rest of the people do, does illustrate difference and separateness rather than the communal celebration of the sacrament.

Paul describes the devastating consequences of practising the Eucharist improperly in 1 Corinthians 11.17–33. The rich ate ahead of the poor; there were people getting drunk. Such acts of provision for the rich and forgetting the poor is equivalent to making the Eucharist inaccessible to autistic people. This may be by demanding a cognitive ability before being accepted as able to receive the Eucharist – and this may be by making a church service sensorially inaccessible, so that the autistic person cannot take the bread and the wine because they can't attend church at all.

There are many ways in which the sacrament of the bread and the wine are made inaccessible to autistic people, or requires a profession of faith that is beyond the capacity of an autistic person; when this happens the church is guilty of 'profaning the body and blood of the Lord' (1 Corinthians 11.27b). To prevent access to the Eucharist for the autistic person is to leave them hungry (v. 21) and that is a dreadful sin. In contrast, to allow access, unconditional and in light of the grace of God for all sinners, is an act of service and devotion by the church to autistic people and to the God who loves and created them.

In the same way as the Eucharist should be made available by the worshipful practice of *access*, so also should baptism be available via the practice of *acceptance*. By accepting all people as made and loved by God, and by recognizing that all who call on the name of the Lord shall be saved, we are able to look again at what is the precursor to the sacrament of baptism. Whether we practise the baptism of infants or the baptism of adults, no one person who honestly and earnestly seeks it should be excluded from this sacrament. Baptism is the recognition that no single person is able to come to God without the love and sacrifice of Jesus Christ. We can do nothing to earn our acceptance by God and this includes earning it by being of a particular and acceptable bodymind. Instead, we come, entirely as we are to stand before the throne of grace and receive as a gift that which God offers to us all. Therefore, there should be no conditions for baptism that exclude the autistic person. No questions should be asked about whether they understand what they are doing, for who can honestly say they fully understand the grace and wonder of God's gift of salvation? Those who seek to die to their previous life and rise again through the beautiful waters of baptism should never be prevented by the oppressive normativity of rationalized neurotypicality.

Finally, the church, and the autistic people within the church most particularly, should seek to worshipfully practise *imagination*. Imaginative practices of worship have been adopted by feminist theologians to creatively reimagine practices that have been oppressive. Elizabeth Stuart notes that feminist theologians must not concede to men – especially men invested in patriarchal systems – the liturgical spaces.[33] These spaces are the ones that allow people to be incorporated into the new reality in faith, she says. Therefore the work for feminists who are interested in the practices of the church is to find access to these spaces that facilitate the reality the liturgy helps us narrate and inhabit. Marjorie Procter-Smith defines spirituality as 'a way of being in the world: a way of living, of knowing, of seeing and hearing'.[34] Thus she says a feminist liturgical practice must account for the being in the world that is specific to women. It is also in solidarity with all women and therefore adopts practices of spiritual disciplines that are emancipatory. I shall list her suggestions and then indicate the ways, perhaps obviously, that these are relevant to the emancipation of autistic lives.

Women's spiritual disciplines should identify with other women, says Procter-Smith, recognizing that there is plurality of oppressions and different circumstances for all women. Women's spirituality should 'name the world' and in so doing make visible the lives of women who have been hidden. Women should learn to love themselves, 'learning to love ourselves as women is our most difficult and our most necessary task as women living in a patriarchal society. It is the necessary precondition to our survival.'[35] Women should recover their collective memory; by so doing, they recognize that other women have struggled to change the world before now and by doing the act of remembering we can continue the struggle. Women should imagine a different world, where the oppression of women does not exist; and women should celebrate the rituals and liturgies of women where women are able to gather together to be in solidarity with one another and to lament and be thankful together.[36]

It does not take a huge imaginative leap to see how these feminist spiritual disciplines might be applied to an autistic theology of practices. An autistic practice of identifying with other autistic people may look like the mutual support of one another, especially in light of the differences of support that are part of the 'spiky profiles' of autistic people. By mutually supporting one another, a critical mass of the autistic church develops in all its glorious diversity. By naming the world, autistic people in the church are able to show, as is the intention with all liberation theologies, the areas where oppression is and to shine a light upon them.

The task of learning to love our autistic selves is not a sinful form of self-love. It is the Christian requirement of recognizing neurodiversity as part of God's creation and loving that which God has made. It would be a sin to dismiss that which is knitted together in their mother's womb even when that is ourselves. The trauma that comes from existing in a neurotypical world means that many (or even all) autistic people have experienced self-loathing. If we believe that autistic people are made in the image of God and capable of being saved by the grace of God, then it is wrong to loathe ourselves. We must make the journey towards accepting ourselves and loving ourselves as a worshipful practice. The collective memory of autistic struggle is a mighty task. That autistic people have always existed is without doubt, but to recognize that existence and to remember the struggle is difficult when the language to describe it is still new. The work of collective remembering is in part the mourning of unrecognized lives that were difficult and painful and are now gone. The practice of remembering necessarily involves lament, a grief-riddled cry for the injustices that are past.

This book in many ways has been an attempt to imagine a different world, as Procter-Smith advocates. It suggests the ways in which the oppression of autistic people must be called out and transformed in light of God's love for all people. This work is only one very small contribution to the significant work of imagination required. Finally, the work of autistic people is to draw together and find autistic liturgies and rituals that encompass all that has been mentioned regarding the imaginative future. The lamentable past has scope for constructive and hopeful worship that identifies the needs of autistic people of all walks of life who live in the light of the glory of God.

Notes

1 Pete Ward, *Participation and Mediation: A Practical Theology for the Liquid Church* (London: SCM Press, 2008), p. 33.

2 Nancy L. Eiesland, *The Disabled God: Toward a Liberatory Theology of Disability* (Nashville, TN: Abingdon Press, 1994), p. 92.

3 Armand L. van Ommen and Topher Endress, 'Reframing Liturgical Theology Through the Lens of Autism: A Qualitative Study of Autistic Experiences of Worship', *Studia Liturgica* 52, no. 2 (September 2022): 219–34.

4 van Ommen and Endress, 'Reframing Liturgical Theology', p. 229.

5 Owen McGill, 'Challenging Behaviour(ists) – Neurodiverse Culture and Applied Behaviour Analysis', in Damian Milton, *Neurodiversity Reader: Exploring Concepts, Lived Experience and Implications for Practice* (Charlotte, NC: Baker & Taylor, 2020), p. 179.

6 Grant Macaskill, 'Autism Spectrum Disorders and the New Testament: Preliminary Reflections', *Journal of Disability & Religion* 22, no. 1 (2 January 2018): 15–41, p. 31.

7 Macaskill, 'Autism Spectrum Disorders', p. 32.

8 Micheal Sandbank et al., 'Project AIM: Autism Intervention Meta-Analysis for Studies of Young Children.', *Psychological Bulletin* 146, no. 1 (January 2020): 1–29.

9 Ann Memmott, 'Autism: Some Vital Research Links', Ann's Autism Blog, http://annsautism.blogspot.com/2019/01/autism-some-vital-research-links.html (accessed 16.10.21).

10 Gail A. Alvares et al., 'The Misnomer of "High Functioning Autism": Intelligence Is an Imprecise Predictor of Functional Abilities at Diagnosis', *Autism* 24, no. 1 (January 2020): 221–32.

11 Sarah Kurchak, 'Autistic People Are Not Tragedies. My Life Has Value and Joy', *The Guardian*, 30 April 2015, https://www.theguardian.com/commentisfree/2015/apr/30/autism-is-not-a-tragedy-take-it-from-me (accessed 25.09.22).

12 Macaskill, 'Autism Spectrum Disorders', p. 31.

13 Gustavo Gutiérrez et al., *A Theology of Liberation: History, Politics, and Salvation*, rev. version of the orig. English-language trans., SCM Classics (London: SCM Press, 2010), p. 174.

14 Flora A. Keshgegian, *Time for Hope: Practices for Living in Today's World* (New York: Continuum, 2006), p. 188.

15 Eiesland, *The Disabled God*, p. 93.

16 David Trementozzi, *Salvation in the Flesh: Understanding How Embodiment Shapes Christian Faith*, McMaster Theological Studies Series, volume 7 (Eugene, OR: Pickwick Publications, 2018), p. 110.

17 Steven K. Kapp et al., '"People Should Be Allowed to Do What They like": Autistic Adults' Views and Experiences of Stimming', *Autism* 23, no. 7 (October 2019): 1782–92.

18 This, as I will later conclude, does not exclude other theological versions and it would be exciting and productive to see liturgical work done in this area.

19 Trementozzi, *Salvation in the Flesh*, p. 114.

20 William James Abraham, *The Logic of Evangelism: A Significant Contribution to the Theory and Practice of Evangelism* (London: Hodder & Stoughton, 1989).

21 Trementozzi, *Salvation in the Flesh*, p. 128.

22 Trementozzi, *Salvation in the Flesh*, p. 132.

23 Erik Varden, *Entering the Twofold Mystery: On Christian Conversion* (London: Bloomsbury Continuum, 2022), p. 139.

24 Miroslav Volf, *Exclusion and Embrace: A Theological Exploration of Identity, Otherness, and Reconciliation*, rev. and updated (Nashville, TN: Abingdon Press, 2019).Otherness, and Reconciliation}, Revised and updated (Nashville, TN: Abingdon Press, 2019), p. 78.

25 This is not to say that all autistic people are relatively more innocent than neurotypical persons. It is entirely possible and likely that many autistic people have proportionately been involved in heinous crimes and sinful behaviour. However, the individual autistic person is sinful only in so much as they are part of fallen humanity.

26 Eli G. Cohn et al., 'Repeating Purposefully: Empowering Educators with Functional Communication Models of Echolalia in Autism', *Autism & Developmental Language Impairments* 7 (January 2022).

27 Max Turner, 'Early Christian Experience and Theology of "Tongues" – A New Testament Perspective', in Mark J. Cartledge, *Speaking in Tongues: Multi-Disciplinary Perspectives*, Studies in Pentecostal and Charismatic Issues (Eugene, OR: Wipf & Stock Publishers, 2012).

28 Frank D. Macchia, 'Babel and the Tongues of Pentecost: Reversal or Fulfilment', in Cartledge, *Speaking in Tongues*.

29 James K. A. Smith, 'Tongues as "Resistance Discourse"', in Cartledge, *Speaking in Tongues*, p. 81.

30 Frank Macchia, 'Sighs Too Deep for Words: Toward a Theology of Glossolalia', *Journal of Pentecostal Theology* 1, no. 1 (1992): 47–73.

31 Eiesland, *The Disabled God*, p. 112.

32 Eiesland, *The Disabled God*, p. 113.

33 Elizabeth Stuart, 'Exploding Mystery: Feminist Theology and the Sacramental', in *Embodying Feminist Liberation Theologies*, ed. Beverley Clack (London: Continuum, 2004), p. 233.

34 Marjorie Procter-Smith, *In Her Own Rite: Constructing Feminist Liturgical Tradition* (Franklinville, NJ: OSL Publications, 2013), p. 152.

35 Procter-Smith, *In Her Own Rite*, p. 155.

36 Procter-Smith, *In Her Own Rite*, p. 156.

Letter to the Peculiar People of God[1]

Dear autistic siblings,

You were my first thought when I began this book. How can I represent such a diverse and wonderful group of people? How can I account for the many different ways in which life can be glorious and difficult, beautiful and disastrous, profound and painful? I wish to do no one a disservice through my assumptions about our lives. Rather, I offer this book primarily as an account of my own experiences but with the hope that there are fragments of correspondence and snippets of similarities – enough that you will perhaps see something of yourself in these pages and find the theorizing I have done helpful and hopeful.

Autistic liberation theology is concerned with the lived experience of *you*, autistic people. This lived life is peculiar, at odds with the world around us. Autistic lives appear in a different stream of humanity's being-in-the-world, out of sync with the majority. This leads to situations where we feel that we are on the outside looking in, unsure of where or whether we will fit. In the worst instances of this we can be rejected body and soul by other people and by the church. This is the true tragedy of autism.

Yet our lives are of utmost value. We read in the scriptures that all people are 'fearfully and wonderfully made' (Psalm 139.14), that the knitting together in the womb was with intention and promise. Something about the tangled, knotted wool of our brains was deliberately cast on and knit with purpose. The pattern of this knitting is sometimes unclear to us, the progress of the work uncertain. Yet there is hope that the God of all creation holds us firmly and tenderly in his hands and, as for all humans, is for us and with us. Autistic liberation theology entertains the hope of scriptural witness and Christian theology and takes these resources into mutual conversation with the autistic world. This conversation might start in the middle of a thought, or interrupt halfway through someone speaking; it might be better framed in a piece of artwork or music or something that isn't hemmed in with words. Autistic communication is unique and beautiful and autistic theology will bear these elements also.

Throughout this book some themes appeared frequently as I believe they are paradigmatic for autistic liberation theology. The book of Ruth speaks of a stranger, someone who is different, who chooses to walk with the people of God and makes great efforts to be accepted. In that book I see something of my own experience: my successes and failures at being part of the community of faith. In the same way, the event of Pentecost speaks of the Holy Spirit's endorsement of difference; God's ability to hear in different languages and to speak to all people in ways that they can understand. This is because of the theological anthropology that is revealed in the Bible – that all, being made in the image of God, are precious. This means that autistic people who worship God neurodivergently, who approach the church and the world in a way that may seem strange or indeed, may seem peculiar to others.

This book has developed along what seems to me a logical path. Starting with the methodological standpoint of this autistic theology it moves directly forwards into concerns with time and eschatology, the base way in which people engage with everything around them, and what may or may not be hoped for in the future. From there, the book turns and the final three chapters follow on from one another. I explain why I believe we can be in solidarity with one another through an identifier that transcends all others; that this solidarity leads to communities of faith that should behave in particular ways, and these communities should practise faith that is radically hospitable and allows for autistic faith expressions.

There is much work still to be done for autistic liberation and this book is a part of what is perhaps the beginnings of a theological discipline.[2] It is important to understand what the barriers are to full participation in the church; this can only be done by asking autistic people themselves and attending carefully to their answers in whichever mode of communication they come. This should be done *by* and *with* autistic people rather than *to* them. We should take account of our siblings who do not speak with audible words. How do they experience the church? How do they know God? My friend J. will speak of being 'trapped in silence' where only God was with him. Is this a common experience? What can J. and others like him teach us about that intimacy with God? Communication only with God, once the common practice of anchorites and solitaries, is seldom seen today. Perhaps autistics have a route to this devotion that is yet unexplored. Much practical change should be made in how churches operate to educate themselves about autism and to dissuade them from 'accommodations' that exclude people rather than include them. Churches need not fear that if they attempt to welcome autistic people warmly and fully they will have to run costly programmes and make significant changes to their buildings. Rather, they should be encouraged to encounter each autistic person as an individual and learn about them.

I also note that there is extended family in this discourse who should have their own work written by them. Neurodivergence no longer simply refers to autism. It encompasses many different ways of being. It is necessary that these ways are accounted for, described and revealed so that they also begin journeys of liberation. What does a bipolar person need us to know about their faith and their church experience? What about the experiences of those with ADHD? The neurodivergence wider family requires research, stories and lived experiences told for the benefit of the church.

I think back to the NHS consulting room in 2018 and my shame and embarrassment. I think further back to my strange and somewhat solitary childhood and I share with you the verse in the Bible that I clung to then and still do now, as the offer and the welcome that comes from Jesus to all who need it:

Come to me, all you who are weary and are carrying heavy burdens, and I will give you rest. Take my yoke upon you, and learn from me, for I am gentle and humble in heart, and you will find rest for your souls. For my yoke is easy, and my burden is light. (Matthew 11.28–30)

If you are wearied or burdened by the world and the church, Jesus offers rest for your tired bones. His gentleness and kindness takes us further on the journey of faith; he does not give up or expect less of us, but instead teaches us. This teaching is not overbearing; it does not oppress you or make you suffer in order to change you. It is life-giving and hopeful. There is hope for autistic liberation, hope that is found at the feet of Jesus Christ who died for all autistic people that they might have life.

Notes

1 See Joanne Limburg, *Letters to My Weird Sisters: On Autism, Feminism and Motherhood* (London: Atlantic Books, 2022), for the inspiration for this letter.

2 For other sources, see Stewart Rapley, *Autistic Thinking in the Life of the Church* (London: SCM Press, 2021); Grant Macaskill, *Autism and the Church: Bible, Theology, and Community*, first issued in paperback (Waco, TX: Baylor University Press, 2021); Armand L. van Ommen and Topher Endress, 'Reframing Liturgical Theology Through the Lens of Autism: A Qualitative Study of Autistic Experiences of Worship', *Studia Liturgica* 52, no. 2 (September 2022): 219–34; John Swinton, 'Reflections on Autistic Love: What Does Love Look Like?', *Practical Theology* 5, no. 3 (January 2012): 259–78.

Index of Names and Subjects

Abraham, William J. 191–2
acceptance 93
  and baptism 204
  in the church 12, 34, 88, 131, 145–6, 148–9, 183–4, 198–9, 201
  and communication 54
  and decency 141–3
  of difference 18, 29, 129, 147, 156–7
  in education 38–40
  and mothers 108, 116, 136
  and multiculturalism 147
  and neurodiversity movement 6–7, 93, 143
  radical 35
  versus treatment 75–6, 79
accommodation, and hospitality 110, 119–20, 140, 143–4, 148–9
actions, repetitive 17, 56, 70, 75, 191
ADHD, and neurodiversity 17, 211
advocates 41, 109–10, 112–13, 135, 179
  self-advocates 111
aid, and othering 25

alone-ness 59
alongsiding:
  and the church 35
  and motherhood 48, 109, 112–18, 122
  in scripture 123–4
  see also solidarity
Alston, William P. 32
Althaus-Reid, Marcella 141–3
Anglicanism, liberal 21
animals 160–3, 164, 166–7, 171
  in scripture 167–8
anthropology, theological 142, 202
  and sin 142, 202
  and solidarity 12, 117–18, 125, 127–8, 135–6, 148, 149
  see also image of God
anxiety 75, 186
  and time 48–9, 66, 69
applied behavioural analysis (ABA) 1, 52–3, 185–7
Archer, Kenneth J. and Waldrop, Richard E. 95
Aristotle 164
Artemisia 53

Asperger's syndrome 77
attentiveness 42, 60, 62,
  67–8, 102, 192, 202
Attfield, Richard 55
Augustine, Daniella C.
  125–7, 129, 147, 154–6
autism:
  advocates 41, 109–10, 135,
    179
  critical studies 7, 9, 80–3,
    101, 104
  deficit model 3, 8, 17, 20,
    27, 59, 78, 80–2, 83, 86,
    91, 115
  diagnosis 2, 4, 17, 22, 77,
    113–14
  as disability 17–18, 75–8,
    90–1, 188
  disadvantages 18–21
  and language 9–10, 24, 75,
    90–1, 111, 155–7, 196–9
  medical model 5–7, 42,
    50–2, 55, 76–9, 80, 112,
    124, 150–1, 185
  as neurodiversity 5–8,
    16–17, 107–8
  ontological status 9, 11,
    74–8, 80, 82, 112
  pathologizing 5–7, 10–11,
    18, 55, 58, 78
  as problem 18, 22, 34, 52,
    74, 77–8
  research into 18–19, 37, 111
  and resurrection body
    97–104
  social construction 7, 78,
    80–2, 84, 90–1, 110, 124,
    133
  as spectrum 16–17
  as tragedy 6, 12, 18, 23, 42,
    76, 109–10, 117, 194
  treatments 6, 51–4, 57, 76,
    79, 115
Autism Speaks 111
autistic liberation theology
  7–8, 9–11, 16–18, 34–40,
  59, 209, 212
  and inclusion 143–5, 159,
    183
  and neurodiversity 7–8,
    34–40, 42, 107–8, 150–1
  and oppression 80, 82, 144,
    205–6
  and practices 178, 179–90,
    194–5, 201–6
  and speaking in tongues
    196–8
autistic theology 8–9, 11–12,
  101
  and community 12, 112,
    140–4
  and creation 160–3, 164,
    166–7, 171–3
  and liberation 16–18, 24,
    25–8, 34–40, 143–4, 171–3

baptism:
  and acceptance 204
  as overwhelming 65
Bauckham, Richard 164–5,
  167
Beckford, Robert 8–9
bedtime, problems with 22–4
behaviour:
  autistic 1, 19, 52–3, 58, 63,
    113

INDEX OF NAMES AND SUBJECTS

and the church 21, 110,
    154–5, 179–90
and decency 142–3
and image of God 128, 136
learned 187
modification 148, 156, 179,
    185–90, 193
normative 11–12, 52, 67,
    76–8, 94, 154, 157, 179
prophetic 183–4
repetitive 17, 19, 56, 70,
    75, 191
and sin 178, 188–9
see also stimming
belonging:
  and inclusion 12, 153–7
  and radical hospitality 178,
    196
Benedict, St:
  and hospitality 147
  and humility 152–3
  and solidarity 129
Bertilsdotter Rosquist,
    Hanna, Chown, Nick and
    Stenning, Anna 19, 21, 79
Biklen, Douglas et al. 54–5
bipolar disorder, and
    neurodiversity 17, 211
black theology 8–9
Bleuler, Eugen 127
body, resurrection 97–104
Boff, Clodovis 25–6, 40–1,
    43
Boff, Leonardo 256, 356,
    401, 43, 17–23
Bonaventure, St 169
Bovell, Virginia 75–6, 78–9
brain, and autism 76–7, 78–9

Brock, Brian 98–100
Brueggemann, Walter 68, 96

Calvin, John 147
Campbell, Eilidh 20, 22,
    41–2
Campbell, Micah 22, 42
Casey, Michael 152–3
change, effects 59, 66, 159
charismatic movement
    34–40, 92–6, 100–1
  and petitionary prayer 83–4
  and speaking in tongues
    197
  and worship 3, 4, 21, 157,
    158, 181–2
children:
  and the future 51–3, 55
  inclusion 202–3
Chopp, Rebecca 61–2
Christ:
  and mutuality 148–50
  and Sabbath 68–9
  see also Jesus Christ
Christianity:
  and autism 2–3, 9, 124–5
  practices 178–206
Christology:
  and anthropology 99–100
  and neurodiversity 35–6
church:
  and accommodation of
    autism 110, 119–20,
    145–6, 148–54
  autistic liberation 35, 40–1,
    43, 113, 201–6, 211
  and behaviour 21, 110,
    154–5, 179–90

as community 12, 13–14,
  40–1, 89, 107–8, 112, 140,
  148–54, 159–60, 192
and decency 141–4
and exclusion 178, 179–89,
  209
and hospitality 147, 160,
  203
and liberation movement
  141
and mutuality 148–50
and solidarity 35, 118, 120,
  122, 126–7, 130–1, 134–7
see also acceptance
Clough, David 163–4
cognition:
  diversity 39–40
  and faith 190–1, 203
common good 124–5,
  127–9, 130
communication:
  and animals 160–3
  difficulties with 16–17,
    19–20, 30, 34, 38–9, 54–7,
    115, 155–6, 196–7, 210
  and resurrection body 98
communities, Benedictine
  158–60
community 140–74
  in autistic theology 12, 67,
    112, 140–74
  boundaries 143, 145, 174,
    196
  church as 12, 13–14, 40–1,
    89, 107–8, 112, 140,
    148–55, 159–60, 192
  of creation 166–7, 168–71
  and discernment 32–4

and language 155–6
and suffering 79, 82
see also hospitality, radical;
  solidarity
conscientization 26, 93, 94,
  95–6, 179–80
contextual theology 16, 27,
  36–7, 39
creation:
  and community 166–7,
    168–71
  and dominion 60, 163
  and humanity 163–6,
    167–9, 170–3
  and image of God 164–5,
    166
crip time theory 40, 57, 63,
  68
culture, autistic 7, 80
cure 6, 75–6, 78, 111, 162,
  186
Cure Autism Now
  Foundation 111

d/Deaf community, and
  academic theology 38
d/Deaf liberation
  theology 26–7, 43, 102
Dalit community 29
Deane-Drummond, Celia
  170, 172
death, and trauma 58
degradation, rituals 180, 183
difference:
  acceptance 18, 29, 129,
    147, 156–7
  and exclusion 179, 182–3
  and language 197–9

INDEX OF NAMES AND SUBJECTS

and neurodiversity 5–8, 11, 14, 77–8, 81, 124
and oppression 24, 79, 205–6
and shame 58
disability:
  autism as 17–18, 75–8, 124
  deficit model 8, 17, 20, 27, 59, 78, 80–2, 83, 86, 91, 103, 115
  and dis/ability 81
  and eschatology 101–3, 190
  and impairment 88–9, 99
  medical model 42, 50–2, 55, 76–9, 80, 112, 124
  and neurodiversity 26–7
  and resurrection body 97–104
  sin as cause 87–8
  social model 7, 78, 80–2, 84, 89, 90–1, 110, 124, 133
discernment, in Pentecostalism 31–4
discipleship, and Pentecostalism 28–9
DSM-IV 540–5

echolalia 197, 199
education:
  access to 55
  and common good 125
  and difference and equality 119, 137
  and home schooling 113–14
  theological 39–40
Eiesland, Nancy L. 88, 180, 182, 190, 202, 203
emancipation, and neurodiversity 61, 80, 82
embrace, and hospitality 150
empathy:
  double 128, 155
  lack of 107, 115, 126–8
employment:
  problems with 1–2, 19–20, 56, 130, 157
  and productivity 51
Endress, Topher 180–1
epistemology, and neurodiversity 31–4
eschatology:
  autistic 12, 74–104, 190
  and healing 94–5, 100–4
  and normativity 97–100
  Pentecostal 33
  realized 86–7, 134
Eucharist, and exclusion 203–4
eugenics 18, 79
evil, and suffering 83
exclusion:
  from baptism 204
  from the Eucharist 203–4
  practices 179–90, 203–4
expectations:
  and employment 19
  neurotypical 20, 50, 57, 63, 69, 120, 122
  and parents 110–12, 114–16, 119
  societal 121–2
  and time 190
experience:
  and liberation theology 35, 93–4, 191–2, 209

and motherhood 41–2,
   108–9, 114, 118–19, 122–3
and practical theology 36–40
eye contact 1, 52

faith:
   and autism diagnosis 2, 4
   and cognition 190–1, 203
   and healing 89
   and knowledge 191–2
flexibility, and time 62–3, 71
Ford, David 64, 66
formation, ministerial 39–40
Francis of Assisi, St 169–71
Francis, pope 169–70
freedom 60–1, 150–1
   and choice 149, 151
Frestadius, Simo 31, 32, 33
friendships:
   difficulties with 1, 56
   and Pentecostalism 181–2
functioning:
   high/low 17, 54, 76–8, 120,
   187–8
   and neurodiversity 17, 76–7
future:
   and hope 50–1, 53, 54,
   55–7, 74–5, 94, 190, 206
   and time 50–7, 60, 70–1,
   190
   see also eschatology

Garnett, Michelle 53–4
Gates, Gordon 19
genetics, and eugenics 18, 79
girls, autistic, and masking
   53–4
glossalalia see tongues

God:
   experience of 66, 211
   and healing 83–5
   knowledge of 3, 13–14, 16,
   31–2, 94, 174, 182, 191–5
   and time 68–71
   see also image of God
Goffman, Erving 180
Goldsmith, Daena J. 110–11
Goodley, Dan 80–1
grand narratives 35, 141–2
Gregory of Nazianzus 173
Grey, Mary 34
Gutiérrez, Gustavo 129–31,
   132–5, 148, 188–9

habitation 190
Hacking, Ian 80
healing:
   and eschatology 94–5,
   100–2
   and Pentecostalism 85–8,
   92–6, 101
   and providence 83–5
   and suffering 74–5, 83–5,
   89, 101–4
health and wealth theology
   88, 94, 96
heaven see eschatology
Holy Spirit:
   and conversion 129, 130,
   191–2
   and discernment 31–2
   gifts 94–5, 181, 196–7
   and healing 96, 102
   as overwhelming 65–8
   and Pentecost 155, 157,
   197–8

home groups 3
home schooling 113–14
hope:
  and Christianity 83–5
  and the future 50–1, 54, 55–7, 74–5, 94, 190, 206
  and memory 60–2
  and the present 65–6, 71, 190–1
Horan, Daniel P. 164, 165, 170–1
hospitality:
  and belonging 178, 196
  and embrace 150
  and mutuality 148–50, 156
  and practice 178
  radical 12, 35, 131, 140, 145, 146–7, 160, 181
Hughes, Jessica 112
humanity:
  common good 124–5, 127–9
  and creation 163–6, 167–9, 170–3
  and dehumanizing of autistics 11, 129
  and liberation theology 34–6, 124–5, 194
  and rationality 79, 145, 164–6
  and sin 116–17, 186–7, 194–5
  see also image of God
humility, and Benedict 152–3
hyper-focus 114, 121

identity:
  and autism 68–9, 74–5, 103–4, 136, 145, 160
  fractured 58–9, 90, 93, 100, 148–9, 186
  person/identity first 10, 17, 79, 91, 111–12
image of God 31, 164–6, 206, 210
  and belonging 12
  and community 140, 147, 148, 166–7
  and creation 164–5, 170
  and disability 88
  and solidarity 124, 127–8, 130, 136
impairment, and disability 88–9, 99
inclusion:
  and autistic liberation theology 143–5, 159, 183, 202–3
  and belonging 12, 153–7
  and healing 102
  and hospitality 140, 143, 145, 150–2, 183
indecency 141–4
instrumentalization 153, 163, 183
invalidation 19
Isasi-Daz, Ada 41

J, spiritual story 13–14
Jesus:
  as friend 13–14, 211–12
  sacrifice 16, 66, 204, 208
  and suffering 61, 125–6
  see also Christ; Christology
Johns, Cheryl Bridges 95–6
joy, autistic 63
justice 201–6

Kafer, Alison 50–2, 54, 57, 60, 62–3
kenosis (emptying) 125–6
Keshgegian, Flora A. 4, 62, 190
Kim, Cynthia 56
kinship:
  creation 163–6
  and liberation theology 171–3
knowledge:
  embodied 190–2
  of God 3, 13–14, 16, 31–2, 174, 182, 191–5

language:
  and autism 9–10, 24, 75, 90–1, 111, 196–8
  and community 155–6, 196–9
  and diversity 198, 210
  and Pentecostalism 30, 155, 158
  see also speech
Lewis, Hannah 26–7, 30–1, 38, 43
liberation theology:
  and animals 161–2
  characteristics 25–8, 34
  charismatic/Pentecostal 28–34, 92–6, 100–1, 191–2
  and Christian practice 178, 190–5, 201–2
  and church 141
  and creation 170
  and eschatology 94
  failures 141–4

  feminist/womanist 30–1, 34, 171–3, 204–5
  and freedom 60–1, 150–1
  and oppression 25–6, 36, 43, 67, 80, 82, 88–9, 95–6, 113, 144–5, 151
  and scripture 27
  and sin 188–9, 194–5
  and solidarity 26, 35, 40–1, 61, 107–9, 124–37
  and suffering 93–4, 125–6
  and time 68–71
life expectancy 2, 71, 135
Limburg, Joanne 10–11, 127
Linzey, Clair 172–3
literalism 121
looping 80

Macaskill, Grant 86, 92–3, 187, 188, 200
Macchia, Frank D. 198, 199
MacKenny-Jeffs, Frances 83
masking 53–4, 143, 148, 184
McGill, Owen 186
McPherson, Aimee Semple 33
meltdowns 23–4, 63–4, 67, 119, 121
memory, of suffering 60–1
Metz, Johann Baptist 60–2
Milton, Damien 128, 155
mimicry, and solidarity 131–7
MMR vaccine, supposed links to autism 6–8
motherhood:
  autistic mothers 112
  as blessing 1

as disruptive 12
and experience 41–2, 108–9, 114, 118–19, 122–3
refrigerator mothers 108, 110
and solidarity 107–9, 112–18, 122–3, 131, 136–7
mutuality 148–50, 156

naming, and overwhelming 67
nature mysticism 171–2, 173–4
neurodiversity 5–8, 10, 12, 16–17, 21, 78–9, 101–4, 211
and autistic liberation theology 34–40, 42, 107–8, 150–1
and Christology 35–6
and disability 26–7
and emancipation 61, 80, 82
example 22–4
and functioning 17, 54, 76–7
medicalized model 5–7, 72–3, 78
and Pentecostal liberation theology 31–4, 88
and time 47–50
and trauma 64–5, 101, 205–6
neurotypicality 17–19, 42, 193
and expectations 20, 50, 57, 63, 69, 120, 122
and inclusion 144

and solidarity 120
noises, loud 1, 66, 119, 121, 201
nonconformity 142–3
normalization 57, 63, 141
normativity:
and difference 156–7, 204
and eschatology 88, 97–100
and liberation theology 143

O'Dell, Lindsay 76–7, 80
O'Donnell, Karen 15 n.5, 84–5
ontology, and status of autism 9, 11, 74–8, 80, 82, 112, 124
oppression:
and autistic liberation theology 80, 82, 144, 205–6
and creation 171–2
and difference 24, 79, 205–6
and liberation theology 25–6, 36, 43, 67, 82, 88–9, 95–6, 113, 144–5, 151
and solidarity 113, 116, 134–5
Ortega, Francisco 82
orthopraxy 190–2
ostracization 19, 90
othering 19, 21, 24, 25, 35, 88, 144, 180
otherness 2, 4–5, 58–9, 126–7, 136, 145, 196
overload, sensory 58, 63–4, 115
overwhelming:

by Holy Spirit 65–8
present as 63–7, 69, 71
trauma as 64–5

Packham, Chris 162
parents:
  autistic 34, 118–19
  of autistic children 6–7,
    22–4, 41–2, 50–3, 81,
    107–37
  and expectations 110–12,
    114–16, 119
  and sacrifice 114, 117
  see also motherhood
past, and time 50, 58–62, 71
Pavlides, Merope 162
peculiarity, and autism 4–5,
  10–11
Pentecost:
  and language 65–6, 157,
    197–8, 210
  and plurality 15, 67, 147,
    155
Pentecostalism:
  and epistemology 31–4
  and healing 85–8, 92–6, 101
  and language 30, 155, 158
  and liberation theology
    28–34, 65
  prophetic role 30, 61, 96
  and speaking in tongues
    196–9
  Word of Faith 86, 96
Plass, Adrian 100
plurality, and Pentecost 15,
  67, 147, 155
Pohl, Christine 146–7
political theology 59–60

poverty:
  and solidarity 132–3
  spiritual 132–5
practical theology 4, 8, 11,
  16, 36–40, 43, 118, 186
practices:
  exclusory 179–90, 203–4,
    209
  liberating 190–5
  as means of grace 192
prayer:
  petitionary 83–4, 89, 93,
    101
  speechless 199
prejudice 179–80
present 63–71
  and hope 65–6, 71, 190–1
  as overwhelming 63–6, 71
process theology 62
Procter-Smith, Marjorie
  204–5, 206
productivity, and time 51–2,
  55–7, 68–9
prophetic role:
  and autism 183–5
  of Pentecostalism 30, 61, 96
prosperity gospel 87–8, 94,
  96
providence, and healing 83–5
PTSD and trauma 58

Rambo, Shelly 58, 59, 70, 92
rationality:
  and animals 164, 165
  and humanity 79, 145,
    164–6
realism, theological 31–2
recognition 146–7, 194

reflection, theological 4,
  11–12, 25, 26, 36–40, 108
reformism 25–6
regression, autistic 56–7
rejection 20–1, 47, 58, 120,
  130, 179, 182–3, 209
relationality, and autism 90,
  126–8, 140
relationships:
  with animals 160–3
  with creation 169
  difficulties with 20, 58–9,
    89–90
  with God 194
  and kinship 163–6
  and speech 20, 56–7, 155–7
  remaining 92–3
  repetition 17, 56, 70, 75,
    191
  and echolalia 197, 199
research:
  into autism 18–19, 37, 111
  by autistic people 38–9
  ritual 49
rocking 63, 193
Romero, Miguel J. 166
routine 121
  and time 49–50
Rowland, Christopher 25, 27
Ruth (biblical book) 123–4,
  200–1, 210

Sabbath 62, 68–71
sacraments 192–3, *see also*
  baptism; Eucharist
sacrifice:
  of Jesus Christ 16, 66, 204,
    208

  by parents 114, 117
salvation 87, 144–5
  and creation 179
  in liberation theology 30,
    191–5
  and neurodiversity 99, 206
  in Paul 145
  in Pentecostalism 94, 173
  personal 189
Sanders, Cheryl J. 94
Sanders, E. P. 145
Schüssler Fiorenza, Elisabeth
  34
scripture:
  and alongsiding 123–4
  and animals 167–8, 171
  and difference 156–7
  and experience 36–7, 40
  and liberation theology 27
  and Pentecostalism 32
segregation, and 'special
  needs' 14, 76, 148–9
self, fractured 58–9, 90, 93,
  100, 186
sensory processing 20, 90,
  121
sentimentalism 132–3
Seymour, William J. 29,
  94–5
shame 19, 43, 58–9, 67, 121,
  125
Shoop, Marcia Mount 91
shutdowns 63, 67
Silberman, Steve 18, 52–3
silencing of autistic voices
  14, 37, 39, 42–3, 54–6,
  102, 109, 112, 130–1
Silverman, Chloe 81–2, 111

sin:
  and autism 99–100, 117–18, 186–7, 194
  as cause of disability 87–8
  and liberation theology 188–9, 194–5
  societal 188–9, 195
Sinclair, Jim 76
Singer, Judy 6, 17
Slee, Nicola 39–40, 64–7
Smith, James K. A. 33, 199
society:
  engagement with 19–20
  and sin 188–9
solidarity:
  and anthropology 12, 117–18, 125, 127–8, 135–6, 148, 149
  with Christ 61–2
  and church 35, 118, 120, 122, 126–7, 130–1, 134–7, 140
  with creation 167, 168–9
  and liberation theology 26, 35, 40–1, 107–9, 124–37
  and mimicry 131–7
  and motherhood 107–9, 112–18, 122–3, 131, 136–7
  and poverty 132–3
  as similarity and difference 118–23
  in sin 194–5
  and spiritual poverty 132–5
  theological 124–37
  see also alongsiding
speaking in tongues 195–9
speech, and relationships 20, 56–7, 155–7

stigma 19, 88–90, 110, 125, 179
stimming 19–20, 58, 75, 115, 119, 184, 186, 191, 192–3
Stone, Selina 28, 29–30, 33, 95
Stuart, Elizabeth 204
suffering:
  and autism 61–2, 74–6
  and community 79, 82
  and evil 83
  and healing 74–5, 83–5, 89, 101–4
  of Jesus 61, 125–6
  and liberation theology 93–4, 125–6
  and memory 60–1
  and prayer 83–5, 89, 93
  redemptive 88, 93
  and resurrection body 97–104
superpower mythos 162
support needs 77, 148–9
Swinton, John 143–4, 151–2, 153–4
Swoboda, A. J. 69

Tanner, Kathryn 152
theobiography 3–4
theology:
  academic 38
  apophatic 84
  community of creation 166–7, 168–71
  disability 8
  and healing 74, 83–5, 89, 92–6

INDEX OF NAMES AND SUBJECTS

and (in)decency 141–3
interdisciplinary 41
of the people 141
and practice 179–90
solidarity 124–37
and trauma 89–93, 100
see also black theology;
  practical theology
therapy, animal 162–3
Tillich, Paul 64
time:
  and anxiety 48–9, 66, 69
  and autism 12, 47–71
  crip time 40, 57, 63, 68
  future 50–7, 60, 190
  as God's time 68–71
  normative 51–2
  past 50, 58–62
  present 63–71, 190–1
  remaining in 92–3
  and routine 49–50
  see also eschatology
tongues, as gift of the Spirit 196–8
tradition 36, 40, 60
trauma 19, 85, 120
  and healing 101
  as overwhelming 64–5, 67
  as peculiar 90
  and theology 89–93, 100, 205–6
  and time 58–62, 70–1
Trementozzi, David 191–2

van Ommen, Armand Leon 110, 180–1
Veil, Simone 84
Volf, Miroslav 145, 150–1, 194–5
Vondey, Wolfgang 86

Wakefield, Andrew 6
Walton, Heather 39
Ward, Pete 3–4, 36–7, 178
Ware, Kallistos 126
Watkins, Clare 37
Wesley, John 147
Williams, Rowan 128–9, 168–9, 172
women, autistic, and masking 53–4
Woods, Milton, Arnold and Graby 78, 81
Word of Faith movement 86, 96
worship:
  access to 203–4
  charismatic 3, 4, 21, 157, 158, 181–2
  and creation 169–70
  imaginative 204–5
  and practices of the church 202–6
  speechless 199
Woznicki, Christopher G. 84

Yong, Amos 29, 88, 101–3

Index created by Meg Davies

www.ingramcontent.com/pod-product-compliance
Lightning Source LLC
Chambersburg PA
CBHW022050290426
44109CB00014B/1052